The Constitution under Social Justice

Studies in Ethics and Economics

Series Editor
Samuel Gregg, Acton Institute

Economics as a discipline cannot be detached from a historical background that was, it is increasingly recognized, religious in nature. Adam Ferguson and Adam Smith drew on the work of sixteenth- and seventeenth-century Spanish theologians, who strove to understand the process of exchange and trade in order to better address the moral dilemmas they saw arising from the spread of commerce in the New World. After a long period in which economics became detached from theology and ethics, many economists and theologians now see the benefit of studying economic realities in their full cultural, often religious, context. This new series, Studies in Ethics and Economics, provides an international forum for exploring the difficult theological and economic questions that arise in the pursuit of this objective.

Titles in the Series

Intelligence as a Principle of Public Economy / Del pensiero come principio d'economia publica, by Carlo Cattaneo
And Why Not?: The Human Person at the Heart of Business, by François Michelin
Faith and Liberty: The Economic Thought of the Late Scholastics, by Alejandro A. Chafuen
The Boundaries of Technique: Ordering Positive and Normative Concerns in Economic Research, by Andrew Yuengert
Within the Market Strife: American Economic Thought from Rerum Novarum *to Vatican II*, by Kevin E. Schmiesing
Natural Law: The Foundation of an Orderly Economic System, by Alberto M. Piedra
The Church and the Market: A Catholic Defense of the Free Economy, by Thomas E. Woods Jr.
The Constitution under Social Justice, by Antonio Rosmini, translated by Alberto Mingardi

The Constitution under Social Justice

Antonio Rosmini

Translated by Alberto Mingardi

LEXINGTON BOOKS

A division of
ROWMAN & LITTLEFIELD PUBLISHERS, INC.
Lanham • Boulder • New York • Toronto • Plymouth, UK

LEXINGTON BOOKS

A division of Rowman & Littlefield Publishers, Inc.
A wholly owned subsidiary of The Rowman & Littlefield Publishing Group, Inc.
4501 Forbes Boulevard, Suite 200
Lanham, MD 20706

Estover Road
Plymouth PL6 7PY
United Kingdom

British Library Cataloguing in Publication Information Available

Library of Congress Cataloging-in-Publication Data

Rosmini, Antonio, 1797–1855
[Costituzione secondo la giustizia sociale. English.]
The Constitution under social justice / Antonio Rosmini ; translated by Alberto Mingardi.
p. cm.— (Studies in ethics and economics)
Includes bibliographical references and index.
ISBN-13: 978-0-7391-0724-9 (cloth : alk. paper)
ISBN-10: 0-7391-0724-0 (cloth : alk. paper)
ISBN-13: 978-0-7391-0725-6 (pbk. : alk. paper)
ISBN-10: 0-7391-0725-9 (pbk. : alk. paper)
1. Constitutional law—Italy—Philosophy. 2. Natural law—Philosophy. I. Title. II. Series.

KKH2070.R67 2007
342.001—dc22 2006026480

Printed in the United States of America

The paper used in this publication meets the minimum requirements of American National Standard for Information Sciences—Permanence of Paper for Printed Library Materials, ANSI/NISO Z39.48–1992.

CONTENTS

FOREWORD

Over the past quarter of a century, a great work of retrieval has been underway wherein sundry documents, all but lost to contemporary memory, are being brought back into circulation and studied anew for the light they can shed upon the synthesis between human liberty in the political and economic spheres and its moral foundation in the Christian moral and theological tradition.

In this regard, one can cite examples such as the recent translation and publication of the economic commentaries of members of the sixteenth century School of Salamanca such as Martin de Azpilcueta, Luis de Molina, and Juan de Mariana's in the internationally renowned *Journal of Markets and Morality*. Pioneering efforts to bring to light the writings of Mariana and other members of the School of Salamanca include the work of scholars such as the recently deceased Marjorie Grice-Hutchison[1] as well as Alejandro Chafuen in his recently republished *Faith and Liberty: The Economic Thought of the Late Scholastics* (2003).[2]

This has been a long needed undertaking, given the neglect and at times distortion of the history of the Christian tradition of thinking about these subjects. In Europe, the intellectual mission to make the case for Christianity as the foundation of the authentically free (as opposed to libertine) society has been underway for a longer period of time, largely owing to the longer memory of most Europeans compared to their American cousins, but also due to a greater familiarity with the languages in which these ideas were first expressed, those being Spanish, French, Italian and Latin.

In the popular mindset, particularly in the modern period, the assumption so succinctly and famously summed up by Paul Tillich—"Christianity is the religion of which Socialism is the practice"—reigns in many circles. As figures such as Grice-Hutchison and Chafuen have demonstrated, plenty of Christians, both now and in the past, would take issue with this claim. One such Christian was Antonio Rosmini.

The pope of the last years of Rosmini's life, Pius IX, is often remembered as the author of the much mocked *Syllabus of Errors*, the publication of which shocked much of Europe. Yet prior to the revolutionary year of 1848, he was widely regarded as a reforming pope, one who even granted a constitution to the people of the Papal States, which soon after descended into anarchy and turmoil in the wake of the seizure of power by Jacobin revolutionaries.[3] It was Rosmini's awareness of Pope Pius' reforming instincts that encouraged him to write the constitution you find in this book.

Like Lord Acton, John Henry Cardinal Newman, and Count Alexis de Tocqueville, Fr. Antonio Rosmini was one of those comprehensive nineteenth-century Catholic thinkers whose breath and depth of thought and analysis may be seen as all the more remarkable from the distance of time. There was barely a topic that Rosmini did not consider worthy of further exploration as becomes evident from scanning the indexes of the one hundred or so volumes that constitute his corpus.

If his name is not as familiar as that of Acton, Newman, Tocqueville and others, one factor may be that until recently very few of his works were available in that contemporary lingua franca of the academy: English. Although *La costituzione secondo la giustizia sociale* was the last of Rosmini's works to be published within his lifetime, this translation by the young Italian scholar Alberto Mingardi is its first appearance in English. It is hoped that the scholarly lacuna is well on it way to being bridged.

Rosmini's decision to present an outline and analysis of the principles that should underlie a constitution designed for a free people afforded him the opportunity to explore a staggering rang of philosophical, social, historical, economic ad theological matters. To present such an array of material in a coherent manner evidences a synthetic capacity rare enough in the academy and perhaps rarer still in clerical circles.

Rosmini, one should remember, was a Catholic priest whose chief concern was human redemption. Yet not only does this ultimate goal *not* impede him from a consideration of more finite and proximate concerns: it actually appears to propel and motivate him. Indeed, it provides the lens through which he is capable of coordinating abstractions into social structures worthy of the human person who, created in the *imago Dei*, has a destiny beyond human society: heaven or hell.

Antonio Rosmini stands within a venerable tradition of thinkers often identified as "liberal." The use of such a word, particularly in a book that will be widely referenced in international and theological circles, requires some definition in order to be clear. When we contend that Rosmini is one in a trajectory of liberal thinkers, it should not be thought to refer to that aberrant, even self-contradictory form of liberalism, which emerged in full bloom in the French Revolution. That form of liberalism culminated in a chaos that was anything but freeing for those whose blood stained the very banners that called for *Liberté, Fraternité, Egalité*. Much less ought the term be employed in its more contemporary and largely American usage, which tends to signify a liberty uprooted from any reference to tradition, culture, or custom (an inheritance from the

French libertine-libertarianism), while simultaneously suppressing economic freedom. This is manifestly *not* the liberal tradition in which Rosmini stands.

As a lover of culture (witness his long friendship with the novelist Alessandro Manzoni, author of *I promessi sposi*) and a priest, Rosmini embraced structure, hierarchy and legitimate authority—even to the point of founding his own religious order, the Institute of Charity. The liberalism which animates Rosmini is one grounded in a love of man, not mere abstractions, and an awareness of his transcendent origin and destiny. In this version of liberalism, the state, along with all other social arrangements, exists for man—not the reverse.

The distinction Rosmini consistently insists upon between society and the state is a hallmark of authentically liberal thought over against the more totalistic conceptions of society that see the state as the embodiment of society's ideals. Likewise in rooting so much of the reality of human liberty in the right to acquire and dispose of private property, Rosmini establishes a prescient bulwark against the socialist and communist movements which would arise with force within decades of his writing.

What is most important for those students of liberty who are also concerned with truth is to grasp the religious underpinnings of Rosmini's approach. The effort to retrieve a theologically based rationale and defense of human liberty in the history of ideas—that is, to continue what might be called Lord Acton's project—is critical, all the more in an age where what Pope Benedict XVI famously called the "dictatorship of relativism" so easily reigns and undermines human liberty, even while speaking of its achievement. As long as the popular mind associates religious authority with despotism and oppression, and free thought with secularism and atheism, the Acton-Tocqueville-Rosmini-Newman agenda remains incomplete. The body of Rosmini's work stands against any dichotomizing of liberty and truth or faith and reason, and provides for the contemporary student a useful model of how to approach such questions today.

—Robert A. Sirico

Notes

1. See Marjorie Grice-Hutchison, *Economic Thought in Spain: Selected Essays of Marjorie Grice Hutchinson*, eds. Lawrence S. Moss and Christopher K. Ryan (Aldershot: Edward Elgar Publishing Ltd, 1993), 9–12.

2. See Alejandro Chafuen, *Faith and Liberty: The Economic Thought of the Late Scholastics* (Lanham, Md.: Lexington Books, 2003).

3. It should be recalled that many of the statements contained in this text were written as a direct response to the horrendous attacks on the Church by leaders of the movements that gathered momentum throughout Europe during and after the French Revolution. As one scholar notes, the most famous denunciation in the Syllabus—that that the Roman pontiff "can and should reconcile himself to, or join up with, progress, liberalism, and modern civilization" was taken from Pius IX's Allocution *Iamdudum cern-*

imus of 18 March 1861, which responded to the extension of Piedmont's anti-clerical laws and prohibitions upon Catholic publications to the rest of Italy. If this were modernity, no pope would welcome it." Samuel Gregg, *Challenging the Modern World: Karol Wojtyla/John Paul II and the Development of Catholic Social Teaching* (Lanham, Md.: Lexington Books, 1999), 1–2.

FOREWORD

Beyond Democratism and Conservatism: The Original Approach of Rosmini's *Costituzione*

The Constitution under Social Justice (*costituzione secondo la Giustizia Sociale*) is probably one of Rosmini's works which better represents the uncommon qualities of its author. In fact, Rosmini was at the same time a man endowed with a strong historical sense and an extraordinarily profound philosopher. This book is an example of these two characteristics.

Indeed, the first and more direct interpretation of the text is historical and political. The very title "Constitution" and a first glimpse of its contents tells us of a politico-juridical text devoted to a very concrete political project in an immediate historical context. In fact, Rosmini conceived the *costituzione* as a response to the extremely complicated political puzzle involving Italy during the post-revolutionary period of the beginning of the nineteenth century.

However, after a more attentive reading, the work reveals a broader significance considering its very deep theoretical foundations. Open to a vast landscape of political and social insights, the text is delicately intermingled with Rosmini's most profound ideas that refer not only to his political works but also to his other anthropological, ethical and even metaphysical texts. In a word, the book is an interesting piece not only as a historical document but also as a helpful meditation still capable of shedding light on our own contemporary dilemmas in the political and social arena.

A Cultural Vision for Christian Modernity

When I try to picture the situation lived by Rosmini in the Italy of the turbulent decades around 1848—the year of the publication of the *costituzione*—what comes to mind is an extraordinary scene in the world famous book *Il Gattopardo* by Giuseppe Tomasi di Lampedusa.[1] Although the scene is situated in Sicily around 1860, that is, a time and a place different from Rosmini's northern Italy of the 1840s, the main elements are the same in both dramas. Lampedusa's story shows us a carriage taking two persons in the midst of an Italian night. Prince Fabrizio, an old representative of Sicily's nobility, and Father Pirrone, the priest chaplain of the prince's family and character representative of the Church, are traveling together toward Palermo, the great city of the island. The last lights of the day still allow them to see the city's great baroque cupolas silhouetted against the horizon. Everything breaths the calm atmosphere of a known world still protected by the comforting shadows of historical tradition and religious mystery.

Suddenly, after a curve in the road, the two surprised passengers open their eyes to the most amazing and frightening sight: Hundreds of fires burn all over the great plain. It is the splendid and, at the same time, terrifying view of Garibaldi's army, the unequivocal symbol of the changes to come: an unstoppable modernity, often ferocious and cruel, intent on raising the flags of liberty and equality even at the sacrifice of all that has always been worthy of respect and veneration for the two paralyzed observers in the carriage.

Rosmini would have understood the conflict presented by Lampedusa perfectly well. Moreover, being a nobleman and a priest himself, he would have probably sympathized with the two passengers in the carriage. In fact, Rosmini saw the dangers that an extremely secularized modernity, as the one represented by the French Revolution, signified both to the Church and the Christian religion and also to the aristocratic values in which he was educated. However, Rosmini's sympathies would not have remained enclosed in the carriage. In fact, his view on the "fires" of modernity was not completely negative and critical. He did not share the opinion of traditionalists who rejected modernity as a whole and clamored for a return to some kind of medieval society.

On the contrary, Rosmini's position represents a very original point of view among the Catholic opinion of his time, including that of very high positioned clergy in Rome itself. In fact, the project started by him during his early years in his natal city of Rovereto and then continued in Padua—at the university and at the seminary—and especially during his years in Milan,[2] included a general restoration of Christian life from a modern perspective. Indeed, Rosmini conceived that the formula for the Church of his time was not to combat every expression of modernity but to try to find in it the elements which could be rescued as part of a new Christian culture. Starting from the heights of theology and philosophy, this restoration would include ethics, education, medicine, and, of course, the vast field of political sciences.

Rosmini was convinced that his task was not to be merely critical or reactive toward modernity but to endow Christian faith with a new cultural vision. To reach this goal, he read everything and tried to assimilate the best elements of every author, every cultural movement, and current of thought. This did not mean, however, that his thought was devoid of any critical sense. On the contrary, Rosmini was always prepared to complete and correct what he judged incomplete or wrong. The text of the *costituzione* is an excellent example of this audacious effort of critical assimilation of modern political thought in the context of his project of a cultural vision for a Christian modernity.[3]

The Sociopolitical Project and Its Circumstances

This grandiose cultural project should not only be carried out, according to Rosmini, on the theoretical level, but also give concrete responses to the new practical problems presented by modern times and particularly in the context of his beloved Italy. In this sense, sociopolitical and economic problems in general and the European, and especially the Italian situation, were a constant worry in Rosmini's intellectual work. The *costituzione*, in particular, has to be understood, in my opinion, in this last context.

As we know, until modern times Italy remained an aggregate of multiple separate small regions, cities, and territories governed by local princes, successive foreign sovereigns (especially Austrian, French and Spanish), and of course, the pope. At the time of Rosmini's childhood, the country had known its last greatest foreign invasion: the one led by Napoleon Bonaparte which, although brief, left a great impression on the Italian soul and also a very concrete political transformation.

On the one hand, the Napoleonic invasion made the Italians aware of an urgent need for unity if they wanted to survive the new era of power politics. Besides, it put into question the political and cultural *status quo* in which they had lived for centuries. It also brought a cultural turmoil of enlightened and romantic ideas that woke up the Italian spirit of freedom and prosperity that had characterized the vast plurality of Italian cities and urged their citizens to break the old feudal and monarchical shackles. Thus, the Napoleonic invasion triggered a huge political, juridical and socioeconomic reform concretely expressed in the several new constitutional reforms sanctioned first by Napoleon and continued later all over the different Italian regions and cities even after Napoleon's defeat.

By the time in which Rosmini started to write his first political texts and constitutional projects, Italy was in the midst of this extremely conflictive process of becoming both a unified nation and a liberal political society which involved at least four actors. The first one was the Austrian monarchy, heart of the Holy League and representative of the political tradition of the Old Regime. Austria did not want to hear about constitutional reforms leading to Italian unity and to liberalism in the regions under its rule.[4] Austrians were afraid that such a process would eventually lead not only to the destruction of monarchy, but also of non-dividable inherited property, considered the only thinkable means to obtain economic prosperity and social order.

The second actors were the Italian kings of the different regions and the powerful local *bourgeoisies* close to them. Although they shared the idea of Italian unity and independence from absolute monarchies—especially if they were foreign—they were also afraid of the quick ascension of an uncultured people that could bring a liberal reform.

The third actor was precisely this ascendant *petite bourgeoisie* and proletariat who saw in a democratic French-style constitution the best instrument to gain quick changes, and in the monarchy, the *grande bourgeoisie* and the Church, the obstacles to these aspirations.

Finally, the fourth actor in the conflict was the Church. Although the pope sympathized with Italian unity and saw the need of a new political and economic regime, he was also aware of the anti-Catholic inspiration of much of French liberalism. From a Christian perspective the Napoleonic reforms led to the absorption of the Church by the state and to a completely secularized and materialist vision of politics. Thus, the pope adopted a dubious position between supporting the changes and at the same time looking for support in the apparently safer power of the Austrian Catholic monarchy.

Although Rosmini had passed most of his life devoted to his philosophical work and his religious activities, he had also always been in contact with the political realm. Thus, by 1848, the moment in which the conflict among these different actors in relation to the constitution of liberal political systems had reached the apex in Europe and in Italy, he was asked to carry out a very delicate diplomatic mission. Being aware of the very solid prestige of Rosmini with the Holy See, the president of the Council of Ministers of the Piedmont sent Rosmini to Rome in order to convince the pope to join his kingdom in a war against Austria. Rosmini accepted the mission but changed its purpose into a general presentation before the pope of a much broader and profound political project.

Indeed, the project included a very concrete proposal of a new political organization for Italy consisting in a confederation of states including Piedmont, Tuscany and the papal states—with a more moral than political presidency of the pope—which could serve both as the basis of a new unified Italian state and also of a peaceful relationship between the Church and the state.

But this was not all. In fact, although Rosmini's mission turned into a complete diplomatic failure and ended in an ecclesiastical conflict deeply painful for a sensitive and profound spirit like his, it had the historical significance of having revealed the extraordinary system of political ideas upon which Rosmini had been elaborating for at least twenty years.

Indeed, what Rosmini presented at the pope's court—and that is contained in the text of the *costituzione* presented here—was a delicate and elaborated corpus of juridical and political ideas that formed what was perhaps one of the first

Catholic interpretations of modern political and economic liberalism. However, it was also too advanced and audacious to be accepted by the Catholic intellectual and political culture of the time. The latter, moved by an anti-modern and anti-liberal mood, rejected the project, failing to make any distinction between Rosmini's liberalism and the extremist liberalism of the French Revolution.

However, the main virtue of Rosmini's constitutional project was precisely its moderation, sense of proportion and, at the same time, its spirit of broad and generous views, a subtle combination generally scarce in times of conflict when everybody tends to stress the differences. The *costituzione* was a politico-juridical instrument so broad and rich that it integrated and brought into equilibrium the different and at many times antagonistic forces of the time.

Critique and Assimilation

From the very start Rosmini's *costituzione* gains our attention as an acid and sometimes violent critique of the constitutions inspired in what our philosopher calls "the French system," very similar to the famous ones made before him by authors like Joseph de Maistre or Edmund Burke. Indeed, like them, Rosmini criticized the French system for writing constitutions which were always "created altogether, emerging complete as theory from the mind, like Minerva from the head of Jupiter," always "written before being enacted" (chap. I), full of "vain abstractions" and of "theories that are inapplicable to social realities" (chap. III). Thus, these constitutions are for Rosmini a product of the "improvisation of audacious and imaginative minds, too much infatuated with too general and too imperfect theories . . . daughters of a philosophy that wanted to break with the past, of which it was so tired, a philosophy that, indignant, trampled upon history and traditions" (chap. I).

Moreover, and also in a very Burkean way, Rosmini begins the text comparing these kinds of constitutions with "the constitution of the Venetian Republic" and especially with "the English constitution," "enacted before being written," "formed passage by passage, without a premeditated scheme, incessantly patched and mended according to counterpoising social forces and the urgency of instincts and popular need" (chap. I).

Following the logic of the argument, Rosmini believes the French-style constitutions, created by an abstract method that disdains historical facts—the opposite of what happens, for example, with the English constitution—contain a wrong interpretation of political liberalism. According to Rosmini, these constitutions articulate an extremist conception of political freedom that divinizes political majority incarnated in the legislative power, despising every other kind of political, economic and religious freedom such as the one of minorities, individual citizens, families, private associations and the Church. As a logical consequence they lead to "promot[ing] in all citizens a limitless ambition to ascend to ever-greater degrees in society," "open the way to corruption in the election of deputies and, especially, of the president if the form is republican," "give such preponderance to the Chamber of Deputies, even for their comparatively excessive number, that the state is kept in the danger of revolution," "do not guarantee sufficiently and in all fullness of law the freedom of the citizens," "do not guarantee the distribution of properties," and "abandon religion to the mercy of political interests, and divest the Church of its liberty" (chap. 2).

In fact, Rosmini believes that this wrong conception of political freedom is very closely related to a wrong conception of *political representation*. Moreover, the issue of political representation is one of the main worries of Rosmini's political and constitutional thought and it is also one of the subjects in which he has turned to the English tradition in search of a solution. In fact, according to Rosmini, the latter has mainly contributed to political thought and practice by always stressing the importance of *economic interests and rights* for the constitution of society and therefore the need for their proportional participation at the level of political representation. This is especially true in what Rosmini calls the present "historical stage of civil society" (very different from the previous historical stage of the "familiar society") in which the economic factor is essential not only for the progress but also for the basic functioning of society. Indeed, for Rosmini it is a big mistake to ignore the economic dimension both of man and of society.[5] The right of property—through which the economic dimension of man can be expressed and defended—is one of the key concepts of Rosmini's political, economic, and juridical philosophy and is, with the principle of liberty, the second principle on which is based the entire organization of society[6] (chap. 2).

In this sense, the reduction of government election exclusively to universal suffrage puts all the power of the state in the hands of an anonymous electoral mass of equal votes without any kind of connection to the different weight of their economic interests and rights.[7] In doing so it leads inevitably to a political despotism of the majority which uses political power as an instrument of quick and easy ascension at the expense of the economic rights of groups and individuals legitimately gained in the economic realm. Therefore, a political representation based exclusively on universal suffrage becomes "an organized theft" (chap. 9), a political despotism, which deforms completely both government's finances and political economy,[8] obscures the possibility of a transparent and just fiscal policy, and eventually destroys every kind of incentive for economic growth.

Rosmini believes that the way out of this situation is to introduce another kind of representation in which "we accept a franchise that is proportional to properties" (chap. 9), "the majority of taxation is approved by those who pay" (chap. 9), so "that there is economy in finances" (chap. 9) and a true "political and economic administration" for the "citizens' properties, the complexities of which form the wealth of the nation" (chap. 2). In a word, Rosmini seems to assimilate and follow the British tradition of "real representation" (based on *res*, that means on property) instead of the "personal representation" (one person, one vote) of the French system. In that sense he argues that "it would be desirable that Italians took greater interest in the study of the British politicians and economists. Some of them understood better than anyone else the function of ballast that property has in keeping the ship of state balanced" (chap. 12).[9]

Natural Right as a Corrective

Although Rosmini assimilates many arguments both of French traditionalism and of English conservatism for his critique of the constitutions inspired in French liberalism and for the proposal of his own project, he is decidedly not another de Maistre or an Italian Burke.[10] Rosmini's original point of view comes from the fact that he has taken an unexplored road which would lead him to a new vision of the political problem not identified with the ones proposed by other earlier authors.

Let us analyze some of his key points. In the first place, although Rosmini criticizes the abstractness of the French-inspired constitutions and appraises the experience and historical realism of the English constitution, he did not share the empiricism and historicism of many traditionalists and conservatives who despised written constitutions and denied any political value to theoretical principles.[11] In fact, Rosmini argues that trying "to submit facts to reason and practicality to theory was a generous thought" of the French constitution "for nothing is more sublime than a true and complete theory. That is an eternal and divine thing and the human and temporal fact must conform to it, as the nature of the intelligent being and the dignity of man demands it" (chap. 1). Indeed, according to Rosmini the problem of the French constitution was not the fact of being based on too much reason and theory but precisely of being based on incomplete and "*imperfect* theories" (chap. 1). Therefore, the solution for the political problem of his time is not for him to reject constitutionalism and accepting blindly, like traditionalists and conservatives, a state of things just because they come from the past. Rosmini was convinced that, beyond the mistakes committed in its name, constitutionalism was the political future of the world and he himself supported a written constitution[12] but one that does not despise theory but is, on the contrary, based on a "deep plan" and on "peaceful meditation" (chap. 1).

As a consequence of his constitutionalism and his belief in theoretical principles, Rosmini does not agree with the traditionalists' and conservatives' reduction of political freedom to a historical product and their rejection of every kind of natural or rational foundations for political, civil, and economic rights. He did not support, for example, Joseph de Maistre's affirmations that "rights of the people can never be written" and "freedom is a gift of the kings."[13] Nor did he agree with Burke's statement that "in the gross and complicated mass of human passions and concerns the primitive rights of men undergo such a variety of refractions and reflections that it becomes absurd to talk of them as if they continued in their simplicity of their original direction."[14]

Contrary to Burke, Rosmini affirms that "the best thing that was done in '89 was certainly the *Declaration of the Rights of Man and of the Citizen*, proposed by Lafayette to imitate the American constitutions" (chap. 7). In fact, Rosmini's most important idea in the realm of political philosophy is perhaps his vindication of natural and rational right as the ultimate basis of social order: "it conforms to the dignity of a constitutional statue that such a statute begins by proclaiming as inviolable the law of nature and of reason" (chap. 7). Indeed, this conviction comes from the very center of Rosmini's philosophical system in which he elaborated a modern and original interpretation of the traditional doctrine of natural law taught by the scholastics.[15]

It is true that Rosmini agrees with conservatives and traditionalists in their idea that government cannot treat every right as if it were an absolute natural right. In fact, many rights are the product of social history and cannot be exerted just by invoking human nature. This is the case especially with what Rosmini calls "social rights," including the economic rights which are in great part a result of a very complex historical process. But even in this case we cannot dismiss their ultimate foundation on natural and rational right. Thus, Rosmini's originality on this point shows that it is a mistake to assimilate his thought to English or any other kind of conservatism.[16] In fact, he disagrees completely with the conservative idea that natural rights have nothing to do with politics, as exemplified by Burke's assertion that "the pretended rights of these theorists are all extremes; and in proportion as they are metaphysically true, they are morally and politically false."[17]

Rosmini has always believed that modernity's main error has been to despise natural right, an error derived from "a philosophy that is utilitarian and based on the senses" (chap. 3)[18] that denies the light of right reason that should preside and regulate politics and reduces the latter to a mere calculus of advantages and disadvantages.[19] In the end, this leads always, according to Rosmini, to absolutism, no matter if the political party is monarchical or democratic: "every despotism has at its root the negation of the rights of nature and reason" (chap. 7).[20]

Politics Based on Rights: The Political Tribunal

There are very concrete applications of Rosmini's ideas about natural and rational right to the realm of politics. The first and most important one is Rosmini's idea of what he calls the "political tribunal." This institution, which Rosmini considers the *most important of the state*, was seemingly inspired in him by his reading of the civil philosopher Giammaria Ortes and perhaps also other authors like Leibniz.[21] The "political tribunal," an expression that has nothing to do with the political fight for power, is the supreme court of the state. In Rosmini's conception, it differs from a regular court of justice because it is not in charge of applying the law promulgated by the legislative power but, on the contrary, it has the crucial mission of "holding the natural and rational right against all other powers of the state" (chap. 7). In fact, Rosmini had not criticized the French Revolution for its declaration of the rights of man but for its lack of "a corresponding tribunal that would enforce it" (chap. 7). Unless there is a "power to judge the justice of the acts of legislation" (chap. 6) there is no possible defense for the citizen against what has become, according to him, the nightmare of modern politics that is, "the specter of an omnipotent civil society" (chap. 7) or, in other words, "the deadly belief in the omnipotence of the law—that is, of the omnipotence of the legislators through the laws" (chap. 9). Thus, the political tribunal was designed to be the institution to which any citizen can appeal when his natural rights have been violated, even by the state itself.

Among these natural rights, Rosmini stresses the importance of what we would call "civil rights" such as the right to life, to a fair trial, to travel freely inside and outside one's country, to express one's own ideas, of association, of disposing of one's property, of exerting freely an economic activity or profession and, above all, of religious freedom. With respect to the latter, it would not be an exaggeration to say that, according to Rosmini's view, his whole constitutional setting would be devoid of sense if religious liberty was not recognized. Indeed, the central position of religious freedom in his constitutional project includes not only freedom for Catholics but also for believers of every other faith.[22] For Rosmini rejects not only democratic secularism, but also theocratic traditionalism, on the basis that history illustrates that both have ended in the absorption of the Church by the state.[23]

In addition, the qualifications for being an elector of the political tribunal's members are very different from the ones required for electing the parliament's members. Indeed, contrary to Rosmini's rejection of personal representation and universal suffrage for the legislative power, in the case of the political tribunal he believes that its members should be elected by every citizen's equal vote: "We have established a proportional vote, but we have not excluded the universal and equal vote. The proportional vote we have kept for the election of the parliaments representing the material interests—and those interests are not equal in all men. The universal vote we have adopted for the election of the political tribunal, representing the interest and the personal rights, which are and must be equal for all" (chap. 12). Rosmini's "constitution admits the universal vote with an extension that is greater than all those that have admitted it so far" (chap. 12) and introduces a fundamental democratic principle in the very heart of his project.

The Institutional Design for a Just Economic Order

Rosmini introduces the political tribunal in part to control what he calls the parliament's laws of "pure justice" that are made to "declare what is just and what is unjust" (chap. 10). However, even the parliament's proper task, that is to make "laws of utility"—or what our author also calls the "political economic administration" in which "no utility and no interest must be excluded"—falls under the area of the political tribunal. In fact, "a power that is turned to utility must be accountable to another power that oversees the preservation of justice, so that the utilitarian instincts that naturally move the parliaments do not damage justice" (chap. 10).

Moreover, Rosmini considers that the danger of the legislative power is not only to become an "unfair democracy" like the French Revolution characterized by "the arrogance of the nonrich who would like to steal wealth from the rich" (chap. 9). There is also the danger of becoming an "unfair aristocracy" like the one established in part in England which has a constitution that "has shortcomings arising from the opposite tendencies" (chap. 9). In this latter system, characterized by "the arrogance of the rich who would like to perpetually tie wealth to their families" (chap. 9), the parliament as a representative of the right of property is changed into a political instrument for the gain of the richest. In the England of Rosmini's time, "the landlords wrote legislation which was to their exclusive advantage" (chap. 9). In fact, Rosmini's proposal that parliament's members should represent economic interests does not mean that the latter should be independent from right and justice. On the contrary, Rosmini believes that the function of parliament is precisely to put these interests under an objective light by which they can be openly recognized, clearly measured in their real size, and subordinated to justice and natural right.[24]

All this explains why Rosmini insists so much upon elaborating his whole political and economic design not on an idea of property as a mere factual "possession" economically useful, but as a right destined to develop the human being as a human person.[25] Precisely around this idea of property Rosmini designs his complex electoral and fiscal system[26] by which he tries to protect neither the *status quo* of some present economic interests nor the excessive ambition of future interests in a certain historical society, but the natural rights of every human person implied in society's economic interaction. Here Rosmini distinguishes socialism, which proposes a complete political control of economic interests in favor of equalization, from conservatism, which tends to a political and even juridical protection of the most powerful interests, from extreme liberalism, which defends a general liberation of interests of every kind, denying any type of political intervention in the economic realm.

According to these criteria, and based also on deep anthropological insights that distinguish and harmonize the moral and utilitarian tendencies in man's heart,[27] Rosmini believes that political economy cannot be reduced to a mere conservation or liberation of private economic interests. In this regard he differs with both Adam Smith's "invisible hand"[28] and with state planning.[29] On the contrary, the economy should have, in the first place, a very strong juridical framework that should provide the channels through which economic competition can be regulated according to principles of natural right.[30] In the second place, it should include a delicate use of some political means in order to induce economic interests to arrive at the most just result possible for society, always taking into account that, according to Rosmini, political means cannot modify the essence of rights, but only "determine the modality" of their exercise according to the prudence required by particular situations.[31]

However, all these institutional instruments are understood by Rosmini always as means created to cooperate with and never arbitrarily replace individual decisions of free individuals. Rosmini believes strongly in economic freedom of private individuals and associations as the first agents of their own prosperity and of the whole country's economy.[32] Besides, he is also one of those who foreshadowed the Church's teaching on the subsidiarity principle, which authorizes the state to engage in economic activities only in those instances where such activities are necessary for the development of the country and not able to be exerted by private agents.[33] When the state goes beyond these limits, it deforms the "natural course" of the economy and creates false incentives, passive attitudes in the citizens and, above all, an unfair distribution of wealth.[34] Moreover, Rosmini clearly foresees the dangers for human dignity of the future welfare state and the decisive role of civil or intermediate associations in relation to social problems.[35] Although he believes that the state must intervene sometimes to help the poor, he thinks that this assistance has to be always "extraordinary and momentary" and not "ordinary and continuous."[36]

These opinions are closely related to Rosmini's idea of common good. According to Rosmini, one of the greatest errors of modern politics is the utilitarian reduction of common good to a mere mechanical satisfaction of needs by government's planning or to a disordered growth of unlimited desires by extreme market competition.[37] Instead, he understands the common good mainly as a moral good—one that is formed by the total sum of personal virtue and of the happiness that comes with it—"produced" with the help of civil society and the economic system but which ultimately is the result of personal freedom and responsibility governed by internalized moral principles.[38]

Rosmini's Lessons for Today

In his book *After Virtue*, Alasdair MacIntyre argues that the main problem of contemporary political debate is that we have lost a common philosophical idea of justice according to which we could discuss the distribution of power and wealth among the different parties and interests engaged in the political arena. In this philosophical vacuum, the discussion between, on the one hand, a conservative politics focused on the defense of individual and property rights and, on the other hand, a democratic (meaning the American "liberal") policy devoted to social rights and equal opportunities, hides what MacIntyre sees as a subterranean political war. In my opinion, Rosmini's *costituzione* goes beyond this classical political opposition but not by means of a more or less eclectic settlement or a superficial "third way" between the two parties. On the contrary, he believes that politics is mainly a moral art that should set in equilibrium the multiple interests and rights but based on a common ground of metaphysical, ethical and juridical principles.

In fact, almost a century and a half before the publication of John Rawls' *Theory of Justice*, Rosmini was aware that modern political liberalism could not be based solely on the notion of liberty but needed a strong conception of justice as its ground. But contrary to those who propose eliminating all metaphysical and moral discussions from the political realm, Rosmini believed that these foundations were an unavoidable condition for society to flourish. From Rosmini's point of view, a society based on relativism does not lead to freedom but to totalitarianism. However, neither did Rosmini fall in the other extreme of holding that a just society requires heavy state control. In Rosmini's thought, strong principles do not mean a diminution of freedom, they are the only guarantee of it.

The first and most important metaphysical principle is the principle of the dignity of the human person, which Rosmini calls "the subsistent human right" on which all the other individual and social rights and duties are grounded. Thus, Rosmini's defense of freedoms and rights of every kind (religious, political or economic) does not mean the simple "liberation" of blind interests, needs or desires. In fact, Rosmini understands freedom as a responsible action of the human person that is independent of any individual interest or social consensus. According to Rosmini, the solution for the social problem does not require an essential contradiction between the individual and society. Society is conceived by Rosmini precisely as a bond by which "a person is recognized as person and never as means."[39] Thus, this union, subject to the demands of the law and the obligations of the common good, should never involve a renouncing of individual rights but rather should be the best means to obtain their defense and expansion. In other words, based on the principle of the dignity of the person, Rosmini is at the same time a defender of personal freedom and of social union.

This becomes apparent when we consider Rosmini's ideas for the practice of politics. Rosmini would disagree with those who deny the very existence of the problem of social justice by a simplistic reduction of the idea of society to a self-organized spontaneous order among self-seeking individuals. He would also disagree with those who conceive social justice as "social engineering" and treat society as if it were a mechanical artifact to be managed by a central rational plan. One of Rosmini's main lessons for our time was his rejection of the reduction of the social problem to a simple formula such as the usual clichés of "laissez-faire" or "equal opportunities." Rosmini believed that the first step to finding a true concept of social justice was to "persuade ourselves that the problem of social organization is naturally complex" (chap. 12) and to overcome the conformism and laziness of the so-called "practical men" who "are so used to handling affairs in such a set way as to not recognize as valid any other possible theory except that which comes from the way they and others always handle things (with good or bad result being irrelevant)" (chap. 12).

Thus, the originality of Rosmini's project is that it asks people "to open a new path" (chap. 12) which arrives at "a reconciliation of all systems and of all parties" (chap. 12). In fact, leaving aside those particular elements that modern people might consider dated in his constitution—such as his support of parliamentary representation based on property ownership—it is still true that it contains an extraordinarily original combination of elements with particular meaning for our time. In fact, we can find in Rosmini's *costituzione* a "human and social rights" policy and a "property and individual rights" policy that we would identify nowadays with separate democratic or conservative agendas, but that our philosopher puts together without contradiction.

Rosmini is thus a supporter of both the importance of "material interests" and of "intellectual and moral capacities" (chap. 12), a critic of the welfare state and of the excesses of market competition, a defender of state intervention within the limits of the subsidiarity principle and of market freedom under juridical and moral rules. His *costituzione* is a sophisticated text and at the same time full of common sense. Its intelligent integration of different political traditions under the light of political prudence offers a very interesting example to follow in our own political and social debate.

Rosmini was perhaps the first Catholic thinker of the modern era who tried to assimilate the best elements of political and economic liberalism and combine them critically with the tradition of Christian philosophy. Criticizing many of the teachings of modern liberal thought, but also accepting many of its insights, he provided strong precedents for Catholic social teaching and the documents of the Second Vatican Council, both brilliantly synthesized in the thought of John Paul II. Thus, he has a very important place among Catholic philosophers and still offers the richness of his great work for those in our time who try to reflect on contemporary society from a Christian perspective.

—Carlos Hoevel

Notes

1. In English it was translated as *The Leopard*, by A. Colquhoun, Collins Harvill, UK, 1988.

2. In Milan he met his best friend, the great writer Alessandro Manzoni, who also became his fervent disciple.

3. "His politics is worthy especially as an effort of rooting a conception of society in a larger religious anthropology of Christian inspiration," Francesco Traniello, *Società religiosa e società civile in Rosmini*, Morcelliana, Brescia, 1997, 354 (author's translation).

4. Rosmini was born in the Trentino, a region under Austrian rule.

5. The importance of the economic factor in the history of society is extensively explained in Rosmini's *Naturale costituzione della società civile*.

6. The theory of the right of property is mainly developed by Rosmini in his *Filosofia del diritto* (*Philosophy of Right*). For the importance of the philosophical concept of "property" in Rosmini see "Uomo ed economia in Rosmini" ("Man and economy in Rosmini"), *Rivista di Filosofia neo-scolastica*, aprile-giugno 1995, 219, 248 and the chapter dedicated to property in Pietro Piovani, *La teodicea sociale di Rosmini*, Cedam, Padova, 1957.

7. "What is, then, the universal vote in this assumption, and what does it involve? It is, and it involves, an equal amount of power in the writing of the laws granted to all citizens regardless of the major or minor groups of rights that each citizen possesses or represents" (chap. 9).

8. "We can expect economy from men who spend their own, but how can we expect it when they spend what belongs to others, and with somebody else's money, which they dispose of by law, they can buy the glory of doing great and beautiful things? For those who have little or nothing, it is of very little importance whether the finances of the state are administered with economy or not" (chap. 9). "These legislators are inclined to let the government into all those enterprises that should be freely left to private industry, and often inclined to reserve to the government itself the monopoly, because they care very little about the damage that is caused to private entrepreneurs and to capitalists" (chap. 9). Eventually Rosmini stresses his point by arguing that universal suffrage leads almost necessarily to economic socialism: "an equal vote in the election of deputies eventually leads to socialism as a result; and that this system tends to convert the whole nation into one gigantic factory, into one immense manufacturing plant where the only entrepreneur is the government" (chap. 9). In this same line of argument he praises the English tradition on the subject: "only England so far has understood well that it is convenient for the government not to substitute itself for private industry" (chap. 9).

9. This phrase is almost literally the same as this one by Burke: "Let those large proprietors be what they will . . . they are, at the very worst, the ballast in the vessel of the commonwealth." *Reflections on the Revolution in France*, Hackett, Indianapolis/Cambridge, 1987, 45. In the *Naturale costituzione della società civile* Rosmini explains the historical basis of real representation that originated in Rome and then continued in European history. He defends this kind of representation against the arguments of the "levelers," "radicals" and other sympathizers of the French Revolution in England who tried to prove that the English constitution was originally based on personal representation, a point that our philosopher considers historically false.

10. On this point we follow the interpretation of Francesco Traniello who believes that "the solutions offered to the problem of authority by the fascinating rhetoric of de Maistre and of the brilliant formulas of traditionalists were not sufficient for Rosmini" Francesco Traniello (1997), (author's translation), 45.

11. "One of the major mistakes of a century that had it all, was to believe that a political constitution could be written and created *a priori* . . . a constitution is a divine work, what is most fundamentally and essentially constitutional in the laws of a nation cannot be written," Joseph de Maistre, *Ensayo sobre el principio generador de las Constituciones políticas y de las demás instituciones humanas*, (*Essay on the Generative Principle of Political Constitutions and Other Human Institutions*)" Dictio Edit., Bs. As., 1980, 215. "The science of constructing a commonwealth, or renovating it, or reforming it, is, like every other experimental science, not to be taught *a priori*." *Reflections on the Revolution in France*, Hackett, Indianapolis/Cambridge, 1987, 53.

12. "And in spite of such fatal experiences, the faith of the people in written political constitutions never declined. Rather, they all rushed on them with growing ardour and hope, and it has become universal that feeling that a civilized nation cannot flourish and reach its natural and godly destiny, or if the organic form of its government is not constitutional. This opinion is what I myself strictly profess and nothing could divert my soul from this persuasion" (chap. I).

13. Joseph de Maistre, *Ensayo sobre el principio generador de las Constituciones políticas y de las demás instituciones humanas*, (*Essay on the Generative Principle of Political Constitutions and other Human Institutions*)," op. cit. 211.

14. Edmund Burke, *Reflections on the Revolution in France*, Hackett, Indianapolis/ Cambridge, 1987, 54.

15. Rosmini's interpretation of natural right, which includes a personal integration of elements that come from the Ancient Greeks and Romans, the Fathers of the Church, Saint Thomas Aquinas, the Catholic and Protestant Scholastics, Locke, Rousseau, and many other authors (especially the Saboyan Segismonde Gerdil and the Italian Faletti) is contained mainly in his *Filosofia della Politica* (*Philosophy of Politics*) and his *Filosofia del diritto* (*Philosophy of Right*).

16. This is, in my view, the questionable interpretation of, for example, Danilo Zolo who affirms that "Rosmini's liberalism shows . . . its aristocratic origins and its classist horizon," Danilo Zolo, (1963), 309.

17. Edmund Burke, *Reflections on the Revolution in France*, Hackett, Indianapolis/ Cambridge, 1987, 54.

18. Rosmini's critique of utilitarianism is one of the major themes of his whole work developed from his early writings up to his mature works.

19. Rosmini rejects the reduction of politics to the utilitarian calculus that is distinctive of both radical and conservative utilitarianism. Cf. Burke *op. cit.*, 54: "The rights of men in governments are their advantages; and these are often in balances between differences of good, in compromises between good and evil, and sometimes between evil and evil. Political reason is a computing principle: adding, substracting, multiplying and dividing, morally not metaphysically or mathematically . . ."

20. "When the aversion of the people to the absolutism of princes exploded in modern times, instead of combating the absolutism itself, only one of its special forms was fought—and thus this radical vice of societies just changed its form" (chap. 7).

21. This is the opinion of Carlo Gray who, on the other hand, believes that Rosmini did not take into account American's Supreme Court to conceive his idea of the Political Tribunal. Cfr.: *Progetti di costituzione*, Saggi editi ed inediti sullo stato, con introduzione a cura di Carlo Gray, Fratelli Boca Editori, Milano, 1952, p. XVII. About the influence of Giammaria Ortes see Francesco Traniello's fundamental article "Una fonte veneta del pensiero politico-religioso di Rosmini: Giammaria Ortes" ("A Venetian source of the political and religious thought of Rosmini: Giammaria Ortes"), *Rosmini e il rosmineanesimo nel Veneto*, Casa Editrici Mazziana, Verona, 1970, 113–27.

22. "Freedom of conscience must be inviolable" (chap. 7).

23. "The Catholic religion does not need dynastic protections, but freedom: it needs its freedom protected and nothing else" (chap. 7). The need for the Church's separation from the state and for her devotion exclusively to her spiritual mission is extensively explained by Rosmini in his famous *Delle cinque piague della Santa Chiesa* (*On the Five Wounds of the Holy Church*).

24. "It is important that the true quantity of wealth of every citizen is known rather than hidden," chap. 9.

25. Rosmini's theory of property is very important to understand not only his political thought but also the principles and point of departure of his economic thought. Beyond all the similarities in the field of political and economic ideas, Rosmini disagrees with many of the *principles* sustained by the founders of classical political and economic liberalism. Rosmini rejects the Lockean idea that the right of property is based just on labour:

"to see solely in work the universal foundation of the right of property is not to take into account that the essence of right is moral . . ." *Filosofia del diritto* (*Philosophy of Right*), n. 368. On the contrary, according to Rosmini, the right of property is based on the physical and moral relation of the human person with economic goods.

26. Rosmini's fiscal philosophy, that goes beyond French democratism and English conservatism "where taxes are decreed by one class of citizen at the expense of the others—whether that class is that of the rich as it is in the English constitution, or that of the small proprietors and proletarians as it is in the French-style constitutions" (chap. 9) is one of the strongest pillars of his whole political and economic system.

27. Rosmini discuses extensively throughout his anthropological, ethical and political works on the subject of the relationships of the utilitarian and moral tendencies in the human being. His point of view is severely critical towards utilitarianism. Starting from his famous early debate with the Italian economist Melchiorre Gioia—a follower of Jeremy Bentham's doctrines—the Roveretan has always thought that the utilitarian explanations of human action ignore the capacity of human beings to go beyond self-interest or subjectivity, despising what Rosmini calls the "objective powers" of human beings. However, Rosmini has also always rejected the kind of moralism that denies the importance of self-interest and utility, especially in the economic sphere. Rosmini's attempt has always been to demonstrate the priority of objectivity and morality in human action and the subordination of utility as a derivative concept from the former. See especially *Society and its Purpose* (1994), bk. 2, chap. 2, "Human Good."

28. It is well known that Rosmini admired Adam Smith deeply: "a man worthy of great praise" (*Saggi di Scienza Politica*, [1933] p. 19, n. 1.) and supported the Smithian ideal of a "natural distribution of wealth": "I believe with Adam Smith that the most useful distribution of wealth is done by the nature of things in itself," *Opere inedite di politica*, (1923), 136–37. In that sense Rosmini shares in *general* Smith's principles of political economy based on free commerce, competition, and a strong critique of an "entrepreneurial state." However, Rosmini has some important differences with Smith in the way he interprets the meaning of this "natural distribution." Rosmini does not share Smith's naturalistic idea that individual economic interests are always necessarily directed to the common good: "Adam Smith, talking about material interests . . . tries to demonstrate that private interest is the one that forms the public interest. There is certainly a true element in this phrase. Smith will always deserve to be praised for having shed light on a fact not sufficiently observed before him. But it is one thing to say that private interests, generally speaking, exert a considerable grade of influence in the formation of the public good and another thing to say that always and without exception both coincide. This is the excess of a true proposition and this is what is false in Smith's doctrine." *Storia comparativa e critica dei sistema intorno al principio della morale*, (1941), 379–80. Rosmini believes that the freedom of economic interests, accepted as a general principle, should be regulated by prudence according to the concrete historical and cultural conditions, which implies a juridical and even a political orientation of economic interests: "the more is the inertness and ignorance of a people, the more has to be the government's action that limits the activity of commerce and industry. Therefore, I cannot accept the opinion of Adam Smith and his followers: that the private interest is always perfectly instructed and does never make any mistake even if considered in an entire nation: it is a fact that sometimes the opposite is the truth when we take into account the people's cultural level. *Opere inedite di politica*, (1923), 139–40. These and other passages show that, although Rosmini

is one Catholic philosopher who admires and follows many of Adam Smith's ideas, it would be nevertheless a mistake to interpret Rosmini's economic thought from an exclusive Smithian perspective.

29. One of Rosmini's most interesting insights was his critique of the totalitarian tendencies he saw incarnated in the expansion of government's planning. This critique can be seen throughout all his works but is especially developed in his *Saggio sul Comunismo e il Socialismo* (1978) (Essay on Communism and Socialism).

30. Rosmini is in favor of economic competition but always within the limits of "rational right" (extra-social and social right): "For juridical competition we understand competition within the limits of right, competition protected by rational right. Do not forget that we never talk about an unlimited competition: we propose the cause of a competition that is limited by rational right, and nothing different from that." *Filosofia del diritto*, n. 1479, note 1. Some of the juridical principles closely connected to economic activity presented in the text of the *costituzione* are: the right of property, the right of acquiring property, and the right of free commerce. All these are helped by other juridical means such as the supression of trusts, the possibility of expropriation in case of abuse of the right of property, etc.

31. One of Rosmini's most important insights is that politics, dealing always with particular situations, needs to "determine the *modalities*" of rights "for the common good," always taking into account that it also has "to preserve the whole value of that right" (chap. 7). For example, although the right of free commerce and free industry is "in general" a natural right, "a just and wise government" should be prepared to "determine the modality" of this right. Thus a temporal commercial protection of the industries and commerce of a country from the competition of others would be justified in the case of a country "where the prohibition system has prevailed," where "local capital investments," management "competence" or even capitalists' "initiative" are not sufficient (chap. 9). Rosmini believes that these kinds of economic protections should be always "temporal" until the country reaches the capacity of fully free competition that is the "natural state of full freedom" (chap. 9). Rosmini uses the same arguments to justify other cases of state economic interventions.

32. "That what the citizens do by themselves is more economical than that which is done for them by others, especially by the government," *Opere inedite di politica*, (1923), 64 (author's translation).

33. See *Filosofia del diritto*, n. 2147.

34. "Profitable enterprises that the state takes over bring two great evils to the nation: they take away branches of industry from the citizens and they make them less productive and sometimes even non-productive or passive. And even in the case when they would yield a considerable income to the state, such income would benefit some but not all citizens, nor would it be distributed in function of individual income" (chap. 9).

35. Certainly in the *costituzione* but especially in his work *La costituente del regno dell' Alta Italia* Rosmini demonstrates that he is well acquainted with the so-called "social question" in which he includes what he calls "the great question of workers," "the great question of pauperism" and "the great problem of employing people." In the second text, he argues against what he considers as "two extremes" in relation to the question. On the one hand, he rejects the opinion of the ones who believe that the government should not give any kind of positive help to the poor or unemployed, limiting its functions just to the sole "regulation of individual rights." On the other hand, he rejects the opinion of the defenders of a welfare state that propose an unlimited "beneficence" of the state to every

possible need or desire of individuals. Rosmini calls his own opinion "a middle term between these two extremes." The state has certainly the juridical obligation of assisting the poor in case of extreme need. However, a continuous assistance beyond this extreme situation would eventually lead to an even worse situation. Rosmini foresees that a welfare state would eventually be unable to pay its costs and at the same time would undermine individual initiative and private associations. But his greatest fear is the degradation of the liberty and moral dignity of the human being. Thus, the best way to help the poor and unemployed is to leave free the "founts of private beneficence" and "civil association" but, above all, to promote access to property by means of genuine jobs created by free competition, moderated by moral values introduced through education.

36. *La costituente del regno dell' Alta Italia*, 266.

37. Both problems are explained by Rosmini in *Society and Its Purpose* (1994), bk. 4 "Psychological laws according to which civil societies move towards or away from their end."

38. Moral virtue as the principle and the end of civil or political society is Rosmini's main idea of his political philosophy. It is precisely on this anthropological and ethical point that we can find Rosmini's main differences especially with utilitarianism—socialist, liberal or conservative—which sees pleasure or material utility as the engine and the goal of society. According to Rosmini, utilitarianism has an external conception of political life that is born from a conception of the human being that forgets man's spiritual and interior dimension which is the real end of politics. For Rosmini's idea of virtue as the heart of society see: *Society and Its Purpose* (1994), especially book 2, "The end of society."

39. See *Society and Its Purpose* (1994), especially book 1, chapter 2 "The social bond."

FOREWORD

Property and Liberty: The Development of Antonio Rosmini's Political Thought

The Constitution under Social Justice is the ultimate contribution of Antonio Rosmini to political theory. A man endowed with great talents—priest, founder of orders, scholar—Rosmini left behind himself an enormous body of scholarship and writings: the still incomplete critical edition of his works will include more than one hundred books. His contribution covered a wide variety of subjects and themes, ranging from religion and metaphysics to anthropology and economics. In this vast landscape of intellectual achievements, political philosophy occupies a small area—but Rosmini's contributions in this field are noteworthy and often illuminating. If their originality is not properly appraised within the community of specialists of this discipline, particularly among those of a classical liberal persuasion, it is largely because of the limited availability of his works within the Anglo-Saxon world—English today being the *lingua franca* not just of business but of intellectual research too.

If the translation of *La costituzione secondo la giustizia sociale* fills a gap, providing English speaking scholars with a synthetic but inspired account of Rosmini's thinking on a variety of important issues (most notably, the nature of constitutionalism, the impact and the importance of the French Revolution, the limits of government action), it is necessary to stress how such a work *intimately* belongs to Rosmini's theoretical elaboration.

This essay seeks to present, albeit briefly, the development of Antonio Rosmini's political thought over time, by providing a sketch of his life and a summary of the major tenants of his thinking, in the realm of political philosophy.

It will therefore not enter into a detailed discussion of Rosmini's contributions in other fields—which are indeed numerous, and should be considered so as to appreciate the global value of his thought. Rather it will trace the key ideas presented in *The Constitution under Social Justice*, showing the consistency of Rosmini's elaboration of a political philosophy. For this purpose, we first examine some of the most relevant moments of his life, in the light of his theoretical elaboration, and will later focus on the persistence in his writings of two particular ideas which are indicative of Rosmini's approach. Given an understanding of the key issues of political philosophy as questions of justice related to the proper definition of government's sphere vis-à-vis civil society, the two central Rosmini ideas upon which we focus are the definition of the institution of private property as central for the maintenance of individual liberty and, the subsequent limitation of popular sovereignty that is implied in such a strong vision of property.[1]

A Brief Life of Antonio Rosmini

Antonio Rosmini-Serbati[2] was born on March 24, 1797, in one of the richest and noblest families of the city of Rovereto (a town of nine thousand inhabitants in Trentino, then part of the Austrian Empire).[3] Having learned to read at home, mainly from the Bible, the young Antonio began school at the age of seven, completing the normal course, and simultaneously educated himself as a polymath in his uncle's library. By the age of sixteen, Antonio had already become acquainted with the classics and may have already matured in the choice of his priestly vocation. "This year," he wrote in his diary, "was for me a year of grace: God opened my eyes on many things, and I understood that there is no other true wisdom than in God."[4] His ordination to the priesthood took place on April 21, 1821. As Clemente Rebora [1885–1957] suggestively noted, "ever since his adolescence, his great faith transformed his inner life into a vast shining sky."[5]

The young man's higher studies were completed in theology at the University of Padua (a notable center of Aristotelian philosophy) where he also studied medicine in some depth, graduating on June 22, 1823. It was in Padua that Antonio met for the first time Niccolò Tommaseo [1802–1874] who was to become a leading Italian intellectual and a lifelong friend.

Throughout his life, Rosmini was not only remarkable for his studiousness but also for his spiritual intensity.[6] It is his faith that motivated him, as a very young man, to be as much of a *doer* as possible, endlessly trying to pursue good projects for the greater glory of God. In particular, in addition to various charitable undertakings, in the university year he envisioned compiling a *Christian Encyclopedia*—a work that could respond on equal basis of scholarship to the Encyclopedia of the Illuminists. But with time, and after seeing many of his projects failing, he realized the necessity of a rule of life to put his dramatic enthusiasm under control and to allow the best of his efforts to bear fruits. Following

Saint Thomas Aquinas [1224–1274]—"anybody easily believes what he likes"[7]—he wanted to avoid "confus[ing] his will with God's"[8] and so decided to focus on his continuous self-amendment, but also to accept social and charitable duties insofar as Providence offered them to him. This rule is his famous *principle of passivity*: the idea that true wisdom dictated immediate attention to his own holiness but also acceptance of mundane work insofar as it showed itself as a part of God's calling. To the judgment of contemporaries and biographers, he succeeded in combining a prayerful life with readiness to undertake whatever work for his neighbor should be placed in his path by Providence.

From 1821 to 1828, Rosmini devoted himself to study first in Rovereto, where he had inherited the considerable family fortune on the death of his father and, later, in Milan where he was able to take advantage of the facilities provided by the great libraries in the city. In 1823, Rosmini went for the first time to Rome where he met Cardinal Castiglioni [1761–1830] (later Pius VIII) and Cardinal Cappellari [1765–1846] (later Gregory XVI). His most enduring memory of the journey was a talk that he had with Pope Pius VII [1742–1823] who encouraged him to persevere in his philosophical studies. As soon as the pope had passed away on August 20 that same year, Rosmini produced a eulogy of Pius VII,[9] which would not be published until eight years later because of Austrian censorship. It is indeed far more than a simple obituary and is also relevant to our analysis, since one of the themes Rosmini touches upon in celebrating Pius VII is the latter's defense of property owners against the Jacobin "illusion of a public good."[10]

Rosmini's life in the Church was profoundly changed by an invitation to collaborate in the foundation of a religious order of men, the "Institute of Charity." This was intended to correspond to the institute for women founded by Maddalena di Canossa [1774–1835]. These efforts came to fruition in a practical sense when he took the opportunity to leave the comfort of Milan in 1828 for an isolated sanctuary at Domodossola, a Piedmontese town near the Swiss border. In May 1829, he again visited Rome, where Pope Pius VIII acknowledged the importance of his studies. "It is God's will," he said, "that you devote yourself to writing books. That is your vocation."[11]

The last twenty-five years of Rosmini's life were marked not only by his literary activity and the governing of his religious institute but also by a crescendo of opposition from political and religious adversaries. The year 1848 was an occasion for a profound turn of tide both for his life as a man of faith and as a scholar. Rosmini very much welcomed the revolutionary uprisings, especially as far as Italy was concerned: "I watch with close attention what it is happening in Italy, and I seem to see, beyond all the manipulations of men, the hand of God."[12] Consequently, he found it appropriate to try to influence events to some extent. In March, as soon as he understood that Pius IX [1792–1878] was willing to grant a constitution to the papal states, he elaborated a tentative project, which he sent directly to the pope on March 11.

The pope granted the constitution on March 14, before Rosmini's letter had a chance to reach him.[13] At the same time, Rosmini, who was a close friend of Gustavo Benso di Cavour [1806–1864], the elder brother of Camillo Benso di Cavour [1810–1861], began to contribute to the latter's journal, *Il Risorgimento*.[14] As soon as Gabrio Casati [1798–1873] became head of the Piedmontese government, he bestowed on Rosmini the very difficult task of trying to negotiate a concordat between the pope and the Piedmontese state and to convince Pius IX of the opportunity to create a confederation of Italian states, to be led by the pope himself. Rosmini seemed to be particularly welcomed by Pius IX. Despite the fact that the government that succeeded Casati's in Piedmont lost interest in these projects, Rosmini became involved in Vatican politics at the service of the pope. At a certain point, he was asked to assume the leadership of the government after the assassination of Prime Minister Pellegrino Rossi [1787–1848]. He refused, however, to do so.

At the pope's request, Rosmini accompanied the pope on his flight from Rome to Gaeta. Here, the relationship between Rosmini and the Roman Curia began to change[15]—so dramatically that he felt obliged to move to Naples. A few weeks later, Rosmini returned to Gaeta and received the news of the listing of his *Delle cinque piaghe della santa Chiesa*[16] and this very *La costituzione secondo la giustizia sociale* on the Index of Forbidden Books. This caused him immense pain. Dismissed by the pope, Rosmini returned to his house in Stresa where he peacefully spent the rest of his life, but the polemics on his writings did not reach an end with his death. In 1887, the Sant'Uffizio promulgated a decree *Post Obitum*, which stated that forty propositions extracted from Rosmini's works were not "conformed to the Catholic truth."[17]

In spite of growing Rosminian scholarship throughout the twentieth century, this condemnation lasted until the pontificate of Karol Wojtyla (1920–2005). In a private audience with the Rosminian fathers on November 10, 1988, Pope John Paul II expressed words of esteem for Rosmini's "intense intellectual work . . . so sensible to the great problem of the harmony between reason and faith."[18] Later, the pope opened the cause of beatification of Rosmini, and in his encyclical letter *Fides et Ratio* mentioned him among "significant examples of a process of philosophical enquiry that was enriched by engaging the data of faith."[19]

Finally, it was on July 1, 2001, that the Congregation for the Doctrine of the Faith, in a *Nota* signed by Cardinal Joseph Ratzinger (later Pope Benedict XVI) and Cardinal Tarcisio Bertone, completely repealed the *Post Obitum*: "The motives for doctrinal and prudential concern and difficulty that determined the promulgation of the Decree *Post Obitum* with the condemnation of the 'Forty Propositions' taken from the works of Antonio Rosmini can now be considered superseded. This is so because the meaning of the propositions, as understood and condemned by the Decree, does not belong to the authentic position of Rosmini but to conclusions that may possibly have been drawn from the reading of his works."[20]

Rosmini on Property, Taxes, and the State

The Constitution under Social Justice is the last political text Antonio Rosmini published in his lifetime. It is true that this book has an evident contingent nature. It is hugely indebted to, and influenced by, the historical context in which it was written.[21] But, at the very same time, this work summarizes its author's political thinking in its most refined stage. *A posteriori*, it is what may be called an "intellectual testament," and rightly so: Here, Rosmini engaged in the heroic effort of marrying the principles he believed with the reality he was living in. He did not escape from a theoretical dimension, but tried to forge a blueprint for a political order based on his fundamental intuitions of justice.

This exercise is far from being uncommon among political theorists—treaties of political philosophy have long taken the venerable form of speculations over the ideal political order. The fact that this literary genre was interpreted by Rosmini as an exercise in "applied constitutionalism" counts mainly for the *Zeitgeist*, as constitutions emerged as an affordable means to define the "genetic code" of a political order. The centrality of private property in this work cannot be underestimated. There is very little evidence that, as F. A. Hayek [1899–1992] apparently maintained, *The Constitution under Social Justice* made "more generally known" the term *social justice* "in its modern sense."[22] In Rosmini's book, very little counts for social justice in its modern understanding—this latter being viewed in light of John Rawls's [1921–2002] writings.[23] Rosmini does not call for social devices developing instruments of *equalization* (solving distributing problems by "equalizing utilities" was a solution "evidently wrong"),[24] either of starting points or of outcomes, nor does he subscribe to any vision of "equality" as something more than equality before the law. Instead, Rosmini belongs to a school that sees social justice in a manner quite opposite to the one Hayek sought to criticize.

This is apparent in his constitution. Next to the guarantee of personal liberties, the writer states clearly that, in the political order he envisions, "each property must be equally protected and guaranteed."[25] Reading article by article the constitution's draft, the importance of property within the scheme Rosmini is constructing strikes the reader as quite self-evident: Article 27 states that "all properties are inviolable" whereas article 30 clarifies the corollary, essential in Rosmini's view, that "all properties share the burden of the state in proportion to their income."[26] As Carlos Hoevel acutely notes in his introduction, political freedom and political representation are seriously related in Rosmini's thinking, even though they are not mingled as it frequently happens with modern conceptions of citizenship. Quite differently, Rosmini sharply distinguishes between basic rights of freedom, with which any citizen is equipped, and the right to vote. As Hoevel explains, "the reduction of government election exclusively to universal suffrage puts all the power of the state in the hands of an anonymous electoral mass of equal votes without any kind of connection to the different weight of their economic interests and rights and doing so leads inevitably to a political despotism of the majority which uses political power as an instrument of quick and easy ascension at the expense of the economic rights of groups and individuals legitimately gained in the economic realm."

Under Rosmini's constitution, on the other hand, franchise is based upon property—it is "proportional," that is, the "voting power" of each citizen is paralleled by the assets an individual owns. The right to vote is restricted to property owners: "no particular qualification is required by law to enjoy the right to vote, except the payment of direct taxation [income tax] to the state" (art. 58). The first chamber is composed of "the major property owners, the second one by the minor ones" (art. 51). This differentiation, between "major" and "minor" owners, is a "function of the direct taxation they pay to the state's treasury" (art. 52).[27]

Later in the text, Rosmini clarifies his thought in an unequivocal way: "the very equality of the electoral vote is itself an offence to property because (. . .) the electoral vote must be considered as an appendix, a portion of property right." As Hoevel's summary demonstrates, Rosmini is clearly concerned that unqualified (universal) franchise may open the door to redistribution and, so, expropriations. Because the *have nots* for any given thing are more numerous than the *haves*, and if we recognize that every individual has the same right to vote, then we give the *have nots* the opportunity to form coalitions, attain a majority, and eventually to exploit the *haves*. "How can the property of citizens be inviolable when those who have nothing or a few things can arbitrarily dispossess those who have a lot?" For him, "the possibility of acquiring property must be open to all citizens, so they can enrich themselves through their industry, through their labour and through their ingenuity—and this is certain. But it is equally certain that after having legitimately acquired possessions through the full freedom of action that has been guaranteed, the citizens must have their possessions kept safe and inviolable. Now, to say it once again, this cannot be achieved unless with a proportional suffrage system in the election of the electors."[28]

A one-man-one-vote democracy orders a civil society in a way in which it becomes "nothing but a big gambling game where some citizens are the house and are certain to win while others gamble all their properties in that house. All civil societies that have adopted a French type of constitution," Rosmini explains, "are just that (. . .) those civil societies are nothing more than *organized theft*. Rights are not truly inviolable if some way—no matter how covert or contrived—exists so that those rights can be violated with impunity by using some pretext, even if that pretext is—or acts on behalf of—positive law."[29]

In his mature political philosophy, Rosmini clearly associates the inviolability of the legitimate sphere of action of any person, with the inviolability of his property. The work in which he better explores this research path is his monumental *Philosophy of Right*, published between 1841 and 1845. Here, aiming to find a solid anchorage for the inviolability of the human person in reality, he looks for a clear-cut appraisal of human rights, inquiring about "a general character" of the human person: "a general character" that can be found in the small child as well as in the strong adult.

This "general character," Rosmini argues, is called "property." "This word *property* indicates the union of one thing (accident or substance) with another individual thing. This conjunction is stable and complete and brought about so exclusively that one thing is bound to another without being similarly bound to anything else."[30] This relationship of dominion between an owner and the thing that is owned is seen by Rosmini as characteristic of that "*personal* principle" that he considers the core of his own philosophy: "The very same act of appropriating something displays that consciousness that is typical of, and only of, the human person. Property represents "an entirely *personal* principle, involving *consciousness* and therefore presupposing an intelligent principle capable of reflecting upon itself and seeing itself objectively. . . . The *personal* principle, therefore, is the principle of *property*; SELF is the principle of what is PROPER TO ONESELF, of what is owned by self. 'Self' must exist before 'his' can exist. But self cannot exist except in an intellective being. Consequently, there can be no true *property*, nothing that is *proper to oneself* . . . except in an intellective being."[31]

Giuseppe Capograssi [1889–1956] explained that "the whole of his [Rosmini's] thought is here, and lies in the fact that the individual is a person. And the whole problem of law for him is enclosed in the concept of person."[32] If the strength of Antonio Rosmini's political thought can be seen in this momentous recognition of the centrality of the individual person, its normative originality lies clearly in this gushing emphasis on the importance of private property—"a sphere around the person in which the person is the center."[33] It is particularly noteworthy that this concern is not just central in *The Constitution under Social Justice*, nor comes to surface for the first time in the *Philosophy of Right*. It is actually one of the unifying characteristics—"substantially unaltered" of Rosmini's political thinking over time, from his very first exercises in the realm of political philosophy.[34]

The Development of Rosmini's Political Thought

Rosmini's thought on political and social issues, such as individual rights, property, the meaning of the French Revolution, and social justice, matured at a very early stage of his career and life. Born into a prominent aristocratic family, son of a loyal servant of the Habsburg Empire, the young Antonio distinctively absorbed and developed a lasting distrust toward the ideals and means of the French Jacobins. A malicious commentator, seeking to reduce an author's theory mainly to its autobiographical context, could perhaps trace Rosmini's eagerness to defend private property back to the fact that he was generously endowed with it by the caprice of fate. Such an approach would, however, pay little respect to our author.

On the other hand, it is quite safe to assess that it was probably due to the popular protests of 1821 (which resembled the French Revolution) that Rosmini began planning a systematic work on politics in 1822. At this point, he was already acquainted with the writings of restorationist Catholic thinkers such as François Rene de Chateaubriand [1768–1848], Luis de Bonald [1787–1870], and, especially, Joseph de Maistre [1753–1821]. Karl Ludwig Haller [1768–1854], among the leading theorists of Restoration, exercised the most relevant and lasting influence over the young Antonio.

Rosmini started working on a major contribution on politics in 1822—his *Politica prima*, which was not published during his lifetime, though it consumed much of his time during 1822–1826. His concentration on the text was rather intermittent, and this fact surely has impacted the completion of the treatise. This work has, however, a great relevance not just because it presents clearly the starting points of Rosmini's philosophical reflections on politics, but first and foremost because it allows the modern reader to see how some themes have always been an ingredient of Rosmini's though and thus can be understood as the central tenants of his thinking.[35]

The intermittent character of his capacity to articulate ideas, in this phase of his life, was well understood by his friend Niccolò Tommaseo, who, writing to him after having read some draft of the *Politica* in July 1823 expressed a severe judgment on the work. "Remove the rhetorical make-up: treat it with alum. It is night, and stormy." Mario D'Addio[36] notes that the *Politica prima* is a "work in progress," that it was written precisely in the moments in which Rosmini was getting familiar with a body of thinking, so its value can be seen as the one of a large *preparatory work* for more ambitious undertakings.

But what cannot be overestimated is the influence Haller exercised on the young Rosmini. "I tasted the great work of K. L. Haller, *Restauration of the Science of the State*. It is summa, you learn more by reading that sole work than by reading all those who wrote about public law."[37] A consistent examination of Rosmini's theoretical debt to Karl Ludwig von Haller was the one provided by Mario Sancipriano (1916–2004).[38] For Sancipriano, Haller's influence is present in the whole body of Rosmini's work, even though he accepts that such an influence almost fades away.[39] If Haller's influence was strong and substantial on Rosmini's first works, it must be stressed that even as a young man, Rosmini, in the words of Gioele Solari [1872–1952], "could not concur with the anthropological pessimism of Maistre, and with the determinism and pantheism implicit in his system, in which, while man and his freedom were diminished in the face of divine action, God was resolved in nature, time, and circumstances."[40] In a manner of speaking, his sympathies for the Restoration should be looked to under a different light than those of the great conservatives.

In many senses, a profound love of individual freedom always pervaded Rosmini's writings. D'Addio notes that the intent which inspires his early writings is to demonstrate the reasons why, explaining thus their expediency, "the power of the absolute monarchies of the Restoration ought to be limited, bringing them back to their original and intrinsic 'constitutional' nature, founded upon the balance of property and power."[41]

The "balance between property and power" is also a critical concern of Rosmini's elaboration. His approach to franchise, which, as we noted before, was his solution to political power's potential imperialism over civil society. Even before accepting a democratic (albeit limited) method of selecting the political class, he saw the individual citizen's property as the check to the sovereign's action. At this early stage, we can observe how Rosmini's concept of social life had property at its centre. It becomes even clearer as soon as we examine the eulogy of Pius VII that Rosmini wrote on the occasion of the pope's death, which is indeed marginally related to his political opinions but embodied the essence of his political thought. Here Rosmini considers the question of property, making the protection of property rights the litmus test of the difference between "a system based upon justice," and one grounded on "universal utility."[42] The first is the tradition of thought endorsed by Pius VII: "It decrees: *Consecrate property!* Everybody's own must be untouchable, not because of the power he may or may not retain but because of his own dignity. This is the only possible equality among men. Do not let charity, nor its name, be associated with crimes. It must not infringe those seals posed by God on everyone's property."[43] Rosmini is openly criticizing redistributive policies, which limit and seize private property in the name of compulsory benevolence.

The second system, which was propagated by the Napoleonic armies all over Europe, was instead "not generated by the experience of centuries, not by the course of human things, nor by the study of the eternal truth; it is rather the product of the fancies of those who nowadays call themselves philosophers."[44] The output of such a system is the attempt to "sacrifice any property to an illusion of public good."[45] Giuseppe Lorizio emphasized the tension between Pius VII and Napoleon in the *Panegirico a Pio VII* as an important element in the shaping of Rosmini's thinking.[46]

In essays composed between 1822 and 1825, and being part of the *Politica prima*, Rosmini enunciates two principles of justice which will be the mainstay of his political thought for his entire life: "Everyone's property must be so sacred as to not be violated for any reason" and "Original appropriation has to be considered a legitimate entitlement of ownership, as long as the appropriated thing was not yet someone else's property."[47]

In the same work, Rosmini closely links the defense of property with the problem of guaranteeing everyone's legitimate right to life. When all the properties are safe, life will never be in danger. The scope of society is thus the protection of property, because once property rights are guaranteed everything follows, and personal security comes as a consequence of the defense of private property.[48] At the time he wrote those words, Rosmini's vision of government was still one that might be labeled "patrimonialism," making a direct reference to Haller. Like Haller, he was indeed convinced of the superiority of monarchical rule but, on the basis that he believed the monarch to be the "owner" of a state, he would be far more likely to care about the development of the nation (it was his own patrimony and the heritage he was leaving to his dynasty) than any republican government, which lacked such an incentive. From the outset, Rosmini believed that government has to be "a property owners' business,"[49] and so he identified the monarch as somehow the owner of the biggest estate in a given country, thus the man who would have the right to govern it in order to achieve the protection of his own.

According to Sancipriano, Rosmini's thought changed in tone around 1826–1827, when he joined the ranks of those advocating constitutionalism. For Sancipriano, the key difference between the prior phase and the newer one was that Rosmini abandoned an argument for political order based upon "the force of the things," à la Haller, to adopt a vision more strictly based upon the natural rights of men.[50] By the same token, Danilo Zolo identified Rosmini's initial approach to politics as mainly "empiricist."[51] This view is shared by Solari, who similarly identified the turning point around 1826–1827. Up to that time, "Rosmini considered politics under a generally empirical point of view. Politics looked to him like a science of the means of government determined with historical and psycological criteria." Later on, "the problem of justice appeared to Rosmini as the problem of individual and natural justice, as a search for eternal principles of justice that neither individuals nor governors could escape."[52] After 1826–1827, the idea such that "governments are judged by the results," meaning that people do not mind being governed by men rather than by law if men govern them well,[53] would be unthinkable in a page of Rosmini. In a manner of speaking, it is at this moment that Rosmini adopts a clearer preference for the *iurisdictio* over the *gubernaculum*, in Charles McIlwain's [1881–1968] terminology.[54] Also, the subsequent *Filosofia della politica* (*Political Philosophy*), the first volume of which was published in 1837, the second in 1837, sees Rosmini burning bridges with any "empiricist" approach. He criticizes the eighteenth century for having been "a century of material subjects" that has "abandoned, vilified and annhilated all the sciences that apply to the spirit."[55] If he does not stop to see a space for a legitimate analysis of the *mechanics* of politics, in a manner of speaking, the investigation on the legitimated *ends* of associate life becomes far more important than any other thing.[56]

If we enter the question of Rosmini's thought concerning the legitimate form a government was to assume, it should be acknowledged that, especially when compared to his *Constitution under Social Justice*, his thinking about constitutional guarantees underwent modifications. In a fragment entitled "Del rispettar la proprietà" (On respecting property), he specifies that legitimate rule over a national territory belonged to the "owner" who had originally appropriated it.[57]

Significantly, Rosmini links the precept of respecting the king's estate to the universality of human beings' duty to respect others' property. "I see the prince as nothing but a great property-owner." Consequently, he states that the sovereign is himself bound to respect other individuals' ownership. If "he does not respect the law of property as soon as it favors someone else, he cannot ask any other to respect it to his own advantage."[58] Rosmini goes as far as to argue that "It was a false belief that the prince *qua* prince is exempted from this obligation [to respect other's property], even to the advance of society. "Salus reipublicae summa lex est" [the preservation of the state is the supreme law], this was the great axiom of these political [thinkers]. I, however, believe that, even for any good for the greater number, even to achieve salvation from extermination, no right can be taken from an individual without his consent, unless he himself caused the evil that is to be avoided."[59]

We can see here that, if Rosmini's vocabulary was different than his later one, his *ethos* was very similar—and if, for him, the king was a "property owner," in considering him as such he constantly underlined the duties of the owner before the people of the country he reigned over. Not surprisingly, his metaphor about property being "a sphere around a person," though in a slightly different formulation, is already present in this fragment.[60]

Solari suggested that "the political and legal conservatism of Rosmini was strictly tied to his economic conservatism founded upon land ownership."[61] Still, Rosmini does not seem to have always reduced property to the estate, and to have contemplated the existence of different kinds of ownerships (this is straightforwardly clear in *The Constitution under Social Justice*, where he goes as far as to defend "intellectual property," in article 33).

It is thus clear that even in Rosmini's early writings it is possible to discover a deep "distrust toward political power and the trust in private property" that, according to Danilo Zolo, "inspired in Rosmini a definition greatly reductive of the duties of the State."[62] Here we should note that Rosmini never subscribed to the vague notion of a social contract (an idea that he vehemently opposed), nor did he ever surrender to the idea of *raison d'Etat*. He always tried, perhaps sometimes unsuccessfully, to provide a realistic account of how political life works and to avoid the naiveté that he thought was prevalent among his contemporaries. But the distance that he was careful to keep between himself and theorists of the social contract is noteworthy. In the fourth book of the *Politica prima*, Rosmini warned that social contract doctrines must always end in revolution, because they prepare the ground for an unlimited vision of popular sovereignty, "regardless of what the princes themselves may think."[63] His arguments against social contract may have changed, but they all fit within the framework of a global critique of the notion of "sovereignty."

It can so be said that, from the beginning of his career,[64] Rosmini nurtured an ambition that was to be characteristic of all his future intellectual work: "the concern to erect a barrier against the modern doctrines of popular sovereignty," in the words of Francesco Traniello.[65] This is not solely a characteristic of those thinkers that we may label as "counter-revolutionary." The name of Benjamin Constant [1767–1830] instantly comes to mind when searching for others that devoted themselves precisely to assessing the impact of the doctrine of sovereignty.[66]

During the years between 1822 and 1827, when he began elaborating his political thinking, Rosmini engaged in a program of wide-ranging reading and thinking—an activity essential for shaping his thought on social issues in a definitive form. He went back to the most important writers of the Enlightenment, studying them in depth:[67] the Italians Melchiorre Gioia [1769–1829][68] and Gian Domenico Romagnosi [1761–1835], also Bolingbroke [1678–1751], Voltaire [1694–1778], Helvétius [1715–1771], Condorcet [1743–1794], and, with particular attention, David Hume [1711–1776]. He also chose to read economists such as Adam Smith [1723–1790], Thomas Malthus [1766–1834], Jean-Baptiste Say [1767–1832], and Jean Claude Leonard de Sismondi [1773–1842]. Smith, Say and Sismondi played a considerable role even in the *Politica prima*, and were a considerable influence in all Rosmini's life.[69]

As far as the development of Rosmini's liberal inclinations is concerned, it appears that a particular friendship played a role in it. Rosmini was close to two extremely important men of letters of his own time. The first was Niccolò Tommaseo, and the second was Alessandro Manzoni [1785–1873], author of *I promessi sposi* (*The Betrothed*), the novel that has become a canon of language and style for Italian writers ever since. Rosmini and Manzoni were enriched by each other's company.[70] Manzoni acknowledged the importance of Rosmini as the only contemporary Italian author worth reading.[71] Rosmini in turn commented on the manuscript of *I promessi sposi*, saying that it was "a marvel" and that "Manzoni is a historian of the human spirit."[72]

Given the extent to which Rosmini mentored Manzoni and helped him to fulfill his potential as writer and thinker,[73] it is also probable that Manzoni also had an impact on the development of his friend's thought, especially as far as economics was concerned. Manzoni spent five years in Paris (1805–1810) where he was a regular attendee at Sophie de Condorcet's [1748–1816] salon. There he had the opportunity to meet with the group of intellectuals known as the *Idéologues*.[74] Manzoni became well-acquainted with philologist Claude Fauriel [1772–1884]; historian Augustin Thierry [1795–1856]; and philosophers Pierre Jean George Cabanis [1757–1808] (officially trained as a doctor and a protégé of Anne-Jacques Robert Turgot [1727–1781]) and Antoine Destutt de Tracy [1754–1836], whose daughter Manzoni was even supposed to marry at a certain point. These authors, whom Manzoni greatly admired, gave him an unforgettable glimpse into eighteenth- and nineteenth-century liberalism.[75]

How important this fact turned out to be for the future development of Rosmini's thought is hard to say. We do know that, as close friends, Rosmini and Manzoni spent a great deal of time together discussing virtually every possible subject. It is also an established opinion among scholars that Rosmini was intellectually engaged with the ideas of the *Idéologues*. He was completely aware, as Francesco Traniello notes, of the emerging new historiography on the French Revolution, whose champions ("Thiers . . . Augustin Thierry . . . Guizot") he followed in their reasoning and perhaps borrowed some ideas from.[76] Of particular relevance for Rosmini was also his acquaintance with the writings of

Alexis de Tocqueville [1805–1859]. He strongly admired *Democracy in America*, and surely the denunciation of the tyranny of the majority by Tocqueville had an impact over him. "In democracies," he wrote in a footnote to his *Political Philosophy*, "it shows itself very terrible and very injust the tyranny of the majority. I refer the reader to the very true and very sensible reflections of Alexis de Tocqueville."[77]

It is not by chance that, after such a *tour de force* of readings (which stands next to a *tour de force* of writings),[78] Rosmini choose a more systematic approach while getting back to political question. Between 1837 and 1844, he published the two volumes of his *Political Philosophy* ("The Summary Cause for the Stability or Downfall of Human Societies" and "Society and Its Purpose"), followed by his *opus magnum*, the *Philosophy of Right*. The *Political Philosophy* is clearly indebted to the studies of anthropology and moral science that Rosmini conducted in those year. This work is best known for the fact it presented Rosmini's doctrine of "anti-perfectionism." His anthropological realism applied to the facts of politics brought Rosmini to reject boldy any ideological "idealization" of social affairs that he saw inherent in some of the leading doctrines of his time. Rosmini characterized perfectionism as a "system that believes perfection to be possible in human things, and which sacrifices today's goods to an imaginary future perfection . . . it consists of arrogant prejudice, for which human nature is judged too favorably."[79] Judging political options from "pure hypothesis," the risk is to elaborate theories that do not rest on a proper consideration of the "natural limits of things."[80] Rosmini's target is represented mainly by the utopianism of socialists, who dream of a property-less society: "all that happiness painted in the human imagination does not find any obstacle in imagination herself (. . .) but the lie, the problem, is met as soon as it [this imagination] is confronted with practise."[81] Getting away with property, however, is impossible because the "law of property" confronts men "with the mere alternative, either to accept it, or to devour themselves."[82] The absence of property will produce misery and need, which in turn will provoke crime and widespread aggression, which is the contrary of society itself.[83] Just ideology, for Rosmini, can "blind" men to the extent of not recognizing the importance of this institution.[84]

It is this very realistic vision of human beings and human societies which is at the core of Rosmini's sentiments toward the state. "Government is made of persons who, being men, are fallible."[85] This polemic against perfectionism resembles, to the contemporary readers, some pages of Hayek against central planning—as it emphasizes the fact legislators cannot be assumed omniscient whereas, on the other hand, it puts the burden of making meaningful decisions over their life on individuals. Indeed, in the essay on communism and socialism written in 1847 after Pius IX's encyclical letter *Qui Pluribus*, Rosmini calls utopians "false sages," and vindicates individualism by saying that "a man is not a machine"—by so meaning that he is not as mechanically predictable as prophets of planning would like him to be. These "monstrous utopias" are "the grave of liberalism and of any desiderable progress": communism and socialism "far from increasing the liberty of men and society, provide for them the most unheard of and absolute slavery, oppressing them under the heaviest, most despotic, most prickly, immoral and impious of all governments."[86]

It is, however, in the *Filosofia del diritto* (Philosophy of Right) that Rosmini's elaborations on property arrive at full completion. Pietro Piovani [1922–1980] eloquently argued that, in Rosmini, "the justification of the right of property can be traced back to what can be defined as the metaphysics of *proprium*, aiming to search within the intimate essence of any existing individuality the reason why each is what properly is, in its ontological origins."[87] But if the most recondite bases of his theory of property lie in his idea of *being*, that we cannot properly examine here, its most immediate foundations are to be founded in Rosmini's theory of the *person*. The human person is for Rosmini "an individual substantially intelligent, for there is a principle that is active, supreme, and incommunicable."[88] It is "the active and supreme principle, the foundation of person, which is informed by the *light* of reason, receives the rule of justice: It is, appropriately, the faculty of what is lawful. But since the dignity of the light of reason (ideal being) is limitless, thus nothing can outrank the personal principle, then nothing can outrank that principle that naturally operates behind a lord and master with infinite dignity. It follows, therefore, that it is a naturally *supreme* principle, thus no one has the right to command Him who commands the infinite. . . . Thus, the *Person* has in his very nature all the constituents of Law: He is subsisting Law, and the essence of Law."[89]

The roots of this fact are solely in man's relation with God. "There is no freedom whatsoever, if we consider man alone, in his relationship with himself and his fellows, and we abstract from his relationship to God. It is the absolute and divine morality what *consecrates* man and gives him the right title to an absolute inviolability."[90] The person cannot be anything different than "the first seat of freedom" for which property has to be a necessary ingredient of this very freedom." In Rosmini's system, "juridical freedom means nothing but the power that the person-proprietor has over his own thing, with which he can morally do what he pleases."[91]

The adjective "juridical" is explained by the fact that he is openly searching for the legitimate sphere of action of the individual in the political realm. In the first volume of the *Filosofia politica*, he is looking for a personal reformulation of the Kantian golden rule, or of the ethical principle, *alterum non laedere*. Rosmini finds the Kantian golden rule unsatisfactory. It does speak of an "arithmetically equal quantity of free action,"[92] but it seems unable to clarify "how much" this quantity must be. It seems to him to presuppose a substantial equality of men, which he finds impossible to conceive.

This is why he proposes an alternative principle, which has to serve as a rule to determine rights and obligations. This principle is summed up in a brief sentence, that has—as we saw—its precedent in the preliminary work of 1822–1826: "Respect that which belongs to others." Through this norm, Rosmini observes, "in the first place the *quantity of free* activity that each can have is assigned; that quantity is all that can be exercised without damaging somebody else's *property*. In the second place, *the quantity of limitation* that each must impose on his actions is assigned; such limitation consists not in one's own calculation, according to which he decides the point at which unimpeded activity is limited by the personal co-existence of others. Such calculation is impossible and without foundation. What matters is the *fact* that someone else's *property* exists, varies, and in its variation limits his own activity accordingly, but always justly. In the third place, a practical *reason* for the justice of the limiting *quantum* that each must impose on himself is to be given, and that reason consists in the universal ethical precept not to harm one's neighbor. Certainly, to harm in any way someone else's property is to harm one's neighbor. Thus, the activity of each person finds in someone else's property the moral limit that cannot be trespassed."[93]

The right to property then resides within "the moral law that forbids others from impeding the free disposition of what a person owns."[94] Rosmini sums up this concept in a metaphor: "property constitutes a *sphere* around the person in which the person is the *center*. No one else can enter this sphere, and no one can separate from the person that which is inherent in him as a result of the connection between him and what is his own. This kind of separation would cause *suffering* to the person. But suffering (considered in itself), when imposed upon a person, is forbidden as evil by the moral law."[95]

As was noted by one of the greatest scholars of Rosmini's political thought, Pietro Piovani, what Rosmini successfully accomplishes here is to translate the principle *alterum non laedere* in a more objective form, which anchors the concept of "harm" (*per se*, vague and indefinite) to the idea of property.[96] According to Rosmini, the very same "concept of freedom does not exist if completely deprived of property."[97] This argument was not tempered, for Rosmini, by the existence of social inequalities. In Piovani's synthesis, for our author property is a "projection of the profound individuality" of the single individual, a "social representation" of him. "Conceiving equality in properties is like conceiving the inconceivable existence of identical individuals, i.e., of non-individual individuals."[98] Respecting property is, thus, respecting the other as a human person: "properties have to be reciprocally respected because *the thing* of the other is *the other* [himself]."[99]

It seems clear that this approach brought Rosmini to adopt positions on social issues that would not have been popular among some Catholic thinkers of the twentieth century. His "intrinsically negative" vision of state interventionism[100] goes hand in hand with an approach to social inequality that is not common. One of Rosmini's greatest achievements is his *Theodicy*,[101] which is a work that, being devoted to exploring divine justice, ends up in reflecting upon social evil and its meaning. Danilo Zolo suggested that it is possible to find in Rosmini "a radical refusal" not just of the socialist doctrines but also "of the Catholic tradition on the theme of social inequality," "from Basil to Aquinas to Cajetan to

Innocent IX to Bossuet."[102] In his *Theodicy*, Rosmini argues that the scope of government is to enhance the overall good of society, which is not by any means to be equally redistributed among the members of the same society.[103] He also specifies that the (individual) "accumulation of goods," far from being immoral, is "the way to bring them [the goods] to bear more fruits."[104] Rosmini quotes the gospel: "Omni habenti dabitur et abundabit: ab eo autem qui non habet, et quod habet auferetur ab eo" (To everyone who has will be given more; but from the man who has not, even what he has will be taken away. Luke 19:26) to explain that "God gives more graces and gifts to him who is yet disposed toward making a good use of them"—Rosmini comes to speak of a "law of the accumulation of goods."[105] But this latter is but part of a refined understanding of human nature (that includes, among others, a "law of antagonism" that accounts for an explanation of conflict and competition alike), which is one of the riches of a complex work such as Rosmini's *Theodicy*.

By way of conclusion, we can underline what Pietro Piovani highlighted in the fifth chapter of his *Le teodicea sociale di Rosmini*, that is entitled *Le conseguenze liberali* (Liberal consequences), implicitly arguing that Rosmini's liberalism is so profoundly rooted in his own thinking that any of his political positions are nothing less than a natural "consequence" of his larger body of thinking. Piovani argued that Rosminian liberalism does not fit into a mere historical categorization within the citadel of "Catholic liberalism." It "belongs to the system of the social theodicy; it demands that social government respects the human individual as the Providential government respects him; it fears that an illiberal proposal of redistribution of temporal goods owned by civil society alters the naturally liberal nature of society itself."[106]

Government should respect the individual person as God does. *The Constitution under Social Justice* is the ultimate device that Rosmini provided us with, as to accomplish this very goal. His emphasis on property reflects this necessity. His political proposal to limit the franchise to property owners, which is a constant *refrain* in his political elaboration, was the instrument by which he was to make sure the government could not usurp property rights and, so, individual liberty.

A deep concern for the institution of private property, and the consciousness of the primary importance of its survival for the freedom of the individual in society, is among the qualifying aspects of Rosmini's approach to political questions. If property is understood theoretically as indivisible from a defense of individual action, on the ground of policy Rosmini constantly argued for limiting the franchise, immunizing property from collateral damage caused by inordinate democracy.

This point has been properly understood and emphasized by many commentators (such as, most notably, Piovani and Zolo),[107] but overlooked by others.[108] This is far from being surprising. Rosmini's contributions are vast and diversified, and people interested in his metaphysics can well be indifferent to his political thought. Also, the twentieth century was an era in which the values of classical liberalism have enjoyed a decreasing popularity, and would be indeed surprising if the community of Rosminian scholars made an exception to this rule. The fate of Rosmini's work within the Catholic Church has also influenced its reception.

The entire body of Rosmini's political thought, is permeated with a consistent understanding of private property that earns its author a prominent place among classical liberal thinkers. This small essay has tried to provide evidence that *The Constitution under Social Justice* should not be understood as an exception to Rosmini's thought, but rather as a completion of it. Whether Rosmini's teaching may or may not still be valuable is a matter of personal judgment. But for those Catholics that advocate freedom in the economic realm, that a Catholic author was so adamant in defending private property should be a reason for comfort, assurance, and pride.

—Alberto Mingardi

Notes

1. Part of what follows is based upon my "'A Sphere Around the Person': Antonio Rosmini on Property," *Markets and Morality*, 7, 1 (2004).

2. The original family name was "Rosmini," "Serbati" having been added by Antonio Rosmini's grandfather. See Umberto Muratore, *Conoscere Rosmini. Vita, pensiero, spiritualita'* (Stresa: Edizioni Rosminiane, 2002), 2.

3. During March 1797, when Antonio was born, Rovereto was actually occupied by the Napoleonic army but was returned to Austria the following October.

4. Antonio Rosmini, "Diario personale," in *Scritti autobiografici inediti*, ed. E. Castelli (Roma: Anonima Romana Editoriale, 1934), 419.

5. Clemente Rebora, *Rosmini*, ed. A. Valle (Rovereto: Longo, 1987), 144.

6. Saint John Bosco [1815–1888] once commented that: "I have never seen a priest saying Mass with as much devotion and piety as Rosmini. It was obvious that he had a tremendously vivid faith, from which sprung his charity, his sweetness, his modesty and his outside gravity." Giambattista Pagani and Guido Rossi, *La vita di Antonio Rosmini*, 2 vols. (Rovereto: Manfrini, 1959), 1:189.

7. Thomas Aquinas, *Summa Theologica*, 2,2, questione 60, article 3.

8. Umberto Muratore, *Rosmini. Profeta obbediente* (Milano: Paoline editoriale libri, 1995), 36.

9. Antonio Rosmini, *Panegirico alla santa e gloriosa memoria di Pio VII pontefice massimo* (Modena: Eredi Soliani Tipografi Reali, 1831).

10. Ibid., 112.

11. Quoted in Muratore, *Conoscere Rosmini*, 21.

12. Antonio Rosmini, *Epistolario completo*, ed. Rosminian Fathers, 13 vols. (Casale: Tipografia Giovanni Pane, 1887–1894), 10:194.

13. For Rosmini's draft of a constitution for the Papal States, see Antonio Rosmini, *Progetti di costituzione: Saggi editi e inediti sullo Stato*, ed. C. Gray (Milano: Fratelli Bocca, 1952), 3–63.

14. These articles have been collected in Antonio Rosmini, *La Costituente del regno dell'alta Italia*, now in *Scritti politici*, ed. U. Muratore. (Stresa: Edizioni Rosminiane, 1997), 273–328.

15. On the reasons that determined an increasing pressure on Rosmini to revise his views, even on political issues, see Muratore, *Conoscere Rosmini*, 30–32.

16. Antonio Rosmini, *Delle cinque piaghe della Santa Chiesa* (Roma: San Paolo Edizioni, [1848] 1997).

17. Quoted in Muratore, *Conoscere Rosmini*, 37.

18. See Giovanni Pusinieri and Remo Bessero Belti, *Rosmini* (Stresa: Edizioni Rosminiane, 1989), 214–16.

19. Pope John Paul II, Encyclical Letter *Fides et Ratio*, 1998, par. 74.

20. *Nota sul valore dei Decreti dottrinali concernenti il pensiero e le opere del Rev.do Sacerdote Antonio Rosmini Serbati*, n. 7, cfr. *Osservatore Romano*, June 30–July 1, 2001:5. See also http://www.rosmini.it/NotaCongrfede.htm.

21. The historical context of Rosmini's book is examined by Professor Carlos Hoevel in his Introduction.

22. Friedrich A. von Hayek, *Law, Legislation, and Liberty*, vol. 2, *The Mirage of Social Justice* (Chicago: University of Chicago Press, 1976), 176.

23. The most immediate reference is surely to John Rawls, *A Theory of Justice* (Oxford: Oxford University Press, 1971). For a very clear and accurate introduction to Rawls, see Chandran Kukathas and Philippe Pettit, *Rawls* (Cambridge: Polity Press, 1991).

24. Rosmini, *Filosofia del diritto*, II, par 1650.

25. *Infra*, chap. 2.

26. *Infra*, chap. 4.

27. *Infra*, chap. 4.

28. *Infra*, chap. 4.

29. *Infra*, chap. 4.

30. Rosmini, *Filosofia del diritto*, vol. 1, par. 333

31. Ibid., vol. 1, par. 338.

32. Giuseppe Capograssi, "Il diritto secondo Rosmini," in *Opere* (Milano: Giuffré, 1959 [1940]), V, 329.

33. Rosmini, *Filosofia del diritto*, vol. 1, par. 341.

34. Writing in particular on the subject of the "qualified" franchise, Pietro Piovani pointed out that Rosmini's positions were "substantially unaltered in the young and in the mature Rosmini." Pietro Piovani, "Rosmini e il socialismo risorgimentale," *Rivista Internazionale di Filosofia del diritto*, 1951, 87. Various commentators, however, pointed out that, if his approach to the issue of franchise and the right to vote remained identical, Rosmini anyhow "changed" (i.e., "enlarged") the class that he identified with property owners during time—from a definition of property based upon the estate, to one that included also merchants and traders. See, in particular, Francesco Traniello, *Società religiosa e società civile in Rosmini* (Bologna: Il Mulino, 1966), 114–16.

35. Rosmini's *Politica prima* is now beautifully available in a new edition edited by Mario D'Addio. Antonio Rosmini, *Politica prima*, ed. M. D'Addio (Roma: Città nuova), 2003.

36. Mario D'Addio, "Introduzione" to *Politica prima*, 15.

37. Quoted in Pagani and Rossi, *Vita*, vol. I, 363.

38. Mario Sancipriano, *Il pensiero politico di Haller e Rosmini*, Milano: Marzorati, 1968.

39. Sancipriano, 237–38.

40. Gioele Solari, *Rosmini inedito: La formazione del pensiero politico (1822–1827)* (Stresa: Edizioni Rosminiane, 2000), 73–74.

41. D'Addio, "Introduzione," 33.

42. Rosmini, *Panegirico alla santa e gloriosa memoria di Pio VII*, 106, 110.

43. Ibid., 106. I have availed myself of some liberty in translating this rather archaic passage, which in Italian reads as follows: "Decreta: *si consacri la proprietà*. Non la potenza congiunta, ma la propria dignità, renda il suo inviolato a tutti: ecco la uguaglianza degli uomini. Non cammini la beneficienza o il nome di essa in su' delitti: non muova un passo, che dopo aver visitati, sarei per dire, e trovati saldi i suggelli posti da Dio in sulla proprietà di ognuno."

44. Ibid., 108.

45. Ibid., 112.

46. Giuseppe Lorizio, *Eschaton e storia nel pensiero di Antonio Rosmini. Genesi e analisi della Teodicea in prospettiva teologica* (Rome: Gregorian University Press, 1988), 58.

47. Antonio Rosmini, *Saggi di scienza politica. Scritti inediti*, ed. G. B. Nicola (1822; reprint, Torino: Paravia, 1933), 88. Now also in *Politica prima.*

48. Ibid., 105.

49. Ibid.

50. Sancipriano, *Il pensiero politico di Haller e Rosmini*, 147–48.

51. Danilo Zolo, *Il personalismo rosminiano. Studio sul pensiero politico di Rosmini* (Brescia: Morcelliana, 1963), passim.

52. Gioele Solari, *Studi Rosminiani*, 162–63.

53. Cfr. Antonio Rosmini, *Politica prima*, 166–67.

54. Cfr, Charles McIlwain, *Constitutionalism: Ancient and Modern* (New York: Cornell University Press, 1947).

55. Antonio Rosmini, *Filosofia della politica*, ed. M. D'Addio (1887; reprint, Milan, Italy: Marzorati, 1981), 116.

56. Ibid., 126–27.

57. Fragment on *Del rispettar la proprietà*, typescript in Antonio Rosmini, *Opere inedite di politica*, ed. G. B. Nicola (Milano: 1923), conserved in the Rosminian library in Stresa, 26ff. Original manuscript available in the Rosminian archive in Stresa (A II—34). This fragment has recently been made available to a wider readership in *Elites* 2 (2003), 138–50, with an introduction by the present author. Now included in the *Politica prima*, 630–49.

58. Ibid.

59. Ibid., 28–29. I have availed myself of some liberty in translating this rather archaic passage. The original reads as follows: "Falsamente pertanto si credette da qualcuni dispensato il principe come tale da questa obbligazione, quando altramente volesse il vantaggio della società: Salus reipublicae summa lex esto; fu il grande assioma di questi politici. Noi all'incontro crediamo che per qualunque bene del maggior numero, anche per la salvezza dello sterminio non si possa togliere un diritto ad un singolo quando egli non lo consenta o quando del male che si teme egli non ne abbia la colpa."

60. Ibid., 5.

61. Gioele Solari, *Studi Rosminiani*, ed. by P. Piovani, (Milano: Giuffré, 1957), 97.

62. Danilo Zolo, "Governo temporale e 'senso ecclesiastico': Critica del temporalismo cattolico in Antonio Rosmini," in *Filosofia e diritti: Rosmini e la cultura della Restaurazione*, ed. Giorgio Campanini and Francesco Traniello (Brescia: Morcelliana, 1993), 192.

63. Cfr. Antonio Rosmini, *Politica prima*, 209–11.

64. Significantly, in his eulogy of Pius VII, Rosmini focuses on the role played by the popes, in their struggle with feudal princes and emperors, to generate those principles of law that constitute the European legacy of freedom. Even on that occasion, he emphasizes the fact that the popes never "consecrated [the doctrine of] sovereignty." *Panegirico alla santa e gloriosa memoria di Pio VII*, 107.

65. Francesco Traniello, *Società religiosa e società civile in Rosmini*, 275.

66. Nicholas Capaldi aptly summarized Constant's "research program" in his introduction to the *Principles of Politics*, "Constant, like Mme. de Stael, sought to explain how Rousseau's notion of the general will had been used by Robespierre and others to transform the French Revolution into the Reign of Terror." Nicholas Capaldi, "Introduction" in Benjamin Constant, *Principles of Politics Applicable to All Governments*, ed. Dennis O'Keefe (Indianapolis: Liberty Fund, 2003 [1810]).

67. On Rosmini's acquaintance with Enlightenment thinkers, see Aavv, *Rosmini e l'illuminismo: Atti del XXI Corso della "Cattedra Rosmini"*, ed. P. Pellegrino (Stresa: Sodalitas-Spes, 1988).

68. Rosmini was a striking critic of Gioia: for the latter, the central moment in economic life was not capital accumulation, but rather consumption—by believing that consumption was the necessary engine of the economy, Gioia was conceiving progress as a consequence of an inflation in the number of men and women's needs. This idea of stimulating material need as to grow society could not be accepted by Rosmini, who confronted it in numerous essays. For example, see Rosmini, *Filosofia politica*, 400–420. For an extensive and illuminating treatment of the dispute between Rosmini and Gioia, see Solari, *Studi rosminiani*, 223–64.

69. In explaining Rosmini's deep grasp of economics, Piovani aptly pointed out how, thanks to his vast readings in the subject, Rosmini rejected "the idealization of the Middle Ages which is customary in Catholic thinking, especially in the 19th century" and the "idyllic [vision of] medieval corporatism." Piovani, *La teodicea sociale di Rosmini*, 67.

70. The intensity of this friendship was clear from the beginning. The first time Manzoni (who already knew and admired some of Rosmini's writings) met Rosmini, "He shook hands with the young man, saying: '*O quam speciosi pedes evangelizantium pacem, evangelizantium bona*' (How fair the feet that bring glad tidings of peace, that bring good news)." Claude Leetham, *Rosmini: Priest, Philosopher, and Patriot* (Baltimore: Helicon Press, 1957), 67.

71. See Leetham, *Rosmini: Priest, Philosopher, and Patriot*, 418–19.

72. Rosmini, *Epistolario completo*, 2:165.

73. In particular, if Manzoni was originally keener to write his masterpiece in "an Italian language formed from every dialect in Italy," Rosmini persuaded his friend to "use the language of Tuscany, where a continuous literature had formed the tongue of Florence until it had become more than a dialect." Leetham, *Rosmini*, 68. Manzoni, also, explicitly paid a tribute to Rosmini's philosophical system his *Dialogo dell'invenzione* (1850).

74. I am indebted to Professor Leonard Liggio for pointing out the important nuances of this fact.

75. On Augustin Thierry, see Ralph Raico, "Classical Liberal Roots of the Doctrine of Classes," in *Requiem for Marx*, ed. Yuri N. Maltsev (Auburn, Ala.: Ludwig von Mises Institute, 1993), 189–220. On the flavor of French liberalism in those times, see Leonard P. Liggio, "Charles Dunoyer and French Classical Liberalism," *Journal of Libertarian Studies* 1, no. 3 (1977): 153–78, and also Leonard P. Liggio, "The Counter Enlightenment," in *An Uncertain Legacy: Essays on the Pursuit of Liberty*, ed. Edward B. McLean (Chicago: ISI Books, 1998), 134–71. For an enlightening account of the economic theory endorsed by the French liberals, see also Murray N. Rothbard, *Classical Economics: An Austrian Perspective on the History of Economic Thought*, vol. 2 (Brookfield, Vt.: Edward Elgar, 1995), 1–45, 439–75.

76. Francesco Traniello, "Letture rosminiane della rivoluzione francese," in Giorgio Campanini and Francesco Traniello, eds., *Filosofia e diritti. Rosmini e la cultura della Restaurazione*, 150.

77. Rosmini, *Filosofia della politica*, 502.

78. Some of his major works between 1827 and 1836 include *Galateo dei letterati* (1827), *Breve esposizione della filosofia di Melchiorre Gioia* (1827), *Constitutiones Societatis a Charitate nuncupatae* (1828), *Frammenti di una storia dell'empietà* (1828–1829), *Massime di perfezione cristiana* (1826–1830), *Nuovo Saggio sull'Origine delle Idee* (1828–30), *Principi della scienza morale* (1830–31), *Antropologia in servizio della scienza morale* (1831–1832), *Antropologia soprannaturale* (1832–36), *Storia comparativa e critica dei sistemi intorno al principio della morale* (1836).

79. Rosmini, *Filosofia politica*, 111.

80. Ibidem.

81. Ibid., 79.

82. Ibid., 80.

83. Ibid., 81.

84. Ibid., 86.

85. Ibid, 174. On this point, Dario Antiseri and Massimo Baldini remark that Rosmini's "anti-perfectionism" is not "a denial of the possible improvements within society . . . but an attempt to deal with the issue of improving society in a realistic way." Dario Antiseri and Massimo Baldini, "Il personalismo liberale di Antonio Rosmini," in *Personalismo liberale*, ed. Antonio Rosmini (Soveria Mannelli: Rubbettino, 1997), 8.

86. Antonio Rosmini, *Ragionamento sul comunismo e sul socialismo*, ed. by B. Brunello (Padova: Cerdam, 1948), 57–58.

87. Pietro Piovani, "Hegel nella filosofia del diritto di Rosmini," in *Studi giuridici in onore di Pietro Calamandrei* (Padova: Cedam, 1956), 10.

88. Antonio Rosmini, *Antropologia in servizio della scienza morale*, ed. F. Evain (1884; reprint, Roma: Città Nuova, 1981), 460.

89. Rosmini, *Filosofia del diritto*, vol. 2, par. 52.

90. Antonio Rosmini, *Storia comparativa e critica de 'sistemi intorno al principio della morale*, in Rosmini, *Principi della Scienza morale* (Roma: Città nuova, [1837] 1990), 376.

91. Ibid., vol. 2, par. 340.

92. Ibid., vol. 1, par. 347.

93. Ibid., vol. 1, par. 359.

94. Ibid., vol. 1, par. 341.

95. Ibidem.

96. Pietro Piovani, *La teodicea sociale di Rosmini* (Brescia: Morcelliana, [1957] 1997), 225.

97. Rosmini, *Filosofia del diritto*, vol. 2, par. 1631.

98. Piovani, *La teodicea sociale di Rosmini*, 205.

99. Ibidem.

100. Giorgio Campanini, *Antonio Rosmini e il problema dello Stato* (Brescia: Morcelliana, 1983), 23.

101. Antonio Rosmini, *Teodicea* (Roma: Città Nuova, [1845] 1977).

102. Danilo Zolo, *Il personalismo rosminiano*, 136ff.

103. Rosmini, *Teodicea*, par. 472.

104. Ibid., par 921.

105. Ibid., par 922.

106. Piovani, *La teodicea sociale di Rosmini*, 261.

107. A critic as acute and unsympathetic as Zolo summarizes as follows the inner tendencies of Rosmini's political positions: "liberal and anti-democratic attitude of Rosminian constitutionalism is confirmed by its aversion toward political parties, by his economic theses in favor of free enterprise, by its vigorous appraisal of the 'freedom to teach' against any state monopoly." Zolo, *Il personalismo rosminiano*, 228.

108. A dispute on Rosmini's approach to property between two prominent scholars of his political thought, Luigi Bulferetti (1815–1992) and Pietro Piovani, should be mentioned here. See Luigi Bulferetti, *Socialismo risorgimentale* (Torino: Einaudi, 1949), 104–99; Pietro Piovani, "Rosmini e il socialismo risorgimentale;" Pietro Piovani, "Ancora sul socialismo di Rosmini," *Rivista Internazionale di Filosofia del diritto*, 1951, II; Luigi Bulferetti, "Socialista rosso il Rosmini?", *Rivista Internazionale di Filosofia del diritto*, 1951, II; Pietro Piovani-Luigi Bulferetti, "Per chiudere una disputa sul Rosmini," *Rivista Internazionale di Filosofia del diritto*, 1951, IV. An analysis of this polemic is in Giuseppe Cantillo, "Pietro Piovani interprete di Rosmini," in Pietro Piovani, *La teodicea sociale di Rosmini*, 429–35.

1

On Constitutions of the French Kind

There are two kinds of political constitution: The first one is formed passage by passage, without a premeditated scheme, incessantly patched and mended according to counter-veiling social forces and the urgency of instincts and popular need; the other one is created altogether, emerging complete as theory from the mind, like Minerva from the head of Jupiter. Those are enacted before being written, these are written before being enacted.

The pre-1789 constitutions belong, for most part, to the former kind: such was the constitution of the Venetian Republic, such is also the English constitution. Revolutionary France, indignant with the past, ignoring all previous history, took the first piece of paper, wrote a constitution on it, and commanded the nation to implement it. The British constitution was indeed the model for it but while the former was a consequence of events, the latter emerged from a speculative work of thought.

The will to submit facts to reason and practicality to theory was a generous thought indeed, for nothing is more sublime than a true and complete theory. That is an eternal and divine thing and the human and temporal fact must conform to it, as the nature of the intelligent being and the dignity of man demands it.

But what is difficult to find is that theory which is true and complete, and the verification of the truth and perfection of a political theory is in the consequential facts, that is, in the effect that is proposed or that must be proposed and that such effect is durable, just, and offers satisfactory coexistence for the citizens of a nation. Let us then consult the facts to know if what was done and what was attempted from '89 onward in Europe proves and confirms the goodness of those constitutions that were thereafter applied to the states and all essentially of one mould, and all based on the same principles.

About sixty years have elapsed since the first experiment. What do these sixty years tell us, and what do they prove to us? They prove just one thing: that the lives of all the different constitutions that were tried were fragile and ephemeral. Not only was there not even one that appeared destined to receive the venerable seal of the centuries, none could resist the test of a few decades and none lasted even a generation. Those that were not extinguished like vermin by some violent disease were transformed with the passage of time, and at the end left nothing but the seeds for other temporary constitutions of the same kind. The history of French constitutions is here before our eyes so that we are convinced: all the nations that imitated them fell victim to the same political diseases and to the same painful histories. No one can ignore how many times those constitutions of Spain, of Belgium, and all of the other nations were broken, or changed, or modified in a short space of years without exception.[1]

And in spite of such fatal experiences, the faith of the people in written political constitutions never declined. Rather, they all rushed on them with growing ardor and hope, and the feeling has become universal that a civilized nation cannot flourish and reach its natural and godly destiny, if the organic form of its government is not constitutional.

This opinion is what I myself strictly profess and nothing could divert my soul from this persuasion. The reason is contained in what I stated at the outset. It is a need for intelligence to will that facts be subordinated to theory.

But what makes me wonder the most is that the people so many times disillusioned in their most beautiful expectations, agitated by cruel internal disagreements, struggling with supreme experiments of political life, without ever being able to reach the advantages of a constitutional government which is stable and firm in spite of its statutes changing form, nevertheless never suspected that in the French system was hidden some radical and deep vice which was the cause of the short duration of the constitutions founded on its principles. So much I wonder that statesmen, profound thinkers, have not seriously applied their attention to such a research, or never came to discover that woeful seed of death that is carried from the beginning in the breast of the new constitutions of the states and that all, after causing excruciating sorrows to the people, are breached by violence in popular uprisings. No, neither the people nor the learned have taken advantage of the hard and repeated lessons imparted to them by what has happened in Europe since the French Revolution. As if the inventive power of ingenuity were dead, nothing was done but imitating what was the work not of a deep plan, of a peaceful meditation, or a thorough study of the centuries, but rather the improvisation of audacious and imaginative minds, too much infatuated with too general and too imperfect theories. As if daughters of a philosophy that wanted to break with the past, of which it was so tired, a philosophy that, indignant, trampled upon history and traditions confident in its individuality and independence, the constitutions of which we speak were born amongst the passions of the demagogues, the fury of the parties, the terror and the clamor of national and foreign weapons. Was it not then likely that a law born amid such circumstances, amid so much upheaval, would carry within itself some vice from its inception? Yet it was embraced, copied, and imitated with civility by almost all European states.

Italians! In the hour of your political regeneration, do not follow this false path. Do not dishearten yourselves and imitate the foreigner in what you have not first examined and discussed, without prejudice, through your straight judgment and approved with your splendid intelligence! The thinker cannot but foresee similar effects from similar causes.

2

The Vices of Constitutions

For twenty years or more, I have been confirmed in the persuasion that in the constitutions given to different people from '89 on and molded *à la français*, a deep gentle disease is hidden—a disease that is spreading rapidly. After having contaminated governments and people, it adduces the extreme need for mutation. In 1827, I tried to demonstrate this in a book by the title *Della naturale costituzione della società civile* [*The Natural Constitution of Civil Society*].[†] But the book could not see the light because then, although intelligence was not extinguished in us, nevertheless our mouth was gagged and the communication of thought impeached.

That research, always continued in painful silence and confirmed by events, showed me that the immediate consequences of political constitutions molded on the French system are inevitably the following:

> They promote in all citizens a limitless ambition to ascend to ever-greater degrees in society.

---

†Tr. note: Rosmini refers here to a philosophical work he undertook in 1826–1827, leaving it unfinished before moving to Domodossola, where he began started pondering the "New Essay on The Origin of Ideas" (Nuovo Saggio sull'Origine delle Idee, completed in 1828–1830). Nevertheless, Rosmini worked on the manuscript again in 1848. He did not complete this work, but the fragment was published in 1887 by Francesco Paoli, in Milan, as *Della Naturale costituzione della Società Civile*. See also Antonio Rosmini, *Filosofia della politica* (Milano: Rusconi, 1997), 665–96.

They open the way to corruption in the election of deputies and, especially, of the president if the form is republican.
They generate extreme parties.
They give such preponderance to the Chamber of Deputies, even for their comparatively excessive number, that the state is kept in the danger of revolution.
They do not guarantee sufficiently and in all fullness of law the freedom of the citizens.
They do not guarantee the distribution of properties, because the small properties are represented as much as the large ones.
They abandon religion to the mercy of political interests, and divest the Church of its liberty, which is the most precious of all the liberties of the people.

Such are the factual consequences, immediate and indisputable, of all modern constitutions. It is evident that such consequences produce others, spreading immorality and irreligion, producing civil dissent and civil discord, separating the clergy from the people, and arming all the passions. With such seeds of disorder, it is impossible that order and tranquility be preserved for long. The time comes when a part of the nation rises up against the other and tears up the constitution. The life of this constitution, therefore, cannot be a long one. So Italy must think twice about it, as she needs unity, stability and peace.

But it is convenient to bring forward the investigation. We need to search for the ultimate causes of such sad effects, to find the primary vices of constitutional statutes; and to see how they necessarily adduce the series of ruinous consequences which ends with the destruction of the statues themselves and sometimes even with the disintegration of the nation.

Society and government have two needs: justice and utility. If the government is so organized as to truly render justice to all, and at the same time it promotes the utility of all, then it is perfect.

All the rights of men can be reduced to two groups: the rights of *liberty*, the free, honest exercise of all faculties; and the rights of *property*.[2]

Each liberty, therefore, must be protected and guaranteed; each property must be equally protected and guaranteed, and furthermore, provided with such laws as to favor the development of national wealth. If the government does all that, it renders justice to all and procures the usefulness of all and, to say it again, is perfect.

Modern constitutions fall short one way or the other. They do not render justice to all, because against political power minorities and individuals have no juridical recourse. There is no tribunal to which they can turn in case of violated justice. The legislative power is supposed to be infallible, and therefore it is given omnipotence. Conversely, justice toward minorities can be violated even during the formation of the laws. For that reason, the freedom and rights of the

Church are sacrificed more in all modern constitutions than perhaps even under the most absolute dictatorships.

Modern constitutions do not sufficiently guarantee or fairly develop citizens' properties, the complexities of which form the wealth of the nation and which need a political and economic administration. Under the political power that presides over usefulness, not all properties are represented in fair proportion. Those that are not represented remain neglected, overcome by those which obtain representation and which make legislation to their own advantage.

Therefore, the two radical vices of French-type constitutions are: first, political justice is not guaranteed in them; and, second, all properties are not all equally favored.

3

Remedy for the Two Radical Vices of the Constitutions Molded on the French Model

For the purpose of healing them from these two original vices, we need to turn to the two remedies that are contrary to those vices, and that are proposed in the following constitutional project:

1. The institution of tribunals of political justice.
2. The franchise proportioned to the direct taxation that each citizen pays to the state.

These are the two pivotal points on which the state machine must turn, as will appear from the explanation of the reasons with which we will furnish with the project; one protects the citizens against any injustice even when it is perpetrated on behalf of the powers that be, on behalf of the law; the other promotes all honest usefulness in favor of all equally and proportionally.

The above-mentioned explanation of the reasons, while shedding full light on those truths and showing the necessity to reform and amend the constitutions in use, demonstrates the incoherence that they carry within them. In fact, they promise to keep freedom for all men and at the same time they violate it in many respects, giving to legislatures the power to violate that freedom, and incline and push this power to such violation. No constitution truly and fully establishes freedom for all. Furthermore, the inviolability of each property is proclaimed. Yet, being incoherent, the constitutions themselves violate property rights in many of their dispositions, and, in general, use violence against property, deviating them from their natural direction and opening the door to land reform and communism, into which societies would sink if it were not for the rebellion of people, prompted by their human nature, who would kill the constitutions to save themselves.

In summary, all the constitutions that imitate the French model are far from being as liberal as they profess, and hide in their breast the most enormous absolutism.

Far from being founded on the principles of law, they are deduced from the principles of a philosophy that is utilitarian and based on the senses, which is a calculation—always wrong—of public utility that sacrifices reason, honesty and justice.

Far from conforming to the nature of man and of social coexistence, they are the *dictat* and the expression of vain abstractions, and of theories that are inapplicable to social realities.

It is therefore necessary to abandon them. Italian ingenuity should trust itself and dare to try other avenues, that it should have the audacity to invent and implement them. It will be the unbounded master and benefactor of the people. It may be destined to heal nations.

This high ingenuity can do anything if it wants. The sublime intelligence of my nation, which cannot have lost through long calamities the knowledge of having been the mother of three civilizations and the ruler of the world, and elected from above to that religious empire of humanity which cannot be taken away as long as the sun shines on human adventure—to this I, her reverent son, entrust and submit the following project of political constitution. May it contain the seed of the internal unity of our ingenuity, its prosperity and its moral greatness!

4

A Constitutional Project

ARTICLE 1. The organic form of the state is determined by the present statute: Every law and privilege contrary to this statute is nullified.[3]

Title I

Fundamental Principles of the State

ARTICLE 2. The rights of nature and reason are inviolable for every man.

ARTICLE 3. The freedom of action of the Catholic Church is guaranteed. Direct communication with the Holy See in ecclesiastical matters cannot be impeached. The Councils are the right of the Church. The election of bishops will take place through clergy and people according to the ancient discipline, and the Sovereign Pontiff's right to confirm is reserved.

ARTICLE 4. The state is held by a monarchic government which is tempered by laws.[4]

ARTICLE 5. The deputies of the people, divided in two chambers and united with the king, represent the nation.

ARTICLE 6. The legislative power is exercised collectively by the sovereign and by the two chambers.

The interpretation of the laws belongs to the legislative power.

ARTICLE 7. The acts of government have no effect if not provided with the signature of a minister.

ARTICLE 8. The territory of the state cannot be changed except through a law.

Title II

Concerning the King

ARTICLE 9. The person of the king is inviolable.

ARTICLE 10. The king convenes the two chambers each year. He can extend the sessions or dissolve them.

In this last case, he must convene new ones within a term of four months.

ARTICLE 11. The proposal of laws is done by ministries and laws can be first proposed to either chamber. Either of the two chambers can propose a law upon request of 10 members of that chamber. The law proposals made by ministries are discussed and voted on before other law proposals.

ARTICLE 12. Only the king sanctions and promulgates the laws.

ARTICLE 13. Only the king holds the executive power.

ARTICLE 14. The king is the head of the state. He disposes of all the powers of land and sea, declares war, makes treaties of peace, of alliance, of commerce, and others, notifying the chambers if the security and the interest of the state allow it, and issuing appropriate communications. The treaties involving finances have no effect unless they have the approval of the chambers.

ARTICLE 15. The king names and makes all the appointments that are not foreseen by the present constitution in a way that will be determined by the law; he has the power to issue currency; he creates decrees and regulations necessary for the implementation of the laws; but he may not suspend, suspend the observation of, or dispense with the laws. He confers honorary titles.

ARTICLE 16. Justice is administered on behalf of the king by the judges that he appoints.

The king can give grace and commute sentences. However, he cannot give grace to ministers who have been convicted, except by explicit request of one of the two legislative chambers.

ARTICLE 17. Neither the king nor his children can marry without the approval of the chambers.

ARTICLE 18. The endowment of the Crown will be set by the first legislature, and cannot be changed except by a law.

ARTICLE 19. The private patrimony of the king is subject to the same laws that regulate the other properties.

ARTICLE 20. The king's successor, in assuming the throne, takes an oath to this present statute before the chambers brought together for this purpose.

Title III

The Rights of Citizens

ARTICLE 21. Each man who is a subject of the king is free and a citizen.

ARTICLE 22. All citizens are equal before the tribunals.

ARTICLE 23. Individual freedom is guaranteed. No one can be arrested and brought to justice other than in the cases foreseen by law and in the forms that the law prescribes.

ARTICLE 24. Residence is inviolable. No visit to a place of residence [by the police] can take place if not according to the law and in the forms prescribed by the law.

ARTICLE 25. No one can be removed from his natural judges.

ARTICLE 26. To travel anywhere in the world is a natural right. Emigration cannot be denied to anyone who demands it.

ARTICLE 27. All properties are inviolable. Forced expropriation is not violation of property when a legally ascertained public good demands it, and through a fair indemnity which conforms to the laws.

ARTICLE 28. The deeds of trust extending to non-existing parties are not recognized by law.

ARTICLE 29. No one can receive decorations, titles, pensions, employment from a foreign power without the authorization of the king.

ARTICLE 30. All properties share the burden of the state in proportion to their income.

ARTICLE 31. No tax can be imposed except when allowed by the chambers that represent the taxpayers and sanctioned by the king.

ARTICLE 32. Every obligation of the state towards its creditors is inviolable.

ARTICLE 33. Intellectual property is guaranteed.

ARTICLE 34. The citizens of legal age have the right to send petitions collectively to the chambers if the object of a petition is the formation of a law. The petition is sent to the executive branch if it concerns the implementation of a law, and to the judicial branch if it concerns the administration of justice.

ARTICLE 35. All citizens can create associations amongst themselves, as long as they are not secret. However, upon judgment of a political tribunal, associations can be dissolved if declared immoral or irreligious, or contrary to the present statute; that is, that after a regular trial, it is declared that an abuse has been committed by its members for immoral or irreligious purposes and/or for the purposes of violating state laws.

ARTICLE 36. The right of peaceful and unarmed gathering is recognized when conforming to the laws that can regulate the exercise of this right in the public interest.

ARTICLE 37. The press is free, but law prevents its abuse. The Church preserves the right to impose censorship, but without the imposition of state penalty.

ARTICLE 38. Public spectacles are regulated with preventive measures established by the laws.

ARTICLE 39. Freedom of teaching is guaranteed. There will be laws that regulate it and repress abuses.

ARTICLE 40. The freedoms of commerce and of industry are fundamental principles of the economic law of the state.

ARTICLE 41. All citizens can aspire to state responsibilities according to their abilities and suitability.

ARTICLE 42. Every citizen is a soldier. Exempted from military service are those who are enrolled in the clergy, and all those who hold a public office which is necessary to the state.

The draft is regulated by the law. The weight of the draft will be equally distributed amongst the citizens.

ARTICLE 43. The National Guard, which will be instituted on the basis set by the law, is part of the army.

The king can dissolve it, and recall and reorganize it within one year.

ARTICLE 44. The army cannot be removed from its dependence on the responsible ministry.

Military ordinances made on behalf of the king are valid when signed by a minister.

ARTICLE 45. Laws and sentences must be carried out. Public force must be used by the state to implement the laws and the sentences of the tribunals and for no other purpose.

ARTICLE 46. Municipal and provincial institutions and municipal and provincial territory are determined by the law. The proportional vote that is established in the following title for the election of the deputies will serve as a basis also for the election of city council and provincial council members in a way to be established by law.

Title IV

Legislative Chambers

ARTICLE 47. The legislative chambers have the power to discuss and vote on laws which have to be submitted, once the majority in both chambers is obtained, to the sanctioning of the king who can grant or refuse his sanctioning at this discretion. The chambers can receive petitions requesting the creation of some legislative disposition while rejecting others. The petitioners must present the petitions directly to the executive or judicial power according to the nature of their contents.

The chambers have the right of consulting and the right of inquiry, which is limited to the end of gathering the necessary information for the creation of the laws, or submitting some accusation to the competent tribunals. The chambers cannot deny the public funds necessary to the implementation of both laws and sentences.

ARTICLE 48. There are two legislative chambers, both elected.

ARTICLE 49. By dividing the population of the state by fifteen thousand the total number of the deputies will be obtained: and if the number is odd, neglecting the fractions, it is to be increased by one.[5]

ARTICLE 50. Both chambers have an equal number of members.

ARTICLE 51. The first chamber is elected by the major property owners, the second one by the minor ones.

ARTICLE 52. Property owners are rated major or minor in function of the direct taxation[6] they pay to the state's treasury.

ARTICLE 53. Deputies are elected by electoral colleges, each one electing one deputy.

ARTICLE 54. Once the total sum of the direct taxes is divided by the total number of the deputies, the quota is represented by an electoral college.

ARTICLE 55. The major property owners gather in sufficient number to form a college, which pays the quota represented by the college to the state as a direct tax. If only one property owner pays the established quota to the state as a direct tax, then only he elects a deputy and can even elect himself. If two property owners pay together the above-mentioned quota to the state as a tax both elect the deputy. In the same way, colleges are united with other colleges in a manner that first brings together those who pay more, and successively those who pay less. Thus, there are more electoral colleges when there are more electors who pay less in the colleges that form them.

ARTICLE 56. The first half of these colleges elects the deputies of the first chamber, the second half the deputies of the second chamber.

ARTICLE 57. The king participates in the elections in proportion to the income of the fixed assets owned by the state, and of that of his private patrimony. The Church and all its administrative bodies, societies, or collective persons that contribute some direct tax to the general revenue of the state, participate in the same proportion.

ARTICLE 58. No particular qualification is required by law to enjoy the right to vote, except the payment of direct taxation [income tax] to the state.

ARTICLE 59. The right to vote is exercised solely by men. It can be exercised through legal representation: fathers, husbands, tutors, and caretakers exercise it on behalf of children who are legal wards, wives, minors, and the interdicted.

The missing votes in each college are supplied by the government in favor of any of the above-mentioned categories.

ARTICLE 60. Those eligible for election must be Italians, of legal age, not outlawed, not overburdened with debt, not criminally convicted. If they have been convicted for political matters, they must have been pardoned. Finally, they must not be, at the same time, employed in a capacity that is incompatible with election.

ARTICLE 61. No employee of the judicial order can be a member of the chambers. The mandate of deputy is incompatible with holding the job of a minister of the state. It is also incompatible with any employment that obligates the deputy to reside outside the capital. Once the mandate of deputy has elapsed, those who have surrendered employment to accept the mandate are to be available for employment in their field.

ARTICLE 62. Deputies of provinces receive a moderate remuneration as a title of indemnity from the state.

They cannot receive any gift from the electors. When it is proven that a deputy has received gifts, he ceases to be a representative.

ARTICLE 63. If for any reason a deputy terminates his functions, the college that elected him will be called to a new election. Any deputy who does not participate in the chamber's activities without a just and acceptable reason will be fined by an amount imposed by the chamber to which he belongs.

ARTICLE 64. Each legislative term lasts six years. Half of each chamber is renewed every three years. The half that is to be renewed first is chosen by the king.

ARTICLE 65. The Italian language is the language of the chambers.

ARTICLE 66. The chamber sessions are public. But when ten members make written request, the chambers can deliberate secretly.

ARTICLE 67. It is illegal for one chamber to be gathered at a time when the other is not. The two chambers can never be united in one assembly to discuss or take any decision in common. Acts taken by the chambers in these two cases are null and void.

ARTICLE 68. Each of the chambers is solely competent to judge the legality of the mandate of its own members. If the legal form of the mandate is recognized, the deputy is admitted. But if he obtained the mandate through means that are forbidden by the law, he must be judged by the competent tribunals.

ARTICLE 69. The chambers in accordance determine, through an internal regulation, the way that is used to exercise their tasks.

ARTICLE 70. After their confirmation and before commencing their duties, the deputies take an oath of loyalty to the king and to the constitution.

ARTICLE 71. The president, the vice-president, the secretaries and the other officers of the chambers are named by the chambers from among themselves at the beginning of every session and for the duration of the session.

ARTICLE 72. The sessions and the deliberations of the chambers are neither legal nor valid if the absolute majority of their members is not present.

ARTICLE 73. The decisions are taken according to the majority of votes.

ARTICLE 74. For the preliminary work, each law proposal is first examined by the committees named by each chamber.

Once approved by a chamber, the law proposal is transmitted to the other chamber. Once debated and approved by the other chamber, it is presented to the king for approval. Debates are carried out article by article first; then the law is voted as a whole.

ARTICLE 75. Votes are cast by the sitting and standing of members, by division, and by secret ballot.

This last means will always be used to vote a whole law, and matters concerning personnel.

ARTICLE 76. If the law proposal has been rejected by one of the three legislative powers, it can no longer be reintroduced in the same session.

ARTICLE 77. The ministers and the government commissioners have free entrance in the legislative chambers and they have to be heard when they demand it. The chamber may demand the presence of the ministers in the discussions.

ARTICLE 78. The chambers cannot receive any deputation, nor can they hear others outside of their own members, except for ministers and government commissioners.

ARTICLE 79. The deputies cannot be held accountable because of the opinions they voice or because of their votes in the chambers.

Title V

The Judicial Order

ARTICLE 80. The judicial order is independent in applying the laws to the cases that occur.

ARTICLE 81. There will be two tribunal orders. The first will judge in matters concerning individual rights that are social and private. The other will judge in matters concerning social civil rights.

The tribunals that are purely military belong to the first order.

ARTICLE 82. The supreme court for political justice has a number of judges equal to that of one chamber: These judges are selected by the people with a universal and equal vote from among candidates from both chambers who are at least forty years of age. Every ten years, the people will be asked if they want to renew the election. The legislative power, by first issuing a law decree, can consult the people even before ten years has elapsed.

ARTICLE 83. There will be lower courts, appeal courts and supreme courts in both orders of tribunal.

For the cases reserved to the supreme court of political justice, there will be a first and a second instance made up of two colleges of judges, one more numerous than the other. In the last instance, the court of justice will judge in plenary session.

ARTICLE 84. Any individual or collective person can appeal to the competent political tribunal in cases where a decision made by political authorities might violate the rights that are guaranteed in this statute.

ARTICLE 85. The organization of the judiciary will be determined by a law for those matters which are not covered by the present constitution.

ARTICLE 86. Ministers are responsible.

ARTICLE 87. Each of the two chambers has the right to accuse the ministers. When a chamber accuses, the other one judges, and the high court of political justice applies the law.

ARTICLE 88. A law will determine the cases where the responsibility of the ministers lie, and the ways used to prosecute them and the penalties to apply.

ARTICLE 89. No deputy can be arrested, except for cases of flagrant or near-flagrant crime, during the time of the session, nor can he be judged in criminal matters without a previous decision handed down by the supreme court of political justice.

ARTICLE 90. The king will name state prosecutors in political tribunals. The prosecutors will, as a matter of course, bring before the competent tribunals the perpetrators of abuses of the press, teaching, or other breaches of the social civil right within the limits determined by law.

ARTICLE 91. After sitting for four years, judges cannot be removed.

ARTICLE 92. The sessions of the tribunals in civil and political matters are public. The debates in criminal matters will be public upon the request of the accused.

5

Explanation for the Reasons for the Constitutional Project: Reasons for the Distribution of the Matters

A good, fundamental law must determine three things: the general principles upon which the state is based, the rights of the people, and the rights of government.

Title I of the project explains the principles upon which the state is founded; Title III describes the rights of the people; Titles II, IV, and V describe the rights of government seen in its three supreme powers, which are the king, the deputy chambers and the judicial power.

The natural sequence of the matters demanded that after discussing the power of the king in Title II, and before discussing those powers that immediately are ordered to promote the people's utility and to administer justice to them—which is done in Titles IV and V—we deal with the very rights of the people, which is done is Title III.

Before moving to explain the reasons for the individual articles, I must caution that not all articles that make up the project belong to the substance of the project. Many of them can be changed as a result of learned discussions. What I present as an essential remedy to the evils that burden civil societies under the constitutions that have existed so far can be reduced to two points: the institution of political tribunals; and the right to elect deputies being attributed to the citizens in proportion to the amount of the direct tax that they pay to the state.

6

Reasons for the Disposition Contained in the Preliminary Article

ARTICLE 1—The organic form of the state is determined by the present statute: Every law and privilege contrary to this statute is nullified.

The fundamental law of the state, since it must be the norm to which all other laws refer, makes evident the need that all legal dispositions contrary to it are abrogated by virtue of it.

Furthermore, this article puts a limit to legislative power, because it removes the ability to create any law that is contrary to the present statute. Every branch of the state, even the legislative branch, must be restricted within its boundaries. Otherwise, the state would be omnipotent, thus arbitrary. Civil society would thus be at the mercy of despotism.

The purpose of the constitution is to determine the boundaries of each branch of the state and of supplying norms to the nation, which must know—whenever the case occurs—that one or another branch of government has exceeded, through its acts, the limits of its authority.

But in such a case, that is, in a case where it is clear that the legislative branch exceeds the boundaries of its limits, what is the nation to do?

There are but two roads: the way of facts and the way of rights.

The way of facts is the revolution: and all the constitutions that have been dictated to people so far have left only this way open to the nation to claim its rights, which have been violated by the powers of the state that, by exceeding the limits set by the constitutions, violated the constitutions themselves.

But this is the way of violence, thus the way of barbarism and incivility. Civility demands that the way of facts yields to the way of rights.

It is therefore necessary that a juridical procedure is established even for these cases. It is necessary that the constitution itself establishes a manner that is legal and peaceful through which all powers are held within limits previously assigned and, if they exceed those limits, are reprehended with neither disorder nor bloodshed, or at least their acts are declared null. As those acts have no effect, they cannot damage citizens. In summation, it is necessary that, in addition to the legislative branch, a judicial branch which acts as a custodian of the constitution and tutor of the nation and of its rights, is instituted.

This deficiency which, more or less, is found in all constitutions known so far, is mended by the present project with the Supreme Court of Political Justice that is discussed in Title V.

When we say that "every law and privilege that is contrary to this statute is nullified," we do not speak only about an adversity that is immediate and material against some article of the constitution; the adversity extends to all the consequences that logically can be deduced from the articles that form part of the constitution. Nevertheless, these articles represent as many principles, which in their breast contain endless consequences, and what is contrary to the consequence is also contrary to the principle that contains it. Thus, this first article of the constitution has a power and a value more extensive than it seems, although it declares null all those laws and all those privileges that turn out to be contrary to any logical consequence that could be legitimately deduced from this or that article of the constitution.

But to deduce from the principles all the logical consequences that could arise is a task that is beyond the common intelligence of the multitude. Therefore, the populace cannot itself know of all the infractions that the power of the state can do to the rights of the populace rights, and it cannot always know those laws that would emanate from the legislative power and that would be contrary to the dispositions of the fundamental statue, to the logical consequence that all are included in the dispositions mentioned. The contrariness of the laws brought to statute sometimes stay hidden under the honest form of the words used to express the law, and only the most remote effects of the law offend and infringe upon the rights that the statute guarantees to the citizens. It is therefore necessary that a knowledgeable assembly of uncorrupted judges exist in the state who take all these rights under their wing and who can, with their wisdom, discover the infractions that could occur as a consequence of even the most remote effects of the laws. Only under this condition are the people protected and safe, and are citizens able to live with tranquility and without fears of usurpation by the legislative branch.

In many cases it is very difficult to know that a law, in its consequences, offends some article of the constitution, that is, cause the people or the minority of the citizens or some of them to be blind in this judgment, and thus become wrongly persuaded that the legislative branch has infringed its rights. Thus, not having a competent tribunal for such a grave issue, the people are inclined to take justice into their own hands, and the people's justice is always hasty and violent. In such a state of affairs, even the most just legislation can be compromised.

All those who become malcontent about laws against which they have no defense not only whisper about them and take sides with the opposition to the government; they also become leaders of groups and mislead the populace with sophisms, with invective, and with all those means intended to instigate popular passions and upset the government and the established laws with tumult. The people, who are suspicious where there is no political tribunal that they trust, easily believe deceivers who show themselves to be zealous for the people's good and make huge promises.

One of the characteristics necessary to a good constitution is to place in the souls of everyone the most firm belief that all the rights are protected and guaranteed and that there is no power in government that can abuse its authority with impunity; that there is no violation whatsoever perpetrated by anyone under any pretext that cannot be referred to a tribunal; and that there is no wrong that cannot be legally righted, peacefully and easily.

When the people are convinced of this, they trust and love their government and trust and obey the law. Then, and only then, are the people peaceful and safe, and agitators lose their influence. To that end, it is best that no law can be written and be enforced that damages the rights guaranteed by the constitution. It is best that there is a powerful authority in charge of vigilance, and that the judicial branch be above the legislative branch in order to judge the justice of the acts of legislation.

7

Reasons for the Dispositions Contained in Title I

ARTICLE 2—The rights of nature and reason are inviolable for every man.

It conforms to the dignity of a constitutional statue that such a statute begins by proclaiming as inviolable the law of nature and of reason.[7]

Such a statement declares that the statute is based on the respect due to humanity. The state is thus safeguarded against national egoism, which always inclines to recoil on itself. Such a statement is a solemn lesson given to people, and a protest against those barbarian or pagan laws that confuse the guest with the friend. Thus, such a statement makes the renewal of those laws impossible, as the rights of the foreigners are also recognized and sanctioned.[8]

Every despotism has at its root the negation of the rights of nature and reason. Those rights are rarely recognized in theory in despotic authority, and even more rarely in fact.

When the aversion of the people to the absolutism of princes exploded in modern times, instead of combating the absolutism itself, only one of its special forms was fought—and thus this radical vice of societies simply changed its form.

Then, among other errors, it was taught that the will of the people could do anything, and that from this will would all rights and duties arise! And since the will of the people could be known by ascertaining the majority, thus monarchic despotism was substituted with popular despotism, which has become the despotism of majorities over minorities, with the rights of the latter remaining sacrificed.[9]

Furthermore, popular majorities were led by a few individuals who, without any legal authority, were dragging these majorities behind them. Another despotism therefore arose which, without a stable place in society and without any legal form, emerged here and there randomly. And that was a de facto despotism against which there was as much possibility of defense as there is against a volcano erupting unpredictably from the earth. Under such conditions, a civil society becomes anarchic.

When the theory of popular omnipotence frightened a world that was already painted with human blood, the legislative chambers were introduced with all solemnity to take the place of that theory. The chambers appeared as representative of the people. It was still the turn of people [to speak], but this time through a representative body; the tumults in the squares turned into legislative debates. Absolutism had changed form, but it lived nevertheless and was dressed in the magnificent vestments of a perfect legality. It was no longer atrocious, but it could be unjust at will, and it could be despotic. Violence moved off, but only by one step, as the injustice of the chambers, against which there was no defense, marshaled behind itself the violence of the people, and in civil societies, revolutions continued. In what manner can we therefore destroy despotism itself in all its forms?

It is advantageous to recognize that above civil societies, above the people, and above all of humanity, there is an eternal justice which all humanity must obey, and that this justice does not emanate from the people, nor from chambers, kings, nor human will. In fact, it does not emanate at all, but simply exists, as does God from whom it has its origins. It is advantageous to recognize and to confess that before all positive laws of civil society, there are others to which social laws must conform under the penalty of being null, just as if they had never existed. It must be recognized that the rights of man come before all those that the institution of civil society can attribute to man. We must admit the existence of a law of nature and reason that precedes civil coexistence, and that must be respected by all civil dispositions, and that against such law no civil power can do nor attempt to do anything. If this is fully admitted, sincerely in all its consequences; if the legislative branch submits itself to natural and rational law, which—like it or not—overpowers it; then and only then will the legislative branch cease to be despotic irrespective of any form taken by the will of the most, the many, the few or the one—as these are nothing but the forms of power, and not power itself. Power itself is what must humble itself before eternal law. Civil power and civil society themselves must recognize that they have no authority whatsoever against the rights that nature assigns to man and consequently to all the associations of men independently from their civil association.

Therefore, besides the *social civil law*, the existence of an *extra-social law*—which is more respected than the former and which in case of collision with the former must always prevail—must be recognized.[10]

The study of laws has so far been mainly limited to positive dispositions, and thus we have the tendency of the man of law not to recognize the whole scope of the extra-social right, to attribute too much to civil society and its legislative power, and to emanate from the good will of this power the most natural rights of man such as the right to own, to rest and even to get married. These doctrines were of immense help in creating the specter of an omnipotent civil society in the minds of people, and still are the firmest support for the deplorable despotism which underlies all the different forms of government established in Europe, without exception.

In order to cut down despotism at the root, I published the *Filosofia del diritto* [*Philosophy of Right*] several years ago, a book still mostly unknown, where I defended all the rational and natural rights of man against the evasions and the usurpations of civil society in whatever form that society takes; to establish the authority of an inviolable extra social right, which is indelible and absolutely paramount over all positive dispositions; and to restrict civil government within its proper boundaries, demonstrating that it has no authority whatsoever over the right of any man—and that it has no other authority than to determine the *modalities* for the common good except, always, to preserve the whole value of that good.[11]

When this doctrine is brought into practice, it destroys any social despotism in whatever form it may hide and behind any mask it would use to cover its ugly deformity.

But if natural and rational law must be preserved as inviolable against the power of the chambers, or of the people or of any other authority, how can we proceed when it is nevertheless violated?

Here again is where the road forks in two ways: the way of facts and violence; and that of legality and peace. If we do not want the latter, we must necessarily be the victims of the former. Now the choice must be in no doubt. It is appropriate, therefore, that civil society institutes within itself a political tribunal holding the natural and rational right against all other powers of the states which would perpetrate its violation. It is necessary that this natural and rational law be recognized as a foundation of the constitution of civil society, such and so much is the importance of this second article.

The best thing that was done in '89 was certainly the *Declaration of the Rights of Man and of the Citizen*, proposed by Lafayette to imitate the American constitution. But what it lacked was a corresponding tribunal that would enforce it. Besides that, the declarations of rights made in France are expressed with many words that have no precise meaning, thus giving birth to the most false interpretations; nor can even a short declaration include all the rights of nature and reason to which men are entitled.

It is therefore more worthy, in a constitution, to consecrate the principle according to which the reason of right and nature is inviolable as we do in this second article, and to mention the main rights of the citizen as we do in Title III, and then commit to a high court of justice the development and the further application of all other rights of nature and reason.

ARTICLE 3—The freedom of action of the Catholic Church is guaranteed. Direct communication with the Holy See in ecclesiastical matters cannot be impeached. The Councils are the right of the Church. The election of bishops will take place through clergy and people according to the ancient discipline, and the Sovereign Pontiff's right to confirm is reserved.

Religion is recognized by all legislators as the primary foundation of the state. The constitutions thus far adopted in Italy declare the Catholic religion as the state religion. But the phrase "state religion" does not express a precise concept. The array of political rights that was attributed with it to Catholic citizens changed according to the times. The Tuscan statute admits non-Catholics to all civil and military employment, but the declaration that the Catholic religion is the state religion is barely understandable.

In a statute such as this, it would have been appropriate to add that in the religious festivities celebrated by a nation, the nation cannot be represented by non-Catholic employees. That a Jewish employee, for example, comes to a Mass for a *Te Deum* is not only inappropriate and immoral, but also a mockery of religious beliefs, an authorized prostitution of consciences which is commanded by law. Then it would be a lesser evil if the nation were represented by statues.

Freedom of conscience must be inviolable. Therefore we should not practice violence on the conscience of a Jewish employee whom, if he is a true Jew, must feel total repugnance in associating himself with the acts of the Catholic religion. By the same token, we must not practice violence on the consciences of the Catholics who cannot, without being sinners, admit non-Catholics to the acts of their religion. We cannot give freedom of conscience unless we allow all to exercise the laws of their religions in their fullness. To obligate people to infringe upon those religious laws with force, with laws, and with acts of government is but intolerance, persecution and despotism.

The fundamental law needs to be without misunderstandings and without vague and improper expressions.

It is of benefit, therefore, to leave to the legislative branch the determination of the political and civil condition of other religions according to the conditions and circumstances of the times, instead of establishing these conditions in the constitution itself, which demands that an undetermined maxim is to be stable and perpetual or, if that maxim is determined, that it can be modified as time proceeds to the disadvantage of both the authority of the fundamental law itself and its solidity.

Yet if it does not seem convenient to declare in the statute that Catholicism is the religion of the state, nevertheless it is practical to recognize Italy as a Catholic nation through the statute, since non-Catholics are an exception and a minimal fraction of the population. Now, in a Catholic nation which is coherent with its faith, it is appropriate that it provide guarantees to that faith, and that it keeps the freedom to practice it inviolate as its most precious good.

The Catholic religion does not need dynastic protections, but freedom. It needs its freedom protected and nothing else. The greatest absurdity is that a free people keep the religion it professes as a slave. This absurdity can be seen in all the constitutions of the French type because of the influence that unbelief exerted in their formation. While the freedom of all religions was proclaimed, with perfidious incoherence a public law that prevented any free action to the Catholic Church was allowed to exist and to consolidate more and more beside the fundamental law.

Religious Italy, now called by God to freedom, also has the mission to become the liberator of Catholicism from the infamous servitude in which, oppressed, it has lain for so long.

The Catholic religion must be free in its dogmatic, moral, and disciplinary decisions. It must be free in its faith, in its morality, in its worship, in its discipline, in its pastoral care, and in the application of all its laws, otherwise it will not have full freedom of action. This must be the first element of the true and accomplished freedom of Italy. Lies must end, as Italian intelligence discovers them—regardless of their mask—and Italian rectitude abominates them.

The third article of the project looks after this supreme national need.

The centre of the nation is Rome, the centre of Catholicism is the Apostolic See established by the author of Christianity in the centre of the Italian nation of which it is the maximum and perpetual glory. The double political and religious unity depends upon free communication with Rome. The foreign power that wanted to extinguish Italian nationality did its best to put a thousand impediments to communication with the Apostolic See in its Italian dominions. It wanted the children to be separated from the father. Italy regenerated to freedom and called to unity must do the complete contrary of what the foreigner did.

Dynastic jealousies were the second cause of the wall of separation that was built between Catholics and the head of Catholicism, in particular between Italy and its august centre.

Such dynastic jealousies, and all the legal technicalities under which they were poorly disguised, have now fallen forever. The princes became close to the people, and the princes and the people shook each others' hands. The interest of the people is now the interest of the princes. The interest of the Italian people is to be civilly and religiously united with Rome. No barrier and no excuse must be built to divide it again.

Gallicanism and the irreligious spirit that it disseminated in the Italian government, systematized and legalized by agitators, victimized and intimidated the faith of the Italian people. But while it harmed Catholic belief in Italy a great deal, it did not extinguish the faith of Italians. Therefore, in spite of what was done to seduce them and to cheat them, amongst the people of our peninsula there still was unhappiness, bitterness, and restlessness at seeing the obstacles that governments erected with thousands of calculated formalities to damage the Church, and to damage relations with the Sovereign Pontiff. In addition, there was the institution of the most captious, insolent and incompetent censorship on all Roman decrees. This restlessness, this discomfort of the Italian faithful must stop forever. The people will have full confidence in their governments if they see them respectful to the Head of the Church. They will fully enjoy their liberty if nothing more will forbid them, hereinafter, from turning directly in each instance to their common Father and to hear the free voice of the Universal Shepherd invested by Jesus Christ with the duty of feeding his flock. The right of the faithful to communicate directly and freely with the Master and Supreme Regent of their consciences is divine, inviolable and impossible to forbid. Nothing can remove it, nothing can attenuate it.

The Church is not free if the bishops cannot gather, as they see fit, in councils according to canon and pontifical laws. Here we are talking about councils, not secret or illegal meetings convened against the will and the laws of the Church. The episcopate is one, in which many bishops participate, first among which is the Roman Pontiff, successor of St. Peter. They must govern the Church in union. The discussion of the bishops among themselves concerning anything that can be of interest to the good government of the Church, and always in agreement with the Sovereign Pontiff, is necessary. Uniformity must be the characteristic of the ecclesiastical government. The Church has been governed in this way since the beginning, and it flourished until despotism obstructed the councils. The weakening of the faith, and all the temporal and spiritual diseases that thus emerged, was due for the most part to the jealousy of despotic governments helped by the barbarism of the times. The union of the episcopate was thus prevented in a thousand ways, as the government saw clearly that such union would have put breaks on their despotism by defending the rights of the people that were trampled on, and the rights of the oppressed nationalities. It is high time that even these tools of tyranny be broken by the hands of the shepherds of the Church. Without this, there is no real freedom for Italy and for the nations. The freedom of gathering and association is granted to all (article 34, 35) and is forbidden to the bishops? Such incoherence! How is it possible to persuade the people to be free when they see their masters, their shepherds, in chains? How can Catholic sentiment not be offended? How will Italians be able to honestly believe that their governments are sincere when those governments proclaim freedom while reserving the right to keep the episcopate in shackles? How can they have confidence in such governments? How will they grow attached to the constitution? How will their hearts and souls become one in the national interest? How will they obey the laws with religious respect when in those laws they can see the seeds of impiety? Is it possible that loyalty and deep persuasion can be infused in a people through legal cavils or with the violence of arms? Let us leave those beliefs to the despots. We Italians, with our common sense, continue to recognize that the loyalty of peoples cannot be bought, cannot be cheated, cannot be imposed by violence; and that the harmony, unity, and brotherhood of the Italian nation cannot have any foundation other than the deep and universal persuasion that its governments are sincere, that its laws are true, and the spirit of both is genuinely and completely religious.

What does despotism do to gain the reputation of being religious? Behind the mask of magnanimous protector of the Church, it interferes in all ecclesiastical dispositions and brings to them its materialistic spirit, its spirit of death. It prevents any disposition contrary to it and its vices. The very value of the canons of the councils must depend uniquely on its goodwill. It removes and corrupts the clergy, which has the natural duty to protect the freedom of the people, the rights of the weak and of the oppressed. I said the clergy—but I should have said a part of it—is miserably changed into being the most guilty instrument of its greedy designs.

What more does despotism do? It pretends to take part in the ecclesiastic business that it completely reserves for its supreme vigilance; it pretends to take to heart the counsel of the clergy itself, but destroys the clergy's hierarchy, a hierarchy essential in the Catholic Church, and without which the clergy neither has authority nor natural strength.[12]

Instead of consulting with the bishops, and in the gravest things with the head of the Church, despotism loves to have as counselors of its government simple priests, who are cautiously divided and removed from any influence of the episcopate; indeed, putting them in a continuous and systematic opposition to it. The despot knows very well—when it is convenient for him—how to ask for the advice of a bishop, but if he does not like the advice, then he will ask another bishop and will find a way to put the former in contradiction with the latter—and nothing can come more easily, since the bishops are kept isolated and thoroughly divided from each other and it is forbidden for them to gather and discuss and concentrate on the needs of the Church.

If, therefore, Italy is to be fully and truly free, if it is to be consonant and united in heart and soul, it is necessary to establish the freedom of the bishops to gather in councils and to communicate on all that concerns the government of the Church.

Article 3 returns the election of the bishops to the clergy and to the people, and with this article it will be beneficial to reach an understanding with the Apostolic See.

The return of this freedom to the Church is of supreme importance, as it is at the same time the restitution of a right not only of the clergy, but of the people as well.

Such form of election, which is confirmed by endless canons of the Councils, belongs to the Divine Right.[13]

In vain it is said that the king represents the people. This is a solemn lie, one of those many lies that overflow from the legislations of despotism, and I mean despotism under any form, including constitutional forms and republican forms.

The great bishops that exemplified the Church in its happy days were always elected by the clergy and by the people.

Experience through the centuries demonstrates well what governmental or sovereign nominations have been. Those favored by the secular power ascend to the chairs of the Apostles. If they are not vile, they are always mediocre. Their conduct may even be normal; but where are the examples of outstanding sanctity? They may have a decent education and an adequate knowledge of doctrine; but where are the Fathers of the Church that painted the world with their writings? Where are the great works by modern bishops? They may have an honest character; but where is the firm stance of an Ambrose, or an Athanasius, or a Basil? They may be prudent and affable; but where is the great contempt for earthly things and dignity, the heroic integrity against any seduction of power? Great men are always feared by despots. Great ingenuity is not desired, nor are great saints, great scientists nor great writers. And there are not to be souls that are generous and sublime. First, the rise of these great men in the nation is impeded; and then, if they rise in spite of all the obstacles, they are put aside with contempt. Only the clergy united with the people can give great bishops back to the Church. This is what the very religious Italian nation demands now of its legislators. This is its most intimate and essential need. Without it, Italy will not believe it is fully free and it will not indeed be free.

The shepherd of the Church is the man of the people. Despotism allows foreigners to govern the Church, those who have nothing in common with the flock, not even a common tongue. The despot wants to divide and not unite. He wants to put a fissure between the clergy and the people which Christ made indivisible. Italy, in its rebirth, must do the complete opposite. Magnanimous princes who have granted your subjects so many freedoms, give them full freedom, then, and give the clergy back to the people who had it for so many centuries, and give back the freedom to choose the shepherds.

All canons give the people the right to refute the shepherd that is imposed on them when he does not have their confidence. All these canons are eluded or violated by governments which reserve the nomination of bishops to themselves.

The canons of the Church give the people the right to veto; to the bishops of the provinces and to the clergy of the diocese the proposal of the new prelate; and the Supreme Pontiff always has the right to confirm. Here there is perfect harmony; everyone takes part in an election that concerns everyone.

The troubles of the times, and the artifices of the despots no less than their violence broke such a beautiful agreement, such a learned order which came from the Apostles. Now that the barbarism of the centuries has passed and the nations are mature in their civilization, it is time to return the ancient form. And religious Italy is called first to set the example.

Only the bishops elected by the clergy and by the people can be called national bishops. Only they can feel the need to give their clergy and their people a national education; united with the clergy that elected them, united with the people they came from and to which they have given and from which they have received commitments of confidence and respect, they constitute the strongest bonds that tie the nation together and tie in a knot of religious affection the people with their government. And to this they are not enslaved, because from the government they have received nothing. And they are not enemies, because the government has stolen nothing. Public opinion, from which the government itself takes its power, is that which put them on their pontifical seats. The very same public opinion that necessarily favors a free government because it is the public opinion that institutes it, chooses the shepherds of the church, and in that way gives the greatest possible guarantee to the government itself that the elected shepherds are truly national. The fear that the bishops are not loyal to government and not committed to its happy and glorious course can only stem from a foreign government which is itself an enemy of the nation; from a despotic government which itself is an enemy of justice.

I have asked the Italian princes to return to the Church the freedom that belongs to it, so that it may elect its own ministers and shepherds, trusting in their magnanimity and civil prudence. Civil prudence must tell these princes that today, more than ever, usurpation of the rights of the Church—although legalized and agreed upon—can do nothing but harm.

Now I will turn to the people and tell them: I grew to hate rightfully monarchic despotism. Yet know that, given that nominations to the bishops' seats were forcibly given to monarchs—and that that was done to avoid worse evils that were threatening the Church—such nominations are one of the most powerful means of a monarch's own despotism. Monarchs, through these appointments, make religion a servant of that despotism; they convert the sacred ministers into instruments of their absolute desires. They derail and deviate from its beneficial and popular institution that Church which, created to be the mediator between governments and governed, was tied and dragged behind the imposing carriage of the dominators. Why was the Church of these last three centuries ever rancorous towards civilization and the freedom of the people? Is this perhaps its nature? Indeed, it operated against its own nature, its own mission, its own life, as was even recently demonstrated by an acclaimed writer.[14]

The principal and root reason was this: almost all the bishops of the Catholic Church were appointed by the princes. Let us abolish such appointments, and the clergy will go back to what it must be, and it will be what Jesus Christ made it for—to be of the people.

ARTICLE 4—The state is held by a monarchic government which is tempered by laws.

ARTICLE 5—The deputies of the people, divided in two chambers, and united with the King, represent the nation.

Article 5 says that the nation is represented by the deputies of the people united with the sovereign; and that is for the purpose of removing the unfortunate error irresponsibly introduced in the other constitutions that defined the deputies as the sole representatives of the nation, almost as if the nation could exist without its head from which comes unity, which is an indispensable condition for a nation.

It was the popular violence and anarchy built into the theories of demagogues that was responsible for deputies being given the title of representatives of the nation instead of representatives of the people in the people's constitutions. When deputies are "representatives of the nation," logic finds anarchy in this, as the head is separated from the body, and a headless nation is then recognized. Thus, logic still finds the germ of popular despotism and of revolution against any form of government. Time is essentially logical and indubitably realizes, sooner or later, the consequences of such an erroneous definition.

For a similar reason, it is preferable to define government as "monarchic, tempered by laws" (article 4) instead of defining it as "monarchic, tempered by national representation" since the government holds all powers including the power of the chambers of representatives.

ARTICLE 6—The legislative power is exercised collectively by the sovereign and by the two chambers. The interpretation of the laws belongs to the legislative power.

ARTICLE 7—The acts of government have no effect if not provided with the signature of a minister.

The legislative power is given to the king together with the chambers because the king and the chambers united represent the nation, and a free nation must give its own laws to itself. The reason why the Supreme Political Tribunal is not called to intervene in the formation of the laws will be explained later.

The interpretation of the law has no place when it is obscure and dubious. Therefore, the current disposition that attributes the right to interpret the law to the legislator[15] does not impede the tribunals in the application of the law to particular cases each time they consider it clear. Nothing more is to be said, except when the law seems very much dubious to the tribunals and they cannot therefore apply it in the most rigorous way but only a benignly general way.

Those who believe that the law is obscure retain intact the right to turn to the legislative branch for its interpretation, and on this interpretation the sentence of the tribunal that has otherwise judged must be reformed.

More reasons for article 7 will be given in article 9.

ARTICLE 8—The territory of the state cannot be changed except through a law.

Territory is one of the conditions for the existence of the nation, as we are considering people that are not nomadic but stable and civil. The territory, however, had to be dealt with in the constitution as one of the fundamental principles of the state, and the ability to change the borders had to be reserved exclusively to the nation.

8

Reasons for the Dispositions Contained in Title II

ARTICLE 9—The person of the king is inviolable.

The inviolability of the royal person is established for the good of the nation. To violate the king is to violate the nation.

A multitude of people is called a nation because, civilly, it is a nation. If the multitude did not have a civil unity it would not be a nation. Now, in monarchies, the multitude is united with the king as its head. Therefore the violation of the head is the violation of the unity, thus the violation of the nation.

By the inviolability of the royal person we do not mean merely that the king cannot be offended in his rights, as this is common to all citizens. We intend that to him society's criminal laws are not applicable. This is a privilege only of the royal person. All the people who surround him, and all the things of the King must be subject to common laws (article 19).

But why is there this privilege? We repeat: this privilege is not in favor of the person of the king but in favor of the nation. Criminal laws cannot be applied to the entire nation as a whole, as that would be absurd. For the same reason, they cannot apply to the person of the king who unifies and constitutes the nation.

It is in the interests of the nation that its centre of unity remains intact. The king is the symbol of justice, order, and national stability. And to remain properly united, men have the need to have always before their eyes this unchangeable symbol, which reminds them of the immutability of their union, and of something that is superior and eternal upon which that union is founded.

It is true that the king is a man like everyone else and as such has the same rights and the same duties towards his peers, but from this we cannot derive that he must be subject to the same criminal laws that apply to other citizens. The reason is that which we have explained, which can also be expressed in another form, as follows:

Criminal laws are instituted for the good of society. If a greater good for society derives from the exception of the king from the compliance in body and soul with such laws, then the constitution of society must exempt him. On this reasoning, the right of grace in favor of other perpetrators (article 16) is also founded. Society turns out to be more defended, more stable, and more consistent by recognizing in its king such a privilege rather than by not recognizing it.

Furthermore, the inviolability of the royal person comes also from the concept of head of the civil society to which the royal person belongs. Without the head, there is no society (article 5). Therefore, there is no social power that can punish the king, since the nation no longer exists if it is separated from him. If there were such a separation, nothing would be left but the extra-social rights which do not belong to the powers of civil society.[16]

The inviolability of the royal person demands that society be protected against the abuse of royal power. This is provided for in the constitution by putting limits on royal authority and particularly prescribing that no act of the king has value unless signed by an accountable minister (article 7).

With this disposition, any abuse by the king is nullified, as he can do nothing by himself, but can do all with his ministers. This induced the French to say that "the King rules but does not govern," which is tantamount to saying that he represents national unity and the principle of order. As such, the king imparts order to the government by appointing the ministers and the other employees (article 15). As the government is immediately exercised by these figures, responsibility falls upon them. The principle of order from which government springs remains superior to government and is purely beneficial because it solely performs a function of order while remaining without accountability in itself.

The above would not be entirely true if this principle of order were not circumscribed in such a way as to be almost necessitated to order matters well by causing a good selection to be made amongst those who actually govern, that is, the minister and the other officials. Thus, the King is induced to make a choice of ministers and other employees that is most probably appropriate (as "most probably" is the best we can aspire to, given the limits to the perfectibility of human affairs) using those expedients established by the constitution to that end, those expedients being:

1. The need that ministers are in such a position as to enjoy the trust of the people who are represented by the chambers.
2. The accountability of the ministers and of all other employees. The bad repute of these people causes injury to the reputation of the power that elected them. From this derives that the king be moved by the weight of public opinion to make good appointments.

3. The immovability of certain officials, that is, the judiciary (article 91).
4. The visibility of certain positions, the holders of which are elected directly by the people, such as the deputies of the chambers (article 48) and the members of the Supreme Court of Political Justice (article 82).
5. Above all, the fact that the sovereign is tied to the appointment of positions in a way that is determined by the law and not arbitrarily (article 15).
6. Finally, by the collectivity and entirety of the dispositions contained in the statue, which places the king in a spirit that is totally national, and that reduces each and every interest that the king has to gaining approval of his acts by public opinion of the nation.

ARTICLE 10—The King convenes the two chambers each year. He can extend the sessions or dissolve them. In this last case, he must convene new ones within a term of four months.

The executive power is extremely important for society: the best law would be useless if there was no executive power that enforced them. Thus, the executive power is what gives life and actions to law.

This power is entrusted to the king by article 13 of the constitution and the king exercises it through the ministers and the other employees.

The limits that, as we have seen, are imposed by the constitution on the executive power, are insufficient to prevent abuse.

However, once society has been equipped against the abuse of this power, it must desire that it be defended and guaranteed against anything that could disturb the exercise of executive power. This defense and protection must be given to each social power by the constitution.

Furthermore, it is necessary for the executive power to be strong, as its weakness would be the weakness of the laws and of society. If the executive power could be easily obstructed and disturbed in its function, civil society would itself be exposed to anarchy.

The greatest obstacles to the regular exercise of the executive power are those that stem from parties organized within the legislative chambers or within the citizen militia. The constitution has special provisions against these two dangers, giving to the king, through article 10, the ability to prolong the sessions of the chambers and to dissolve them and, through article 43, giving him the ability to dissolve them along with the National Guard. These abilities are, at the same time, limited by the obligation that the king has, in a case where the chambers are dissolved, to convene them again within the term of four months; and if the National Guard is dissolved, to reconstitute it within one year.

The power to prolong the sessions of the chambers has a further motive: that of not obligating them to sit beyond the time that is necessary for dealing with affairs.

ARTICLE 11— The proposal of laws is done by ministries and laws can be first proposed to either chamber. Either of the two chambers can propose a law upon request of ten members of that chamber. The law proposals made by ministries are discussed and voted on before other law proposals.

In Article 11, preference is given to the law proposals made by ministers, because otherwise some party formed in the chambers could obstruct the regular business of government, preoccupying the chambers with continuous law proposals and by impeding the course of those proposed by the ministers.

For the same reason, ten deputies are required to propose a law. This is also beneficial to the purpose of not consuming precious time in the chambers with vain proposals.

The law proposals can be presented to either one of the chambers by virtue of the principle that the two chambers are perfectly equal, and each represents an equal amount of interests.

This also applies to taxes and economic laws in general, since each chamber has the same interest, and each represents an amount of wealth that pays the same amount of tribute to the state (article 30).

ARTICLE 12—Only the king sanctions and promulgates the laws.

A nation cannot exist without unity, and the unity comes from its head. The laws must be written by the nation. Therefore, they must be made the representatives of the people united with the king (article 5).

The king gives unity to the nation as a principle of order of the powers (article 9). All powers must submit to the principle of order as their fundamental principle. It follows, therefore, that even the laws must be sanctioned by the king, otherwise there would be anarchy, as happens when social powers deprived of unity do not submit to the common centre.

Furthermore, since the king has the duty to implement the laws, it is appropriate that the laws be sanctioned by him, so that the king is not obligated to implement laws that he himself has not approved and that could be in opposition to his intimate convictions.

ARTICLE 13—Only the king holds the executive power.

The executive power must be strong so that social order is safely preserved and laws are implemented. To this end, it is very beneficial that executive power is concentrated in the hands of one with the precautions that we have indicated to prevent abuse.

ARTICLE 14—The king is the head of the state. He disposes of all the powers of land and sea, declares war, makes treaties of peace, of alliance, of commerce, and others, notifying the chambers if the security and the interest of the state allow it, and issuing appropriate communications.

The treaties involving finances have no effect unless they have the approval of the chambers.

Since the chambers are instituted with the main purpose of protecting and properly administering the real rights of all citizens, it is their job to make sure that the finances of the state are not improperly burdened. Therefore, this article establishes that the approval of the chamber is necessary for the implementation of treaties that carry with them a burden to state finances.

For the same reason, it could be asked, perhaps, that even commercial treaties must be submitted to the chambers before being concluded. It seems, however, that this would obstruct and remove the necessary secrecy of diplomatic negotiations. On the other hand, this power granted to the king to make commercial treaties is regulated and limited by article 40 of the constitution, which states: "The freedoms of commerce and industry are fundamental principles of the economic law of the state."

There is also another limitation imposed by the constitution on the peace treaties that the king can make and it is that which concerns the territory of the state (article 8).

Furthermore, the nation has a guarantee against the abuse of royal power in concluding treaties in the obligation imposed on the king to notify the chambers—providing that the security and the interests of the state allow it—through the appropriate communications. This disposition attributes to the chambers the right to examine the treaties that have been made and to censor them, and to bring to justice, when the case warrants it, the accountable ministers (articles 7, 86–88).

Finally, it must be noted that where national unity has the form of a confederation of states such as the one described in the appendix of this modest work, many of the rights granted to the king by this article should instead be exercised by the federal Diet, and therefore this article would have to be modified appropriately.

ARTICLE 15—The king names and makes all appointments that are not foreseen by the present constitution in a way that will be determined by the law; he has the power to issue currency; he creates decrees and regulations that are necessary for the implementation of the laws; but he may not suspend, suspend the observation of, or dispense with the laws. He confers honorary titles.

The appointments foreseen by the present statute other than through sovereign appointment are the deputies and the judges of the Supreme Political Tribunal elected by the people (articles 51, 82).

It could even be demanded that even the judges of the inferior political tribunals be elected by the people. But this did not seem necessary because, since those judges are appointed in the manner prescribed by the law, this will be able to determine the manner of their nomination in such a way as to avoid abuse. For example, the law could prescribe that they are appointed by the sovereign overseen by a triad proposed by the Supreme Political Tribunal. The limitation imposed by this article to the sovereign power over the nomination, the promotion and the appointments must be well noted.

It is prescribed that the sovereign nominates and promotes in the way that is established by the laws.

This is a limitation that is lacking in common constitutions, although it seems of maximum importance for the purpose of guaranteeing the smooth functioning of public affairs. Such smooth functioning depends on the wise nomination and just promotion of those holding offices. If both were left entirely to the whim of the sovereign, the nation could not rest assured that its interest would be properly protected, and that article 41 of the constitution—stating that "all citizens can aspire to state responsibilities according to their abilities and suitability"—would always be fully executed.

Everyone knows how much favoritism and recommendations prevail in the courts of the princes, and how much the means of corruption are practiced in the ministries, as well as the use of manipulation by the parties in the republics. On the other hand, an optimal election to the different offices of the state is a very difficult thing to achieve. However, it is desirable that the sovereign is helped in this election by precise norms, set by law by national wisdom. To take just a small example, who does not know to what level of poverty and pettiness our Italian universities have descended for the lack of great men? If the election of the professors were subordinate to a wide norm, it is clear that our schools would shine with the brightest splendor. The same can be said of all the other branches of public administration.

ARTICLE 16—Justice is administered on behalf of the king by the judges that he appoints. The King can give grace and commute sentences. However, he cannot give grace to ministers who have been convicted, except by explicit request of one of the two legislative chambers.

That justice is administered on behalf of the sovereign is consequent to the disposition that entrusts to him the executive power (article 13) as well as his quality as head of the state (article 14). This is tantamount to saying that he is the principle of order for all powers.

One could raise a question—more subtle than it is important—about the fact that the Supreme Political Tribunal elected by the people nevertheless administers justice on behalf of the king. It is not absurd to answer affirmatively to the question, since the king—being inviolable—is not personally subject even to this tribunal. By electing the members of the supreme political tribunal, the people do not at all elect their representatives, but simply ministers of justice—that justice which the people venerate in the person of its living symbol, the king. Nevertheless, it seems to us that this is a rather idle issue.

The right of grace may seem to be contrary to the intention of the preceding article (article 15) that denies the king the power to suspend compliance with laws and to eliminate laws; but this is rather an exception authorized by the fundamental law to which other laws must yield. It is the constitution in this case that creates the exemption to those laws.

The right of grace is not admitted by the constitution as an arbitrary power, but uniquely as a power that must be exercised for the purpose of the public good or equity; and the same can be said of the right of commuting sentences. The good use of such a right is guaranteed in the same way as all other sovereign acts through the accountability of the ministers.

The fact that this right is limited with respect to ministers who have been convicted is a consequence of the very disposition that makes them accountable, as without such a limitation, it may seem that there is only apparent rather than true accountability. It is clear that the highest loyalty and sincerity must appear in the constitution of the state.

ARTICLE 17—Neither the king nor his children can marry without the approval of the chambers.

The marriages that occur in the royal family are of the utmost interest to the nation. The king and his family must be consecrated to the nation if they want to correspond to the supreme duties of the position they occupy, and a king moved by this spirit will not feel burdened by this obligation to consult the people in the choice of his wife and in that of the wives or husbands of his children. In the constitutional system, he is the first citizen, and the interest of the people that he governs is his own. The king must trust his people, as the people trust their king. The king and the people are not two things but one nation.

This disposition seems also a guarantee that is necessary for nationality. Alliances with foreign families may divide the hearts and the customs of the king and of his house, and it is of benefit that the representatives of the people exercise vigilance over the king and his house.

In other times, sound political thinking mixed with dynastic pride induced the tradition that the princes chose spouses uniquely amongst the people of other royal houses. The political view used in the introduction of this practice, which became part of the public legal tradition in Europe, was to prevent the overwhelming power of some noble family in the state that would become a relative of the king to the detriment of other citizens, endangering the security of the state and the Royal family. Such occurrences, especially the atrocious fights between small tyrants and their people in any other time and circumstances other than the present ones, and in all forms of government, suggested the adoption of this precaution.

Furthermore, the authority of the sovereign was more whole and respected, as in this system his family was placed at an unreachable height.

Perhaps nothing better could be imagined in a period when sovereigns were and had to be absolute, but this practice is not in harmony with the attitude of a constitutional sovereign, who is nothing more, as we said, than the first citizen of the state. If he is citizen, the fact that he becomes a relative of other citizens is not alienating. With the acceptance of the constitution, he has abdicated part of his sovereignty in favor of his people, as his people enjoy now a portion of the sovereign power. Therefore, it is not repugnant that the king becomes a relative of his people. That may be equally useful to the sovereign as well as to the nation.

The weakening of the races of the princes must be attributed in great part to the limited sphere from which they are forced by tradition to choose spouses. It is a proven thing that the crossing and mixing of the blood preserves the dynasties and renews them when they become weak. It is convenient to give back even to the royal houses this freedom of choosing spouses in a sphere greater than the tight one in which, so far, they have been strictly confined.

The arrogance of the nobles who are related to the king is not to be feared in a good constitutional government in which laws reign more than people. Constitutional laws are established to put a brake on the arrogance of those who reign; if much efficacy is conferred on the laws, it is much more credible that they suffice to curb the smaller arrogances.

A sovereign tied to his people even through family links would have a much greater interest in the nation, as he would consider it almost as his own family and he would feel towards it the affection of a father.

Furthermore, in that nation, an illustrious aristocracy would rise that would try to make the nation stronger and more respectable outside of its confines. Such an aristocracy would also serve as a link between the sovereign and the lower classes, which are now divided by an unbridgeable gap; it would be a true support for the throne, as all citizens from first to last would form one chain. Wealth would flow from the top to the bottom without accumulating at the top of the social pyramid, as has so far happened, and is happening more and more. All the state would turn out to be harmonious and one.

May the reader forgive me if, although I do not conclusively state that it is prudent to add some article to the constitution regarding the above matter, I submit my thought to his good judgment and consideration. I will only add that in the special case of a nation having to select some new dynasty, the dynasty surely could not find a tighter knot with which to bind the new king than to obligate him to establish some blood tie with the most illustrious families of the nation. That does not mean, however, the establishment of an absolute prohibition on his descendants from ever joining blood with other royal houses, even when the chambers believe it appropriate. In this way, the foreigner called to hold the destinies of a nation would himself become truly national. Otherwise, who could be certain that all his family alliances would not be foreign? Who could be certain that the very sovereign families would not form, amongst themselves, almost a separate nation—a caste with altogether special interests that are not the interests of the people?

Is not this the origin of all the injustices, all the tyrannical dispositions, and all the crimes of the old diplomacy?

There was only one cause: a purely dynastic diplomacy. Since over three hundred years ago, such a diplomacy had no duties other than best accommodating the interests of some privileged families[17] that were totally separated from the people; the interests of this caste or generation of demigods whose blood would have been profaned and stained if mixed with that of mortals. From this stemmed the concept that the interests of the people were considered irrelevant in war and peace treaties that constituted the modern public right. No voice was heard in favor of the people in the secret congresses of the ministers. The people, assets of those few dominating houses, were divided like actual flocks of sheep. Nationalities were insulted, violated, destroyed. Entire Catholic populations were put under the exploitation of heretical or schismatic sovereigns. That is, they were torn to pieces, divided and ripped up for the profit of dynasties that were partially Catholic and partially heretical. By the same token, entire non-Catholic populations were given to Catholic princes. We Italians, in particular, had to abide by the laws of the Germans, of the Moravians, of the Bohemians, of the Croatians. From the dispositions of such diplomacy it was impossible to expect reason—and even less, guarantees—without being accused of rebellion, treason, or *lèse majesté*. In virtue of the justice of the treaties, cries were answered with guns. In virtue of the public right made to prevail in Europe by the treaties amongst the few prevailing families of the princes, justice became injustice, and the people, whose sacrosanct rights were sacrificed, became the unjust ones. The sovereigns who sacrificed and abolished those rights became the only just people on the face of the earth. When will this state of affairs end? Indubitably, it will happen when the old, purely dynastic diplomacy will have yielded to another diplomacy, a just and truthful one—that is, to a national diplomacy where the rights of the people are represented no less than the rights of the king, and that will happen when the king and the people become a nation that is an indivisible whole. This union, on the other hand, is now more than ever what still can save the royal families from the vindictive reaction of the people. As I speak these truths, I treat with equality the cause of the people and the cause of the kings.

But I believe that to get to this point, one of the fastest and most reasonable means is to obtain that the royal families no longer form a caste segregated from the rest of humanity. These families, by stepping down from their ambitious and harmful height, and establishing blood ties with other families, go back to being themselves a part of humanity, thus recognizing and enjoying the priceless good of universal and evangelical brotherhood.

ARTICLE 18—The endowment of the Crown will be set by the first legislature, and cannot be changed except by a law.

The fact that the nation sets the endowment of the Crown is consistent with the constitutional system. It is also a new guarantee for the nation as to the wise use of power by the king.

ARTICLE 19—The private patrimony of the king is subject to the laws that regulate the other properties.

What is set out in article 19 is a sequitur to the principle that the constitutional king is also the first citizen, and the fact that the private patrimony of the king is also subject to taxation consistent with article 29 is useful to the king himself, as with that he acquires the right of intervention in proportion to everyone else when electing the deputies.

ARTICLE 20—The king's successor, in assuming the throne, takes an oath to this present statute before the chambers brought together for this purpose.

This disposition is common to all constitutions. As the oath is a religious act, it would be appropriate that this pronouncement by the Head of State is completed with religious solemnities.

9

Reasons for the Dispositions Contained in Title III

ARTICLE 21—Each man who is a subject of the king is free and a citizen.

As the word "citizen" has become indispensable in constitutional governments, signifying no longer just membership of a municipality but of the state itself, and the citizens are now subject to the same laws, the use of the word *citizen* in this article seems to correspond to the true condition of things and of the times.

That does not prevent us making a distinction between the laws of the municipality or province and those of national citizenship. Rather, the status of citizen, which cannot be denied to anyone who is governed by the same laws and under the same head, conforms to the spirit of a wide constitution.

The rights of citizens are reduced to the two poles of liberty and property.[18] Articles 22, 23, 24, 25, 33, 34, 35, 36, 37, 38, 39, and 40 protect that group of rights that concern liberty, and regulate the modality of liberty. Articles 26, 27, 28, 29, 30, 31, 32, 41, and 43 protect that group of rights that concern property and, in the same way, regulate their modality. Finally, articles 42 and 44 protect and regulate both groups of rights.

ARTICLE 22—All citizens are equal before the tribunals.

Here we are dealing with *juridical equality*, which must be thoroughly distinguished from *constitutive equality*.[19]

Juridical equality consists in the fact that the rights of all are equally inviolable, regardless of the person who possesses them. Constitutive equality consists in the fact of having the same quantity and quality of rights.

The constitution must guarantee the first type of equality; that is, it must establish an equal protection for the rights of all citizens: both those who have many rights and those who have fewer rights. This [kind of] equality is demanded by justice.

Conversely, the constitution must never establish constitutive equality; that is, never establish that all citizens have the same quantity and quality of rights, as that would mean the destruction of any justice.

That would be the destruction of all rights; although, if we recognize the existence of a particular right, we must also recognize the existence of the title upon which such a right is founded—and this title must be recognized to all those who possess it. But the titles of the rights are equal for both those citizens who have much and those who have little. For example, if we recognize as a legitimate title that of a buy-sell contract, this title is the same for both the citizen who through that title becomes the owner of a piece of land of a few square feet and for the citizen who through the same title becomes the owner of a huge estate. Each owns land of very different sizes in virtue of the same title. If, therefore, we recognize that title as a good foundation for the right of he who possesses the tiny parcel of land, we must equally recognize it as a good foundation for the right of he who possesses the vast land, because the title is identical. If this did not happen, the juridical equality of citizens would be offended, as different laws and different measures would be applied to them. We would recognize as good in favor of one the very title that would be no good for another. We would be dispossessing people, as it would no longer be true that a right is recognized, since it is not the recognition of a right to attribute it to some according to one's whim while disregarding the title upon which that right is founded. It would not be true that we recognize the title upon which the right of the owner of the small land is founded, because that title is not recognized for the right of the owner of the vast land. To acknowledge and not acknowledge the same title at the same time is to not recognize any title of right at all, but, as we said, is the substitution of a right with a whim.

We cannot therefore maintain juridical equality of the citizens whenever we want to destroy their constitutive inequality, as juridical equality necessarily brings with itself inequality in the quantity of the rights that each possesses—which is, in fact, constitutive inequality.

Therefore, the socialists, the communists, the levelers of all kinds destroy the equality of the citizens and their true and legitimate equality, which is juridical, as they apply their principles and measures differently. They substitute right with whim.

It is easy for those people to deceive the populace by trumpeting constitutional equality instead of juridical equality; and it is easy to gain trust by promising that the arbitrary government that they want to institute intends to operate in favor of the people. Thus, through the destruction of all rights, maximum despotism would be established.

The constitution according to justice must do the exact opposite, and it has to guarantee its rights to all and to protect the juridical equality of all citizens.

This equality is guaranteed by article 22, which states: "All citizens are equal before the tribunals."

To state that all citizens are equal before the tribunals does not involve that misunderstanding that would result if we said that citizens are equal before the law. In fact, not all laws are written directly for all citizens, but many are written for a class of them, that is, for those who have the title to which [some particular] laws can be applied. For example, there will be laws that regulate the exercise of medicine, and they cannot concern anyone but doctors. Their universality, therefore, consists uniquely in the fact that they are applied to all doctors, and that all the citizens with the necessary qualities can become doctors. The same can be said of almost all laws: There will be laws for soldiers, lawyers, tavern keepers, etc. In this sense, the citizens cannot be all equal before the law; rather, they will be equal before tribunals, which use the same principles in the application of all laws without distinction to all citizens.

Furthermore, to state that citizens are the same before tribunals does not mean that tribunals for certain classes of citizens cannot exist when they are considered necessary for the better administration of justice for all. So there can be tribunals for the military, for private right, commercial, ecclesiastical, etc.—and at any time it is considered that special laws for those classes of citizens are better applied through special tribunals. These tribunals are not and should not be considered exceptional tribunals, but only special ones because they apply special laws.

ARTICLE 23—Individual freedom is guaranteed. No one can be arrested and brought to justice other than in the cases foreseen by law and in the forms that the law prescribes.

All individual rights of nature and reason cannot be touched by the actions of civil society (article 2). Yet, up to this time, such rights have been sucked into the vortex of the actions of civil society, as if by an inexorable machine that has crushed them. I am not referring just to monarchies, but also to civil society in all its forms.

It is therefore fair that civil society gives hereinafter guarantees that protect those rights from the blind behavior of its powers; and one of these guarantees is this article.[20]

ARTICLE 24—Residence is inviolable. No visit to a place of residence can take place if not to enforce the law and in the forms prescribed by the law.

This is a guarantee offered by civil society in protection of the rights of domestic society. Civil society must never obstruct domestic society; rather it has to serve it as a means to an end.[21]

ARTICLE 25—No one can be removed from his natural judges.

If the power of government, whether monarchic or republican, could change the judges and the tribunals in accordance with the accused, it would no longer be true that the citizens are equal before the tribunals (article 22), and juridical equality would be compromised.

For the same reason, in order to remove the danger of political power influencing the administration of justice through splitting people into different classes before the law, the independence of the judicial order from the political one (article 80) and the immovability of the judges (article 91) is also here established.

ARTICLE 26—To travel anywhere in the world is a natural right. Emigration cannot be denied to anyone who demands it.

Up to now, governments have in different ways violated the two natural rights that each man has of traveling and emigrating; that is, to exit the civil society to which he belongs.

These violations stemmed from considering civil government as a seigneurial rather than as a civil government.[22]

It is now certain that Christianity today has brought the nations to a state of civil society and has brought to an end the seigneurial element that was mixed in them, which was of violent or pagan origin.

Men freed by Christianity have returned to exercising all their natural rights. Our planet has been assigned to the human species and each man must be able to travel in any direction in any way and establish domicile wherever he wants, save the rights that have been acquired through just title by his brothers.

With the pretext of the security of the state, governments invented passports and used them as a tool for despotism, molesting citizens in a thousand ways and forbidding or obstructing their most innocent journeys and those that were most useful to their education and interests.

Even the right to emigrate was unrecognized. It is false that a man must, in virtue of being born in a place and under a certain government, be perpetually ascribed to that civil society in which he finds himself. Each special civil society is voluntary. When the citizen no longer wants to belong to it, he can demand to be untied, and that must be granted to him—as long as he surrenders the advantages of that society and satisfies the special obligations he has contracted with it or with its partners.

ARTICLE 27—All properties are inviolable. Forced expropriation is not violation of property when a legally ascertained public good demands it, and through a fair indemnity which conforms to the laws.

This article declares all properties inviolable, and it is so clearly just that it is admitted by all constitutions. However, there are laws that, at least indirectly, offend property and thus violate the constitutional law without possibility of appeal. Indeed, in the very constitutional statutes are introduced certain dispositions which, with their inevitable consequences, violate the wholeness of the right of property.

And that is necessarily bound to happen in all those constitutions where the properties are not proportionally represented in the chambers, as will be discussed later. Here is the true reason for the unhappiness that those laws leave in the people, and of the continuous fighting they give rise to.

The inviolability of property written into the constitutional charter is not, nor can it become, a de facto truth, unless we accept the franchise to be proportional to properties. The very equality of the electoral vote is itself an offence to property because, as we shall demonstrate later, the electoral vote must be considered as an appendix, a portion of property right. Hence, with the attribution of a vote of equal weight to all electors, the charter contradicts itself and violates the article through which it intends property to be inviolable. It lays the seed for all legal violation of property and by that I mean those violations that are later consummated on behalf of the laws and then sanctioned by those very same laws. Wherever there is contradiction in the ideas there is conflict in facts—and the conflict that begins with restlessness ends up with revolution.

In the chambers that arise from such corrupt constitutions, the very deadly belief in the omnipotence of the law—that is, of the omnipotence of the legislators through the laws—is insinuated. In this belief, the violation of property regularly perpetrated through a law that has been voted by the chambers and sanctioned by the king is no longer a violation. The possibility of acquiring property must be open to all citizens, so they can enrich themselves through their industry, through their labor and through their ingenuity—and this is certain. But it is equally certain that after having legitimately acquired possessions through the full freedom of action that has been guaranteed, the citizens must have their possessions kept safe and inviolable. Now, to say it once again, this cannot be achieved unless with a proportional suffrage system in the election of the electors.

To understand this truth it is appropriate to put aside abstractions and embrace calm attention and reckoning.

When a thief steals a purse, robs a house, or rips the clothes off someone else, then everybody understands that a theft has been committed. But if a gambling game is instituted, such as lotto, *rolina, bassetta, faraone*, etc., where the house has thousands of times more chances of winning than those who play, and which has a real value immensely greater, how many are those who clearly recognize that this is a hidden theft? How many can understand that in that game there is such inequality that it is unjust? The populace—and even many of those who do not belong to that ordinary populace—get caught in that net, and leave their wealth in it. Their thoughts are locked on the chance they have of winning. They do not calculate that the probability is all against them; and even seeing that the loss to which they are exposed is extremely probable, they do not fear it, as they hope to avoid it. But you ask a mathematician, and he will tell you that greater probability has a real value, and it is equivalent to the certainty of losing. Therefore, the good laws condemn such games as unjust, as frauds, and as real theft. And how many cheats and hidden booby traps exist that can be used to steal somebody else's property? Ask the usurers. Penetrate into the nature of many contracts that have the appearance of being honest and you will find inside them the art of robbery. You will find some artifice used to obtain someone else's property without just title. These are robberies done without the resentment of the robbed for the only reason that he is ignorant and cannot see the rope used to catch him.

Now, if all properties must be inviolable as this article 27 of the constitution establishes, it is better that society acts in such a way as to defend all properties not just against the theft that is open and obvious to all, but also against the theft that is hidden and full of artifice and which hides itself from the eyes of those—and that means the majority of the citizens—who do not know how to calculate.

Now, what should we say of a civil society which is ordered in such a way as to be nothing but a big gambling game where some citizens are the house and are certain to win while others gamble all their properties in that house?

I will now proceed to demonstrate that all civil societies that have adopted a French type of constitution are exactly that. I will demonstrate that those civil societies are nothing more than *organized theft*. My demonstration will have mathematical certainty, as it is based on the calculation of probabilities.

It is either better to delete the article "All properties are inviolable" from constitutions or, if we keep it, then we have to make it become a truth. To that end, we have to configure legislative chambers in such a way that they never come to steal the property of anyone with their laws. To achieve this, it is better that in those chambers each property, each portion of property, has its own voice that defends it and guarantees it so that each portion of property enjoys an equal probability of being preserved unharmed.

Rights are not truly inviolable if some way—no matter how covert or contrived—exists so that those rights can be violated with impunity by using some pretext, even if that pretext is—or acts on behalf of—positive law.[23]

Expropriation for the common good and under the conditions established in this article is not an exception to the principle of the inviolability of property. The concept of an exception to the inviolability of property is instead what is proposed in some of the Italian constitutions published so far.[24] The reason why expropriation as configured by this article is not an exception is because, through it, we merely replace one value with another equal value. Therefore, with this disposition, we only make a change in the implementation of the right without altering the substance of the right itself, and that does not exceed the powers of civil association.[25]

ARTICLE 28—The deeds of trust extending to nonexistent parties are not recognized by law.

With this declaration, the legal principle that those who do not yet exist cannot acquire rights is established.

It is beneficial to highlight this concept to prevent the unwarranted obstruction of the free exchange of property. As we have mentioned already, the constitution must do two things. The first is to remove all the obstacles that impede property and prevent it from flowing into anyone's hands as the rights of reason and nature demand.[26] The second is to prevent property from being usurped or invaded, with any excuse, against what the right itself establishes.

The first of these two maxims prevents unfair aristocracy—that is, the arrogance of the rich who would like to perpetually tie wealth to their families. The second one excludes unfair democracy—that is, the arrogance of the non-rich who would like to steal wealth from the rich. Let us stop the hatred against the rich and let us stop the hatred against the non-rich. There must be hatred for no one and justice for all. May those who are not rich become rich, but with a fair title and without violence or fraud. May the rich become poor, but again with fair title; but if there is no fair title, may they preserve the wealth and goods they possess in all safety. As long as civil society is not ordered along these norms, it will not be free because it will not have learned to be just, and thus it will be neither peaceful nor happy.

Only in article 28 do we say that deeds of trust are not recognized by the law in order to allow families to freely observe the disposition of the father who orders the trust, thus respecting in this way the family right.[27]

This article does not destroy the natural right to possess that even perpetual societies have.[28]

Civil society must recognize and possess this right like all other natural rights (article 2). If it did not recognize it, it would be in contradiction with itself, since it too belongs to the group of perpetual societies[29] and thus it would declare itself unable to possess.

A perpetual society never dies; however, the kind of trust that it forms is not of the kind that extends to those who do not exist.

The entrance of a new member in a long-lasting or perpetual society, when it is done according to the conditions established by the end and by the statutes of that society, becomes the juridical title through which the new member becomes entitled to the personal and real advantages related to that society.

But what would happen if the members of a long enduring or perpetual society were to establish a pact among themselves through which society could acquire but no longer sell or alter what had been acquired?

Such a pact would obstruct the free exchange of properties. However, that would give government the right to undo such a pact, yet not to forbid it, since it is not illegal and it is even an exercise of the natural right of property. Yet the government should not recognize it, and should treat it as if it had never occurred, so that citizens could not found any legal action before the state tribunals on such a pact. In such a case, the sales, donation and, in general, the alterations affected by such a society would be considered valid before the tribunals as if the pact had never been established. In that way, the government would save the principle, useful to all, of preserving properties free in their natural course, without offending in the least natural and extra-social rights.

In the past, governments offered the Church a false protection, and with the pretext of such protection they usurped the administration of its goods—where they did not manage to openly steal them. This false protection tended to make immobile and almost inalienable the properties of the Church and of the ecclesiastic orders, interspersing a thousand difficulties to the free expropriation of those properties. The enlightened solicitude of governments must do the very opposite: Let free even the course of these properties so that they can pass into other hands whenever the Church itself finds that to be appropriate. Ecclesiastical benefices, although sometimes they may seem a sort of prodigality or dispersion, are far from damaging to the public good; rather, they turn out to be advantageous and are themselves sufficient to remove all the problems that could arise and still now partially arise from the stagnation of ecclesiastic properties.[30]

ARTICLE 29—No one can receive decorations, titles, pensions, employment [appointments] from a foreign power without the authorization of the king.

The intent of this article is to give one further guarantee to the preservation of nationality. What this article establishes about the personal advantages that are not appointments is something that could be controversial.

One could ask: What is the guarantee given by the sovereign that this power will not be abused by depriving some citizen of an advantage to which he could legitimately aspire? Is the right of this citizen endangered?

First of all, I answer that I do not consider this article to be very important, as I believe that even without it, nationality is sufficiently guaranteed by the rest of the constitution.

For the same reason, I would not disagree—if that is found to be appropriate—with the idea of adding an obligation on the part of the sovereign. That obligation consists in—before denying a citizen the authorization to accept honors or proceeds from foreign powers—to consult some special jury or commission, and to make a decision on the opinion of these bodies; alternatively to turn to some other means that can offer the desired guarantee.

But at the same time, I do not regard it as probable that the sovereign would want to abuse such a right, as his own interest and the nobility of his regal soul incline him to help citizens rather than to disgust them with injustice and inappropriate duress. At the same time, I also believe that the nation must demonstrate a certain trust in its head without pushing to the extreme the principle, which is useful and necessary in more important things, to demand that for every act of the sovereign (even one of minor importance) there must rigidly be precaution and guarantees. As for everything, even in this case we must apply the maxim: *est modus in rebus*.

Concerning the need for an authorization before the acceptance of employment from foreign governments, there can be no doubt. Then the law will have to establish that those who accept employment without authorization remain suspended from the exercise of their civil and political rights or also, depending on the case, deprived of citizenship, which is tantamount to saying they are excluded from the civil society to which they belonged.

ARTICLE 30—All properties share the burden of the state in proportion to their income.

The justice of this article needs no proof, as it proceeds from the universal social law.[31] As we state that all properties contribute to sharing the burdens of the state, any privilege of immunity is excluded, as the juridical equality of the citizens demands.

It is not difficult to understand that the distribution of taxation must be done in proportion to the income of each property rather than from the properties themselves, as, since taxes are collected each year, they have to be considered as a passive annuity that weighs on properties almost as a equalizing fee to be subtracted from the profits of those properties.

However, what deserves the most consideration is that this article establishes the basis upon which the state finances must be regulated.

And this, generally speaking, seems to be admitted by all constitutional states; but when we get to the actual facts concerning applications, even this article, like many others, remains a lie.

So far, finances have not been regulated on firm principles of equity and justice. They have been almost solely regulated by considerations of utility for the state. The treasury was filled in the easiest way, which was least considerate of the subjects and of least damage to industries and commerce. The ideas behind this method are excellent, but they have to yield to the justice of a fair allotment, that is, be competently subordinate to that value.

There are two reasons for which such a clearly just principle does not become fact with that near completeness that might be possible. The first reason is the already-mentioned vice concerning the equal vote granted to electors, in which the deputies that write the financial laws and establish tributes are not interested in the equal protection of all properties. Thus, they are inclined to distribute taxes and burdens on certain properties rather than on others, and convince themselves that what they do is fully legitimate and justified for the mere reason that they do it through a law.

The second reason is the extreme difficulty experienced in the distribution of the burdens in such an equal way as to truly be able to tax all the property incomes in a fair proportion.

We will briefly deal with both these reasons, starting with the first.

We believe that public taxation will never be imposed and distributed with justice in the nation as long as the equal vote prevails in the electoral system. Even less, since the equal vote system does not give any guarantee to the nation, should we expect justice to prevail in the imposition and distribution of taxes. Here are the proofs of our belief.

The equal electoral right system is divided into two parts. One is called universal franchise and the other is a system that imposes a property qualification on the electors.

We reserve for later the proof that the system called *universal franchise* does not merit this denomination, as it is very false to say that such a system grants all citizens the electoral right, as it cheats with its misleading name. We shall fully prove that, as we shall also prove that the system we propose is much closer to a truly universal franchise. But for now, we will assume that the universal franchise is truly universal.

What is the equal vote given to those citizens that have a certain amount of property, and what does it involve? It is, and it involves, an equal amount of power in the writing of the laws granted to all those citizens who have that established amount of property, regardless of the major or minor groups of rights that the property possesses, as the property represents each of those citizens.

What is, then, the universal franchise in this assumption, and what does it involve? It is, and it involves, an equal amount of power in the writing of the laws granted to all citizens regardless of the major or minor groups of rights that each citizen possesses or represents.

That this is the situation and that the electoral right involves an influence, a degree of power in the writing of the laws, and that the vote is equal, is an incontrovertible truth accepted by all revolutionaries—it is recognized by universal sentiment. In fact, why does everyone aspire to the power of giving his vote in the election of the deputies? And why do those who still do not have that power fight so hard to acquire it? And why to solve this problem are there not only discussions but insurrections and even massacres? Obviously, because much importance is attributed to the possession of this electoral right, and why is it so if not because this vote influences the choice of the deputies and thus the laws that the deputies must write?

We have therefore to admit as an incontrovertible political axiom that each citizen has an influence in the writing of the laws in proportion of the vote that he casts in the choice of the deputies who are in charge of writing the laws.

From this axiom immediately follow the two consequences that we mentioned.

1. That, in the universal franchise system, each vote (no matter what the group of rights that he has is) has equal power in the formation of the laws.
2. That in the equal vote system with a certain property qualification, each citizen possessing that qualification (no matter what the quantity of his rights is) has an equal degree of power in the formation of the laws.

Proceeding with the consideration of the consequences that stem from these two electoral systems in the formation of those special laws that concern public taxation, we state that, having constituted the legislative power of the chambers with one or the other of those two methods, we will never have fair laws concerning public taxation, as taxation will never turn out to be distributed according to the aforementioned principle of social justice written in the constitution, which states: "all properties share the burden of the state in proportion to their income."

That principle will only be a beautiful maxim on paper and it will never become a reality. It will be a lie and not a truth.

Even if I were to limit the proposition only to the statement that the nation in the two electoral systems that we have mentioned has no guarantees ensuring justice in the vote and in the distribution of taxation—and rather, the nation has good reasons to fear the lack of that justice—I would still come to the same conclusion, as the lack of guarantees is equivalent to abuse of power, and a probability of damage is tantamount to damage.

I will begin by demonstrating the hypothesis on the universal franchise. After that, it would be easy to demonstrate the hypothesis on the equal vote of those with property qualifications, since the same arguments can apply to both systems—although that which establishes an equal vote for a certain property qualification has shortcomings of other kinds.

In the system of universal franchise, all citizens, regardless of their means, have an equal influence in the laws that establish a tax, and that determine the distribution of those laws.

It is natural that each citizen is inclined to burden himself as little as possible; the powerful stimulus of his own interest pushes him to that. Is it not true that their own interest generally moves men to tip the scale in their own favor rather than in somebody else's favor? To deny that would be to deny daily experience; it would be to deny the obvious. Where do all the private and public injustices that fill the world come from? Certainly from one's own interest; and to state that with a more general word, from the selfishness of each one of us. This inclination is so strong that it throws men into such injustice that even the criminal laws, no matter how strong, are inadequate to fully prevent injustices and crimes of all kinds. Can we therefore hope that men abstain from those injustices towards which their own interests push them in those cases where they can be unjust without fearing any punishment? In those cases when they can freely commit injustice because they are protected by a public power with which they are invested while having full legal title? This is the shortcoming that is now universally recognized in systems where there is absolute power—and to avoid this, constitutions are invoked.

The universal and equal franchise in the election of the representatives puts the majority of the citizens in just this predicament. It puts them in a position where they can exercise an injustice for their own profit in the formation of the laws concerning taxation with a very legal title. They can do this on behalf of the very same legislative power, the supreme power of the state, to which no injustice can be legally imputed, as the state in such systems is considered the source of justice. The law in societies as they have so far been constituted has always been considered to be justice itself.

Now, that this is the true situation must be clear to any man who thinks impartially about the fact that in the majority of European civil societies, the number of those who possess considerable substance can be calculated to be at most 1/400th of the population, and those who possess average substance to be 1/100th of the population.[32] From this calculation derives the legitimate consequence that in the universal vote system, the taxes are established and distributed so that those who possess the most can only intervene with one vote—and they have 399 against them, while those whose possessions are average intervene with four votes, and they have 396 against them. If we want to add the vote of substantial owners to it, we would have five votes in the interests of those who possess average substance, against 395 other votes. This enormous majority granted to the minor possessors and to the proletarians against the great and average fortunes demonstrates sufficiently, so as to constitute evidence, that in the universal franchise system the laws concerning tax are made entirely according to the free whim of tiny proprietors and of those who own nothing. These, therefore, are actually the only holders of the power to make laws on taxation, which is tantamount to saying that we can draw annually on the wealth of all citizens the necessary amount—more truly, the amount desired by the legislature—for the expenditures of the state. From those who own little or nothing, and from them alone, the large and medium-sized property owners receive the law concerning what they have to pay to the state regardless of what that law is—without the ability to influence it, form it, and even without recourse after the law has been formed.

Now I ask each man of fairness and common sense: Do we not we have here 399 tiny property holders and proletarians who hold in their hands all the wealth of the rich? Are they not put in such a condition by the electoral law in which they can fully second the instincts of their won interest and with impunity, by violating justice at the expense of those who possess more than they do? Can they do that not only with impunity but also with the authority of legislators, on behalf of the nation and with the greatest legality? How, then, can all properties of the citizens be inviolable (article 27) when those who have nothing or little can arbitrarily dispose of the properties of those who have much? Will not this article of the constitution continue to be a lie? And what guarantee can we ever have that can ensure the contrary?

I do not believe that there are any supporters of the universal franchise who would dare oppose me were I to say that I trust the probity of this majority of tiny property holders and proletarians; yet if one were to trust the probity and the disinterest of men to such an extent, it would then be useless to establish guarantees, to demand a constitution, and to demand a government where even the people have a share and can intervene in the handling of their interests. I ask all that because we know too well—and experience has demonstrated it and demonstrates it every day—that the whole of mankind does not possess such a high degree of virtue, and it is therefore necessary to reduce peoples' temptations, and to put them in such a condition that they do not commit injustice against their peers for the greed of their own advantage, or at least not with impunity.

I can easily convince those who would oppose me of their errors, as I can demonstrate that they are in contradiction with themselves. Why do they feel such repugnance when faced with the idea of surrendering their system? Why would they be—and rightfully so—unhappy if we were to propose to substitute for their system another system that would go to the opposite extreme and that would accord the electoral right to no one except the biggest property holders? Would they not protest—and as I said with good reason—that in such a way the people are sacrificed, that the small proprietors and proletarians are oppressed, tyrannized, and burdened with all the burdens of the state? Certainly it would be that way—but why? Because in that case, only the rich would impose and distribute taxation (among other things—but taxation is our subject here). Now, would my opponents be happy if I were to give as an answer that they have to trust the probity of the deputies that would arise from such elections? That they have to entertain no doubt that those deputies will do everything with justice and humanity? That those deputies represent the nation and thus it is the nation that imposes upon itself? Would not such an answer be an insult? But I am far from giving such an answer.

One answer for another, then: If you do not want such an answer, then do not offer it. If you find it unjust in the mouth of the aristocracy, then recognize it as unjust even in your own mouth. If small properties are inviolable, then recognize that for the same reason and with the same title, the large properties are also inviolable.

But history explains only too well how the universal franchise system was born and had to be born. It was born in virtue of that law which dominates in nature no less than in society, for which to an action corresponds a reaction, and balance does not result if not after the oscillation of many actions and reactions that continuously decrease in intensity. In virtue of this law, the society that goes to one extreme—when it realizes this and experiences the sinister effects—instead of going to the middle, rushes towards the opposite, which is, in fact, reaction.

The extreme that was reached by society in the Middle Ages through to the French Revolution was the unjust aristocracy. The grand seigneur made the law and consequently the taxes, and all the other onuses of the state mercilessly weighed on the shoulders of those who were not grand seigneurs. Such a cruel and prolonged injustice excited the resentment of the oppressed, and they shook off their unfair yoke without them realizing that they were falling into the opposite extreme. I say without realizing, because I assume that everybody is in good faith. The constitutions that establish an equal and personal vote are, in their intimate substance, nothing but a revenge of the modern age against the Middle Ages—a revenge that took legal form. Now, the small proprietors and the proletarians tell the grand seigneur, "You have oppressed us so far, now we want to oppress you as well; you have made the law as you wished so far, but hereinafter we will make the law and we will make it as we wish."

To be convinced that this was really the way things were, it is sufficient to take a look at England's situation in 1838. In this nation, which was more attached than any other to the aristocratic customs of the Middle Ages, to be eligible for the House of Commons, it was necessary to possess £600 as an annual fee for the counties (15,000 francs) and £300 pounds for the cities in those counties (7,500 francs). What happened under the weight of such a high wealth qualification? What had to happen: Landlords wrote legislation which was to their exclusive advantage. With the Corn Laws, the import of foreign grains was almost forbidden and the extremely high price of this first essential good, which they were selling to the people without any competition, was sustained, and on top of that they kept their lands almost completely sheltered from tax! It is enough to say that the lands in England do not pay any fee, any municipal taxation, any tax on transfer of property; nor do they pay inheritance tax. In short, of the gross income of the British treasury, which is £52 million, indirect taxation contributes no less than £38 million while direct taxation on land including the property of the Crown contributes only £1,532,000.[33]

There was a time when Europe was in a similar and even worse condition, as it cried under the weight of a conqueror aristocracy. How many privileged properties in France did not pay tax of any sort even in 1789? All the major ones. That was a flagrant and enormous injustice.

Let us now turn the page and observe the reaction. The French Revolution started with the proclamation of the sovereignty of the people, which was a vague expression without a precise sense,[34] as were all the expressions used in those times; anarchist expressions because they assumed sovereignty before the existence of social organization; expressions that, by retaining the ancient concept of sovereignty do nothing but transport the ancient despotism of the king into the people and, in fact, the populace. So the multitude was invested with regal omnipotence, but with one difference: While the acts of the kings always were somewhat restrained by the force of the people that the king faced, the omnipotence of the people had absolutely no limitation, as the force of the king was annihilated. I will not even discuss the violation of property, of the appropriation of the goods of the clergy—which are always the easiest to pillage, as they are the least guaranteed and most endangered—nor shall I mention the countless other events that damaged property. Those events would certainly not have occurred if it had been for the will of the property owners themselves, and if others had not possessed the power to put their hands into the purses of the owners rather than into their own. If all proprietors could have had a voice, if they could have kept an equal protection, what would have happened? There is no doubt that all the needs of the nation would have been met and debts would have been paid equitably and without blood, as this was equally advantageous for all proprietors. It would have been useful to all if finances had been restored; in that way all credit would have been relieved at the cost of any sacrifice. But at first, this concept was opposed by prejudices founded in the long possession of power by the nobility, the court, and the clergy. The Revolution started from an act of justice, from the abolition of privileges and exemptions. But when the Revolution had in its hands the power to do this act of justice itself, then it felt that with that power it could do much more with impunity, it could shape laws as it pleased and make justice a tool of its whim. Instead of adopting the principle that "all properties share the burden of the state in proportion to their income" this was completely forgotten in practice, and was substituted by the fastest expedient, that of grabbing the goods where they stood and where it was easiest to do, saving the purse of those who made the law, as that purse was the only inviolable one. This fact is so clearly true that that principle of justice concerning the distribution of taxation was not even seriously mentioned in the debates of the time, as the most privileged part of society spoke of generosity while the least privileged part spoke of pillage. The middle way which would have been the just one was not conscientiously considered by anyone. The most generous was the clergy, and for that it was pillaged first and completely, and what is worse, it was put under salary. There was therefore an offence on the one hand and revenge on the other, while passion was everywhere and justice nowhere at all. The Revolution had only one man who thought calmly and deeply, the Abbé Sieyès, praised by all and followed by no one.

Let us put aside all that happened afterward in France, and consider the effect over the course of a few decades of the adoption of personal instead of real representation; that is, the electoral vote as given to people instead of things, and consequently the legislative power to impose taxation that was put into the hands of those with little or no property. This effect is visible both in the way of thinking of that nation and in the acts of its government.

The French people were so much influenced in their way of thinking by the principle that was established—that is, that each citizen, regardless of his properties, had to have an equal degree of power in the election of the deputies—that we ended up having the creation of those systems of socialism and communism that now trouble the entire world. But that was what had to happen. Socialism and communism are the logical consequence of the equal and universal vote in the election of deputies. Because if this electoral right is just, then it also is just that those who have little or nothing have the right to put their hands into the purse of those who have much and dispose of the contents as they see fit, without control or restriction of any sort. And if this is just, then it is also just that all properties are leveled by removing them from those who have more and giving them to those who have less. Thus, any disposition of the wealth of the more affluent citizens wished by the small proprietors and by the proletarians is also just. This is, in substance, what socialism and communism are.

If we consider the acts of government concerning taxation when it is established by the small proprietors or by the proletarians, we see that taxation increases without control, since those who pay the most are not those who write the law in this predicament. Such governments, therefore, are not the inexpensive governments that were promised. The facts are there to prove the consequential truth. Never before did France pay over 1.5 billion in tax, which is what it had to pay under such governments.

And assuming the principle that each citizen, regardless of the mass of rights that he enjoys, must have an equal degree of influence in the legislative power, and then establishing an electoral property qualification, is a contradiction—and contradictions do not last. The universal vote was demanded by France with logical coherence, and finally obtained through the last revolution of February, 1848.

There are still few facts about the new assembly obtained through this electoral mode, as the assembly has just been constituted. However, we can examine through reason if such a system is able to correspond to the principles of justice that, in a free country, must preside over the regulation of taxation; and through the little the assembly has done already, we can deduce what it is really willing to do.

The regulatory principles of taxation in a nation that has conquered its liberty are three, and are universally recognized as political axioms:

1. That the nation is that which taxes itself; that means—and it can mean nothing else—that the majority of taxes are approved by those who pay them.
2. That there is economy in finances; however, taxation must be as light as possible, having regard for the needs of the nation.
3. That taxation is distributed over all properties without exception in function of what the properties yield.

The first of these three principles needs some explanation. With this principle, it is established that the nation is that which taxes itself when at least the majority of taxes are approved by those who pay them. In fact, it would be absurd that the nation tax itself if the majority of taxation was not approved by those who pay, and if there were approval only by those who pay only the smaller quantity of the tribute that goes into the state treasury. In any system it is impossible to obtain that all taxes are always approved by those who pay them; it is sufficient that this happens for the majority of taxes in order for us to state that the nation taxes itself. But if the largest share of the taxes is collected against the will of the taxpayers who are forced to pay through the will of other citizens, it is a blatant lie to state that the nation actually taxes itself.

Now let us see if, in the French universal franchise system, it is possible that the majority of taxation is approved by those who pay or if, instead, it is decreed without their slightest participation in consent. If consensus exists for the majority of taxation, we shall say that the nation decrees taxation itself. If consensus does not exist, or if it is not possible for it to exist, we shall say that a decree of taxation on behalf of the nation is a blatant lie and that the nation actually is under an absolute government from which it receives the tax law in the same way that, in the past, the people received absolute monarchies. It is wise not be deluded by the form, but to look for the truth in the substance of things.

To simplify our calculation and make it clearer and more secure, we will restrict it to taxation on land, which so far has been, as it turns out, the most regularly distributed.

In the French universal vote system, we calculate the electors to be 10 million.[35] Amongst these, 150,000[36] belong to the largest property holders, who possess one-fourth of the land but contribute one-quarter of the whole territorial tax, while 9,850,000 are medium or small property holders who share three-quarters of the French agricultural land and pay three-quarters of the land tax. Therefore, the contribution is imposed by the 10 million electors through their representatives, and each elector has an equal influence.

If the 150,000 electors who pay a quarter of the total tax were to have a quarter of the influence in establishing the tax, and the other 9,850,000 who pay three-quarters were to have an influence equal to three-quarters, then it would always happen that each time the contribution is decreed, the majority of it would be approved by those very same people who pay it and in that way we could say that the nation taxes itself. This is evident because the property itself would have the vote, and a majority of the votes would indicate the largest amount of the property. This is what is obtained in the real vote system which is proportional to the tax paid by each.

But a completely different result is obtained by the universal franchise system, which is the French system. In fact, those who pay a quarter of the tax—that is, the 150,000 electors who belong to the families of the largest property owners—instead of having a quarter of the influence in the chambers of deputies, have only 1/66th. Therefore they have one vote for themselves and 65 against.[37] Thus, those who pay 3/4 of the tax and thus, once the tax is divided into 66 parts actually pay 48, have instead the power to give approval for the 65 parts; that is, they give approval for the 48 parts that they pay and for the other 17 parts that they do not pay for—as those 17 parts are paid for by the major property owners without their consent, and even against their consent. It is therefore evident that each time we put together a number of small owners and proletarians, which, put together, end up paying only 25 of the 66 parts into which we have divided the total sum of the tax, since they have the majority of the personal votes, they are able to make the law prevail that establishes the tax which is imposed on the nation for the 25 parts of those who pay and for the 41 parts of those who do not pay.[38]

Now, if for 41 over 66 parts the contributors must pay the contribution without their consent, against their consent, without any possibility of appeal, how can we truly say that the nation taxes itself? How can we say that this nation is free? A freedom under which the majority of the contributions is imposed with force and by the whim of those who do not pay, is it not an illusion? Are not the small owners and the proletarians absolute sovereigns? Absolute sovereignty does not change its nature whether it is in the hands of one or many, as it still operates arbitrarily and has the ability to use somebody else's goods without limitation, without guarantees, and without any possible appeal. Such, when it comes to taxation, is without question the result of an electoral system that attributes an equal vote to each citizen without taking into consideration what the citizen possesses. Figures do not belie themselves; rather, they belie undetermined and vague words. The demonstration is mathematical.

From this result, we can argue whether in the universal franchise system, we can better observe the second principle, which must preside over the good distribution of tax: "that there is economy in finances; however taxation must be as light as possible, having regard for the needs of the nation."

We have already mentioned that the governments under the equal vote constitutions are anything but inexpensive: This fact is inarguable. It is a natural thing. We can expect economy from men who spend their own, but how can we expect it when they spend somebody else's money, which they dispose of by law, with which they can buy the glory of doing great and beautiful things?

For those who have little or nothing, it is of very little importance whether the finances of the state are administered with economy or not, whether there is squandering and prodigality. Rather, they like that, because of what is wasted, each can grab a bite. They approve of great works of public utility, and even of luxury, without any problems, because the expenditures come from the coffers of the rich and those expenditures are imposed on the rich with the most absolute of commands, which is the command of the law. These legislators are inclined to let the government into all those enterprises that should be freely left to private industry, and often inclined to reserve to the government itself the monopoly, because they care very little about the damage that is caused to private entrepreneurs and to capitalists. If they care, it is not out of respect for private property, but uniquely because they fear the repercussion that would be felt by the small owners and the proletarians, which is the class those legislators belong to.

Even now, I read in a newspaper what follows: "The number of people subscribing to the registers of the national work houses in Paris is little less than 120,000: the expenditures that their unproductive work causes are over 4 million francs per month in Paris alone. But the institution of national work houses, which is already bad in principle, was made even worse by the abuses that infiltrated it. There were many people under the program who, although they claimed need, actually had other means to sustain themselves. Many participated fraudulently under different names so as to take more payments from the state."[39]

Things that have been reduced to this condition in France confirm with facts and evidence what we have stated—that an equal vote in the election of deputies eventually results in socialism; and that this system tends to convert the whole nation into one gigantic work house, into one immense manufacturing plant where the only entrepreneur is the government. What troubles France so deeply—the problem of the organization of work—is due primarily to its electoral system.

Only England so far has understood well that it is convenient for the government not to substitute itself for private industry. The work houses of France did not execute any real and productive work. The worst of workers refused by private factories are admitted to those laboratories; in this way the government amasses an imposing brutal force that has no restraint and that aspires to looting and to revolutions. The newspaper I mentioned before observes in all truth that: "when the workers are dispersed they feel the influence of their employers and of the most thoughtful and well-intentioned of their friends, and thus they can resist more easily the seductions and the threats of those who are more turbulent. But when they congregate in a great number they no longer have any restraint and the growth of discontent becomes a function of immorality." With things in these conditions, can we ever have a peaceful and safe, prosperous and happy society? Could the rights of all be protected? Is this the desirable state or nation?

The deputies of the people elected through a universal franchise are not, for the same reason, much adverse to loading the state with debts. This is because—not being themselves the creditors of the state—they have no great interest in making sure that the debts are covered in any way, since they know that they will not be the ones that pay them. Under such governments, public funds are always vacillating, and they necessarily decrease the state's credit. This is also something that keeps the state in continuous instability and certainly does not contribute to the true prosperity of citizens. Thus, the speculations of the bank, the frauds of rigging the market, and bankruptcies are the plagues always present in constitutional governments that are set up this way, especially in certain periods. In the meantime, England, which has a constitution, and which certainly has shortcomings arising from the opposite tendencies, gathers to itself the wealth that runs from governments constituted according to the French system. It is therefore impossible that in governments that have adopted the principle of universal franchise there is economy in finances and good administration of the public revenues.

However, the representatives elected with equal vote and who decree very abundant taxes are always covered by the name of the nation. It is the nation that draws wealth to itself; it is the nation that draws to itself the gains that, in another system, would be deserved by private speculators. It is the nation, they say, that gets rich. Truly, this nation's word has a magical ring. Damned is he who speaks anything against it! Such a person is backwards; he is an enemy of the nation. Is it no longer legitimate to bring the words back to their proper meaning? Will it be thus a crime to unmask the hypocritical lies of the smart conmen who spin people around, or the lies spoken without knowledge by ignorant fanatics? We are looking for the truth—and know we are never happy with beautiful slogans, brilliant abstractions; we want to see the truth of facts; we want freedom in reality. We want real juridical equality, real inviolability of property, real prosperity. We are not happy with words because no one can live on words emptied of reality. Those who pay tax, are they not the nation? Those private citizens who are prevented by invasive governments from accessing lucrative industries, do they not belong to the nation? You then make two parts of one nation: Proletarians and small owners are one part and large property owners the other. And then you cancel the latter from your agenda and expect that the nation is made only of the former and that this nation of yours must live with the substance of those whom you have separated from the nation. Here is the artifice; here is the legislative theft. This is how to put a rift between the citizens—and the permanent hostility, the disagreement rooted in the law, never produces good for anyone.

Do we perhaps fear that if we gave to all what belongs to them, that if we were to grant to the owners an influence in the imposition of tax that is proportioned to the quota they pay, so that taxes are mainly decreed by the contributors; are we then afraid that those contributors would be too tenacious and in order to save they would deny the necessary funding to the government? What an empty fear! Give me the contributions that are equally distributed over all properties within the nation and in proportion to what they yield. Act in such a way that the owners who pay more have the compensation of the greater influence that comes with their larger contributions and their power to decree. You will see that many divisions between citizens are removed and you will see that everyone will take an equal interest in the common good, because everyone knows in this case that they are equal in their right, while no one feels sacrificed to the unjust supremacy of the others. You will see that everyone is interested in prosperity, in the glory of the homeland, in the cessation of parties, in the generous payment of tributes without complaint, because the people themselves have decided they want them. At the same time, you will see the appearance of the strictest administration of public funds and on a smaller budget, while public works will be executed to improve all parts of the nation equally and to aggrandize the splendor of the nation itself. It is through justice that concord and peace is achieved, and it is with concord and peace that great works of public utility are done.

But this distribution of taxes proportioned to the revenue of all properties which I demanded as a first condition, and that constitutes the third principle of good financial laws, is that which so far has never been obtained, because there was insufficient participation in the formation of the laws by the interested parties. Those laws were always written by the absolutism of the monarchies and also of constitutional governments.

Absolutism mainly consists in commanding the purse of others. If the absolute ruler is a monarch, he decrees the taxes and makes them fall where he deems best, where he finds less resistance: on the rich and on the poor, without caring much for fair distribution. If the absolute rulers are the extremely rich, they make taxes over the less rich and on the poor. If the absolute rulers are the proletarian or the small proprietors, they unduly aggravate those who are richer than they are. Such is the case of the universal franchise system that has taken root in Europe over the last sixty years.

But in this system, there is even less guarantee to the nation for a just distribution of the burdens because those who hold brute power are in command and make law. If they do not turn to the most manifest injustice right away, it is only because legislators still retain some habits of action left to them by their predecessors, and because they have not yet come to the full realization of what they can do with impunity in the name of the law.

However, it is certain that sooner or later they will do anything they are allowed to do—and here we come back to the example of the contemporary French assembly. The assembly has at this time fully demonstrated that it refuses to recognize the principle of equity and social justice that demands that "all properties share the burden of the state in proportion to their income." United by those people to whom it was preached for sixty years that each citizen has the right to have an equal vote in the election of the deputies; united by those people who, as a legitimate consequence, demanded of the justly congregated assembly that one billion francs be taken from the purses of the rich (and let us note that only two hours for the pillage were granted); that assembly, far from recognizing the principle of clear social justice that all citizens share the burden of the state in proportion to their income, adopted right there and then a tax which, instead of being distributed in proportion to income, progressively, and as the income grows, progressively elevates the rate at which it must be paid. This concerns the nobles of Paris; and the rate of this tax grows in the following proportion:

Rental Income		*Tax and Percentage*
From 201 to 400	. . . .	2½ per cent
From 401 to 500	. . . .	3½ per cent
From 501 to 800	. . . .	4½ per cent
And from 801 to	any greater sum	5½ per cent

In such a way, a rental income of 400 francs pays, as we can see, 10 francs, 1/40th, and a rental income of 1,000 francs, if it had to pay proportionally, should pay only 25 francs; instead it is progressively taxed at 5 ½ per cent, that is 65 francs, which means 1/18th.

It is peculiar that the progression stops at 800 francs of rental income, as if to spare the richest, almost as if the progression is recognized as fair for the small proprietors—but not for the large proprietors. But going further in this way would have been impossible, and that itself demonstrates the erroneous nature of the principle, since a true principle has consequences which are always possible.

Now, not keeping the same hand with all citizens in the distribution of tax administered to these with one measure and to those with another, and not tax all properties equally, that is with the same rate—this is to destroy *equality* among citizens, an equality that was so highly proclaimed: the equality of rights. We have said it already: the law based on constitutive equality, such as that of equal electoral right, destroys *juridical equality*; which is tantamount to saying that it destroys justice.

The progression of this tax contradicts, openly and directly, the evident principle of social right that all properties of citizens share the burden of the state in proportion to their income, and therefore it is a masked theft perpetrated by the legislative power on behalf of the law. The progression therefore violates the other principle of natural right which states that all properties are inviolable. If the constituent assembly of France is to be consistent with itself, it will be very careful not to write these two principles of social right and of natural right into the new constitution that it is forming; because if it did write them, the flagrant contradiction between words and facts would demonstrate that the new constitution began to be fraudulent even before being written.

So, the history of the governments that have existed to date demonstrates that the unjust action of the rich was followed by the equally unjust reaction of the non-rich; that governments wanting to avoid one extreme fell into another; that an offence was followed by revenge; that the organization of society was born from the fight between classes of citizens; that when the class of the rich prevailed with force, that class alone created and conceived social organization for its profit; and that when, after a fierce fight, the class of the non-rich won, that class in turn wanted to imagine a social organization that was to its exclusive advantage.

But now it seems to me that the time has come to put an end to such a selfish war; a time when we can come to a conciliation between two opposite interests, and when finally we desist from attempting to organize society according to the principle of the force of the one or the other class prevailing at the moment—as if social organization were a field of conquest, a domination of that class that was able to subjugate the others. Italians! This generous and holy enterprise of peace now belongs to you, as you are in the process of organizing yourselves into a government. Be the first to let the world hear that word not yet pronounced—and not yet pronounced with the truth of action, that word which says and does this: The unique principle upon which a civil society must be organized is social justice and not the brutal predominance of one class of society over another. To each, what he owns. Part of this justice is the inviolability of all properties. Part of this inviolability is the concurrence of all citizens to pay the tax in the exact proportion to their income.

Thus, tell the privileged classes: no privilege, no exemption. Regardless of the property that is protected by the state,[40] it will pay its tribute in proportion of what it yields.

Thus, tell the class of small property owners: You shall pay less because you have less income, but you shall pay as well the same quota that has been assigned to you in the identical proportion.

Thus, tell all classes to proclaim loudly the principle that tax is illegitimate if it is not approved in its greatest part by the property owners; and that in order to make this so, it must not be decreed by any random number of citizens who pay more. To that end, it is better that each portion of property is represented, that it has its vote in the imposition of tributes, which is tantamount to saying that the electoral vote is proportional to the tax that each pays to the state. Those who pay little must give their assent for the little they pay, and their assent must not count for a greater amount. Those who pay much also must give their assent for the much that they pay, and their assent must be worth much.

To make an example (because it is a good thing that there are many examples), let us assume that the total contribution is equal to one hundred and that the contributors are four. Each of the first three pays a value equal to two and the fourth pays a value equal to ninety-four. If we are giving to these four people a personal vote of equal value, and we assume that all four agreed to pay the tax, each one of them would have given consent to payment for a value equal to twenty-five. Thus, the first three would have given a consent that can be expressed with these words: "We accept to pay out of our pockets a value of six and we consent that our companion pays out of his pocket a value of nineteen." Therefore, these people would have given a consent they are not entitled to, since we are talking about a payment that they do not have to take out of their own purses, but out of the purses of others. Now, in our case, this consent is a law: The fourth person must pay a sum of nineteen—a sum that he did not impose on himself, but that was imposed by others against the principle upon which, in a free government "each must tax himself." To further clarify the issue, let us assume that the three people, each one of them paying two, gave their vote for the proposed tax of the value of one hundred, and that the fourth person who must pay ninety-four gave a negative vote. As there would be a majority of votes, the tax would be decreed. It follows that those who pay six have had the power to establish a tax equal to one hundred: In fact, they have had the power to impose on themselves a tax for the value of six, and to impose on others a tax for the value of ninety-four. Can we then say, in such a case, that the contribution has been imposed by the contributors on themselves? Certainly not, as it is exceedingly evident that the largest portion of the contribution was imposed by some citizens on one other citizen against his will, and that, furthermore, those who imposed the tax imposed it just for a minimum part on themselves. Therefore, if we have certain citizens who can arbitrarily impose on other citizens the largest part of contributions, it is evident that the principle that citizens tax themselves no longer applies. Now, let us assume that the number one hundred that we have taken to express the total amount of tax is one hundred million écus, and that the four who decree the tax through the majority of votes are the four hundred deputies of a nation. Can we say that in this nation taxation is voted by the taxpayers? Certainly not, but it turns out that it is clearer than the sun that only six million are voted by the contributors and the other ninety-four million are not voted at all by the contributors, but are voted by other citizens on the shoulders of the contributors without even knowing whether these consent or do not consent—and probably against their will. Let us say it one more time: This is clear despotism. Each time the tax is voted for its most part by those who do not contribute, it is not a free government but an absolute one—because it depends on the arbitrary actions of some citizens approving, more or less, concerning the others, and not on a true majority approval.

We cannot therefore reasonably hope, as long as the people's deputies are elected on an equal vote, that inviolability of property and the good government of finances will become facts. The same applies to article 30 of these constitutional projects, which states: "*All properties share the burden of the state in proportion to their income.*"

We have said that there is yet another reason for which this article of such clear justice has so far remained out of reach in all governments, none excluded, when it comes to its actual implementation. The reason is the extreme difficulty experienced in distributing the tax burden in such an equal way as to get it to hit all property incomes with the right proportion.

This difficulty seemed to be so great in the eyes of certain economists, they declared the hope of overcoming it a utopian idea[41]—so little was their faith in justice!

We are firmly convinced that whatever is just is also possible, and possible to the extent it is useful and necessary. We therefore believe that such difficulty can be absolutely overcome, and furthermore, that it would be overcome in a short time, if those who decree the taxes were all interested in overcoming it. But it is sure that in the equal electoral right, all are interested instead in not overcoming it. Only when the proportional vote system is adopted will we have legislators that have, all equally, the maximum interest in studying such a difficulty and in overcoming it. Thus, then and only then, will it be overcome—if not all of a sudden, at least gradually and with an ever-growing approximation.[42]

It is true that in order for the situation to come to a head, the entire financial system that has been used so far must undergo radical changes, and it has to be entirely refuted, as it is just a superficial construction randomly propped up and without any foundation in justice, and against any justice. But what does it do? And why will we be afraid to do what we must do? Why will we hesitate to free the nation from this enmeshment of arbitrary and unjust laws that entangle and torment it?

We shall proceed to sketch briefly the financial reforms that are indispensable to achieve, as much as possible, the implementation of this very important article of the constitution which establishes the principle that all properties share the burden of the state in proportion to their income.

The whole structure of taxation should be contained in only two laws.

The first one, to be voted each year, should have as its only task the establishment of the percentage to levy equally on all incomes. This law would be very brief since it would be composed of only one article which could be expressed in two lines.

The second law—which would not need to be voted each year but could be reviewed by the chambers each time an improvement was thought possible without touching the fundamental principle—would determine the way of collecting [taxes].

This would be naturally extended, and it is on this point that we have to stop for some time and consider how much should be changed in the system that has been used so far in order to replace it with a new one. Let us review the different kinds of taxes.

The taxes presently used are either direct or indirect. Direct taxes are those that the state receives as a straight tax. The indirect ones are all those the state collects under any other title, for example to protect state manufacturing, or as title of compensation for public services provided by the state, or as a title of gain for industries of which the state holds the monopoly, etc.

Indirect taxes are distributed randomly rather than according to justice, as it is impossible to calculate exactly who the proprietors are who are hit with the tax, and in what proportion they are burdened.

Let us take some examples, the first of them concerning taxation on consumption.

I. Taxes on Consumption

A poor family with many children may consume and thus pay to the state more than a stingy grand seigneur who lives alone. Two families with the same number of members and the same means end up contributing to the state very different amounts uniquely for the circumstance that in one of them the head of the family is generous and in the other, he is stingy.

The tax should be levied on what comes in and not on what goes out, and consumption is what goes out and not what comes in. Nor is it valuable to state that those who consume must have something to consume and also have income, because this supremely general principle does not answer the question in the slightest. In order to answer the question, we should be able to affirm that consumption is always proportional to the income of each person, which is not so. Rather, the contrary is true, since a part of consumption is necessary—such as what is necessary for survival—and that is determined by need, and not by income. Other consumption is determined by the will of consumers and since that will is arbitrary, the consumption is not all proportional to the income.

And here an important question arises: "Should taxation be applied on all income, or should taxation be applied on income only when the income exceeds the needs for survival?"

I have no doubt that taxation must only be levied on the income that exceeds the needs of survival, since neither justice nor humanity allows that the government taxes the governed on what they need to survive.

Here we can detect another vice of the tax on consumption, as it falls indifferently on both what is necessary for living and on what is superfluous.

So, the tax on consumption can never be equally distributed; but when it falls on first necessity goods such as bread, salt, etc., then not only is it unjust, but I think it is also barbarian and inhuman!

We have seen that a stingy rich person can consume less than a large, poor family. But let us also suppose that all families were equally large and that they were somehow obligated to consume almost the same. Still, this tax would be unjust because all, both rich and poor, would pay equally, where it is just that the rich pays more in function of the greater income that he gets.

Therefore, taxation on consumption, if we want to fully satisfy this article 30 of the constitution, must generally be abolished.

I say *generally* since an exception should be made for those goods that, when abused, are detrimental to the state. For example, in China, where opium is abused, there would be nothing unjust with a tax on this good. In countries where alcoholism dominates, a tax on inebriant liquors would be commendable. And what is stated for merchandise also applies to related arts and professions, such as, for example, that of the tavern host and similar ones. Such tax weighs, so to speak, on the vice and it is an indirect penalty used in the attempt to hit and diminish it. In that case, such tax loses its nature as tax and therefore the need for its distribution in proportion to the income ceases.

Nevertheless, I believe that similar taxes should be municipal or provincial, as it is clear that they should be higher in some places and lower in some others—and not universal.

One can ask if taxation on luxury items is allowed. But I equally answer: If consumption of luxury items threatens the morality of the people either for their excesses or for their quality, in this case the government is authorized to charge people with a tax that becomes some sort of a fine—the ability that government has in such a case does not proceed uniquely from the right it has to impose taxes, but much more from the right it has to improve public morality and prevent its corruption. These measures are useful to the whole nation, but especially to those who are taxed; therefore there is no injustice to them.

But if we are talking about an innocent luxury in a country where luxury is held within certain limits, it would be unjust to impose taxes on luxury items, firstly because these contributions would not be equally distributed and would deprive some citizens of those innocent satisfactions that they are entitled to. Furthermore, such taxes would fall in the end on the poorer classes, such as that of the workers, since the manufacturers would have to sell at a higher price and thus try to decrease the cost of manpower or to restrict the number of the workers—and that would be a wound to industry.

II. Capitation or Head Tax

What should we say about capitation, that is, head tax? That it is an unfair tax!

1. Because it is not equally distributed, as it falls equally on all, rich and poor.
2. Because it takes that part of substance which is necessary to the sustenance of the citizens, and that is reason enough for their sustenance to be immune from any burden, as we said before.

Here the question arises as to who are those who have no other income other than what is sufficient for their sustenance.

We answer that such are those who are manual workers, that is, they work for daily wages and only work as laborers. It is a maxim that is generally accepted by economists: The employment of manual labor obtains no other gratification than what is sufficient to the sustenance of life.

On the other hand—and rather, in consequence of this principle—if one wanted to impose a tax on the earnings of manual laborers, that would necessarily increase the cost of labor, and so that tax would obligate property to engage in a useless circle, imparting artificial motion on property, which is always inconvenient and harmful because it is against nature.

What we have said about capitation applies to all equal taxes. Equal taxes fall equally on the rich and on the poor, thus they are unjust and must be abolished.

III. Immoral Taxation

There is no need to say that those taxes must be abolished. The lottery was rightfully listed amongst immoral taxes. Lotteries and gambling are amongst those activities forbidden by the law when they are run by private individuals. However, the state appropriates the right to profit from them—as if what is unjust and immoral becomes just and moral when perpetrated by governments and their laws. Such is the opinion that governments have so far had about themselves—at least for those things the injustice of which they could cover with some appearance of justice. The lottery is immoral because it betrays poor ignorant people and deprives families of the indispensable by raising empty hopes that very often change into most disgraceful passions, fermenting irresponsibility and disinclination to work by promoting superstition and empty observances.

The lottery is unjust because it is a contract between uneven partners, that is, between those who hold the house and those who play, but leaning in favor of the former with a probability that is immensely greater and in fact turns into certainty. The chambers that are elected with equal vote are also a lottery, as we have seen—a lottery of a kind that is immensely more disastrous where the proletarians and small proprietors hold the house and the rich play their fortunes.

Every lottery, large or small, under this or that form, must be forbidden; and it is even more absurd to convert the entire civil society into a great lottery.

The tax received through any form of lottery can never be equally distributed according to the income of the citizens.

IV. Public Utilities Provided by the State

There are public utilities that, according to the principles of a good government, must be provided by the states, whether because private industry would not have the means and could not guarantee the service, or because they bring changes to the national properties, or because it is demanded by public security. Examples of those services are: the mail, bridges, roads, canals, etc. Now, the state financial authority has taken possession of these public services for a gain to the public treasury.

The state financial authority, in this as in other areas, had no respect for the principle of social justice according to which citizens cannot be forced to pay more than the amount of their respective income. It is evident that the profits made by the state for those public services that it offers are unjust, because they do not turn out to be distributed equally to all citizens in proportion to their income.

Thus, we need even on this point to return to justice. It is just that those who make use of these public commodities pay the expenses that the state sustains in their favor. But it is not just that the price becomes inflated because of profit-making on those services, services which the public is obliged to make use of.

Getting a net profit out of public commodities maintained at the expense of the state is something that contains within it yet another injustice, which is that of depriving many citizens of the use of those services—all the citizens, that is, who cannot sustain the higher cost. That is directly opposed to the purpose of instituting public commodities. It offends the juridical equality of the citizens, and has the taste of unjust aristocracy.

It is therefore appropriate that the taxation established for horse and hand-delivered mail, for the maintenance of bridges and roads and similar services, are decreased to the level where they are sufficient to cover the expenditures that the state must sustain and nothing more.

V. Import and Export Duties

Generally speaking, these duties are contrary to the liberty of commerce and industry, the principles of which are recognized by article 40 of this constitutional project.

Export duties can be admitted only temporarily and as an exceptional measure in case of first necessity merchandise and when there is reason to fear that these could threaten the sustenance of the citizens. In that case, the export of those goods could be totally forbidden.

Another exception could take place when it involves the safety of the state—present or threatened—in war time, when it concerns weapons, horses, and anything that could increase the forces of the enemy.

Such exceptional cases, however, should be recognized by a law or by a vote of confidence issued by the chambers to the ministry.

The import duties on foreign merchandise cannot be established as a tax, either, since they can never be distributed in a mode that is proportional to the income of all citizens—which is the principle of justice that is to govern taxation. Therefore, all customs duties established as a tax are unjust.

If these duties are so heavy as to create contraband, they also contain an extreme immorality. Through those duties, the government is the reason why many citizens abandon honest professions and turn to illicit profits that instigate denunciation. The government is then obligated to punish the crimes that it itself has created; so, to the children of the guilty fathers nothing is left but the inheritance of vice, which has become their only means of sustenance.

Export and import duties as a tax are therefore an injustice and sometimes have also the effect of depriving the people. Furthermore, they harm commerce and national industry because they deprive both of the necessary liberties.

The advantages from these liberties seem today beyond any controversy. I will not enter this discussion as I yield to the economists who have dealt with it in great depth. I will only say here that, although the customs duties cannot be generally recognized as tax, I do, however, recognize two exceptional cases where a just and wise government could be authorized to temporarily raise some duties. These two cases are:

1. In a state where the prohibition system has prevailed and thus industry and commerce have taken an exceptional course and shape, we cannot—without damaging many—all of a sudden destroy that status quo which is against nature by suddenly allowing a full liberty of industry and commerce. It is wise to allow time for industry and commerce to back out of their false direction and return to their natural and free ways. It is therefore appropriate that custom duties be gradually decreased until the natural state of full liberty is reached.
2. The condition of a people could be such as to benefit from some ramification of commerce and industry that cannot flourish in that nation—and that for several reasons:
    - —Because the first investments need capital that cannot immediately yield sufficient profits because of the competition from foreign merchandise coming from countries where the businesses are already organized.
    - —For the incompetence of those who start a new industry for the nation.

— And because of the lack of initiative of the capitalists.

In this case, a customs duty that protects against foreign merchandise, and an export duty on raw material that is imposed judiciously and moderately, could encourage the whole industry by allowing the birth in the nation of workshops and factories which, once they have been well started, could sustain themselves and maintain competition with foreign products. At that time, any protective customs duties should cease so that those very enterprises do not grow unnaturally in opposition to the free course of industry.

These customs duties that cannot be justified as tax can be perfectly justified instead as being in the interests of national common utility. But considering how easily state financial authorities could perpetrate abuses in this case, it is appropriate that each case of their application be discussed in great depth by the legislative chambers, and be recognized by a law.

IV. State Monopolies

Amongst all financial laws, the worst are those that tend to fatten state treasuries with monopolies. It is a paramount principle of England that the state is never to become the entrepreneur for speculations that by their nature belong to private industry.

The government of a civil society must not convert into a mercantile or industrial agency. This goes directly against the purpose of its institution, which is that of protecting the liberty and competitiveness of the citizens for profit and never to invade this, or enter into competition with it.

Rarely can the government realize from those enterprises the same profit that is realized by the private sector, which exercises vigilance over those enterprises because of its own interests. Thus, monopolies or even simply profitable enterprises that the state takes over bring two great evils to the nation: They take away branches of industry from the citizens and they make them less productive and sometimes even non-productive or passive.

And even in the case when they would yield a considerable income to the state, such income would benefit some but not all citizens, nor would it be distributed in function of individual income.

Hence even this way of taxing must be abandoned, as it is unjust.

VII. Taxes on Paper and Newspapers

Even the tax on paper does not allow an equal distribution, nor does it fall on all citizens in function of their income. The tax on newspapers and other publications is not quite as unjust—although we believe that it is beneficial to apply a license tax, as we explain later.

VIII. Taxes on Transfer of Properties

It was thought that with this tax, property could be "caught" with a lower tax at a moment when the citizens were aggrandizing their fortunes with the transfer of property. But here too we can see that not even the introduction of such a tax was dictated by a principle of justice, but suggested by secondary views of political prudence. We believe that the mission of a wise government is not that of surprising citizens with cunning, by squeezing money out of their pockets in any which way so long as the citizens do not complain. We rather believe that the government must honestly tell citizens: "You pay me so much, and you pay me that much because it is just that you pay me—as you can see from the law which explains the reasons to you."

On the other hand, concerning mortuary taxes, it is true that when those taxes are imposed, that is the moment when the heir who pays them increases his patrimony. However, the same does not happen in buy-sell transactions. Indeed, in this case, sales tax weighs on the seller, as the worth of the good for sale decreases as the tax to be paid to the government increases. Instead, even the vendor should be spared, as this benefits the buyer.

To conclude, we can add that these taxes also become a useless obstacle to the transfer of properties.

IX. Taxes on Windows, on the Wheels of Cabs, on Dogs, Horses, and Other Animals

These types of taxes have the same shortcoming of not being distributed fairly. Nevertheless, taxes on dogs, horses, and other animals could be justified by a moral end, that is, they could be considered as luxury laws in the case when the legislator wants, with the use of them, to moderate the exorbitant luxury of the rich. In this case, what we have said before about luxury items applies to them.

Under this aspect of public morality, those taxes are even more just because they are voluntary and are at the advantage of those very same who pay them—and this is a moral advantage that must be supremely appreciated by the whole society and its government.

We have so far spoken of indirect taxation, and we have seen that all of these taxes must be either abolished or greatly modified if we want to reform public finances according to the principles of justice, which is the only basis considered indisputable by society. What we have examined is the negative part of the above-mentioned reform, and now we have to pass on to the positive part, which concerns direct taxes which, generally speaking, are susceptible to a fair distribution, that is, a distribution which approximates as much as possible the exact ratio of the income of the citizens. But before getting into this second part of the financial reform, we would like to prevent some objections, as we know well that the novelty of the proposal will elicit against it the repugnance of the old prejudice.

The first objection will be: If you want all taxes to be levied directly on incomes, the citizens will feel the weight more and they will complain. It is therefore convenient to make them swallow the bitter drink without them realizing it.

I respond that governments must stop treating the governed with cunning, taking advantage of people's ignorance. Rather, it is necessary to enlighten people about their own interests so that they know how to exercise a reasonable surveillance on the acts of the government itself.

Which government feels that it is necessary to use such cunning and scheming with the governed?

Only the government that wants to cover the injustices that it exercises against them; that government that wants to pull the wool over their eyes and cheat them with the distribution of tax. Thus it is so in all those forms of government where taxes are decreed by one class of citizen at the expense of the others—whether that class is that of the rich as it is in the English constitution, or that of the small proprietors and proletarians as it is in the French style constitutions. In any case, it always turns out to be necessary to use cunning to cover injustice from the eyes of those who suffer that injustice; and it turns to be necessary to keep the people in ignorance of their interests as well as finding indirect ways to tax without the people realizing it so as to prevent complaining as much as possible. But if the government really wants to do justice, that justice must essentially be liked by the whole nation and it is the duty of the government to enlighten the people. In such a way, the nation no longer resents those taxes that are voted in the greater part by those who pay them, and those who pay them recognize them as necessary and justly distributed. Those who pay them also recognize that they are the smallest possible and that they are administered economically and that they weigh less just because everyone contributes proportionally. Those who pay have compensation in the electoral right, as they carry more votes in proportion to the tax they have paid. And finally, less expenditure is required to collect the taxes. A civil nation cannot desire to pay more through cunning rather than pay less through honesty. The second objection is that wanting to harvest all the incomes of properties would make necessary a hideous inquiry into the possessions of every citizen. This is a prejudice, as the objection states that avoiding this problem is impossible even before trying to avoid it.

Whenever we admit the proportional franchise system, property—wherever it is—has an interest in coming forward rather than hiding. It has an interest in gladly accepting that tax which ensures to it a greater influence in the state and in the formation of laws, as property pulls behind it a higher degree of electoral right. Those sums of money that in contemporary constitutional states are spent in corruption to buy out votes with extreme damage to morality and justice would instead tend to flow into the coffers of the state. Instead of generating processes of corruption which are expensive and flawed in their success, it is more likely that we would have, instead, denunciations to the political tribunals against those who tried to force a greater tax as a payment to the state than that which would be due from the size of their income.

The way to establish approximately the income of properties is a matter that we will examine now, and we shall see that it does not require detailed or intimidating searches. At any rate, I ask: Is it licit for a government to be obviously unjust at the expense of some citizens with the pretext of not molesting them? First of all, citizens demand full justice from government, and it is to render justice that the government is instituted. The government cannot subtract itself from this first and universal duty using captious excuses or subterfuge, claiming inability or ignorance, because for that the government would be damned.

A third objection will be brought forward, and it is that citizens' credit would suffer if their properties were highlighted in public too much. This is very false. We must distinguish between two ways of credit: that based on truth, and that which is exaggerated and misleading because it has no foundation in a corresponding wealth. The government, which knows the economic administration of the state well, must be respectful of the credit that has its foundations in real wealth, but it must consider a credit greater than that produced by the fortune of citizens a fictitious credit, and thus an immorality and a public calamity.

This last type of credit is founded on appearances and cunning, while the government must not favor anything but the truth.

When some entities can easily acquire a credit that is not in the right proportion to their financial substance, what happens? They abandon themselves to enormous speculations in which they end up losing themselves and dragging behind those citizens who entrusted them with capital. Thus we see numerous bankruptcies, never absent wherever the credit goes beyond those limits established by the laws that govern the course of wealth. With bankruptcies, the illusory structure of excessive credit crumbles. Then it is replaced with the absence of credit and panicky fears, the stagnation of commerce and industry, shock to the state and its finances, and the loss of the private fortunes of many innocent and honest citizens.

The government must protect the property of all against any method that could be used to threaten it. It must not make the way for imprudent and reckless people with the pretext of favoring certain families who aspire to become extremely rich by risking everything. Therefore, the wise government must not favor the birth in the nation of a credit that is unlimited but momentary, but only of that credit which is firm and supported by real wealth, and which, through regular and constant behavior, allows the progress of the nation towards an evergrowing prosperity. Now, to this end, it is important that the true quantity of wealth of every citizen is known rather than hidden. This is the most effective means of preventing the disgrace of the great bankruptcies and ensuring that all citizens own what they own, as well as what they can industriously acquire. For example, the credit of a national bank is born when the capital which is destined to the insurance of its business is known. If this capital were to stay hidden from the eyes of the public, its credit would go up in smoke. The same can be said for the credit of a nation and of the commercial or industrial firms that exist in it.

Let us now proceed to sketch the sources of those direct taxes that are susceptible to being distributed amongst the citizens, more or less according to the established principle of the individual income.

It is appropriate that the taxation hits both fixed and liquid assets equally. This derives from the principle of justice that is adopted.

The tendency to spare industrial and commercial properties in favor of others is an injustice, a violation of property exercised by means of the law. The cause of this tendency is not just the difficulty of hitting those properties, but one that is much deeper. If we consider that the consequence of the equal vote granted to the electors is that industrial and commercial property ends up having a greater number of representatives in the chamber than any other property; and that the small proprietors who are truly those with power in the chamber of deputies are necessarily more interested in favoring industrial and commercial property than any other, the explanation of the phenomenon is complete. This paramount cause is present even more in the universal vote system.

Now, if the election of the deputies with equal vote brings with itself this injustice which seems to favor industry and commerce—but which truly damages even these sources of public wealth because it damages the nation—then in a nation such as Italy, which is mainly agricultural, the indecency and the damage is even greater.

Industry and commerce must certainly be protected and encouraged—but not through injustice, which never brings to the state any true and solid good. Rather, they have to be protected and encouraged through the principles of freedom sanctioned by article 51, and through any other reasonable means.

Therefore, direct taxation—which is the only one that can be equally distributed—must hit all incomes. Those taxes can be reduced to what follows:

1. *Lands and houses*—the taxes on buildings are those that offer fewer difficulties and they are already universally adopted.
2. *Mortgage capital*—this also is known by its registration in the mortgage office, and thus is easily taxable.
3. *State obligations*—the state which pays the interest to the creditors must retain the percentage established by the law on any income.
4. *Public banks, insurance companies, and any other enterprise of public interest which is managed by private individuals*—the percentage of the tax must be levied on the annual balance.
5. *Personal credits*—I would like to see established by law that even personal credits brought about by a private or public act must also be registered in public ledgers that are especially established. This must happen at the moment those credits are granted, without the possibility of any action in front of the state tribunals. On this registration, which is established as a necessary condition for the validity of the mortgage contract according to the civil law, it would be possible to know what tax must be paid by the creditors.

6. *Private bankers, wholesale merchants, and heads of factories*—these should be taxed as a block after an approximate estimate of their income in each city or in each province, and each of these blocks should then distribute the tax amongst its members through an assembly.
7. *The same can be said about the retail merchants and the heads of stores*—only the laborers must be exempt from any tax, since they do not contribute anything but the strength of their labors to social work, and thus we cannot assume that they earn more than what is necessary for their survival.
8. *Each mechanical art* must have its license taxed on an approximate calculation of the art's income, and those taxes must change according to the provinces, the districts, and the municipalities, since according to those circumstances the exercise of such arts turns out to be more or less lucrative.
9. *Even on all the pay checks issued by the state to its officers* it is appropriate that a certain percentage be retained as tax.

These nine categories of direct taxation have to embrace all properties. It is appropriate that even the municipal goods pay the state's general treasury the percentage of tax that has been established, since the goods of the municipality are enjoyed by the citizens that belong to it, and it is not fair that a rich municipality be put in the same condition as a poor one.

Only in this manner do we believe that the article of the constitution that states, "all properties share the burden of the state in proportion to their income," may become true.

One must reflect upon the fact that, since there is no longer tax on first necessity merchandise—neither directly nor as customs duties (because they have been abolished)—that decreases the price of manpower, which comes as an advantage for the nation's commerce and industry, which can produce with less expenditure and be more competitive on the universal market. This is a just and wise way to favor national industry.

Since in this way the consumption of things that are necessary to life is facilitated, a greater number of citizens get a benefit from being catered to, and the difficulty posed by the great problem of employing people decreases. It is a problem that we do not believe can be totally solved through dispositions, which create an artificial economic environment, but rather with the protection of the natural course of property and with the simultaneous help of moral means.

We make an act of faith in the fact that all these questions are discussed with rectitude by legislators who have a true will to turn into practice the principles of justice written in the constitutions, and that they have the courage to do so. And they will have this courage if inspired by their own interest, and this interest will exist when they are elected with a vote proportional to property and not with equal vote.

This manner of structuring taxation is not oppressive; it cannot be called so unless the government forces the citizens to show the details of their own private administration. In the way we have described, the government does not descend to minute investigations, as properties are verifiable through public acts, or they are apparent by themselves.

Another advantage that is a consequence of this system is an enormous savings in collection expenditures. Those expenditures are enormous whenever we want to "catch" property that has an interest in eluding and hiding, while the government engages in and keeps alive a fight of cunning and violence with the citizens. Rather, we put citizens in such a condition that they are inclined to present themselves to pay the tax, to which is connected the advantage of the proportional electoral right. From the above—besides the gain of the public treasury, considered to be a gain for all and recognized by all as such—the tax burden that is equally distributed amongst all would turn out to be much lighter and, what is most important, voluntary. Every reason for complaint would be removed.

At any rate, writing in the constitution the principle that all properties share the burden of the state in proportion to their income is useful in any case as a limit to the arrogance of those chambers that would want to deviate from that principle of justice. Furthermore, it gives support to the proprietors that would be unjustly burdened and would like to appeal to the supreme tribunal of political justice, as they would be able to base their appeals on this article of the constitution. Such an appeal would become at the same time an ongoing stimulus and a school for the legislative branch—a school that would be very helpful for finding the expedients necessary for giving the fullest and truest implementation of the article of the constitutional charter that prescribes the equal distribution of the public burden amongst all citizens.

ARTICLE 31—No tax can be imposed except when allowed by the chambers that represent the taxpayers, and sanctioned by the king.

This article is not at all contrary to article 47, which limits the power of the chambers to the legislative branch, since to determine the quantity and distribution of the tax is a matter appropriate for a law. The collection of the tax is the execution of that law, and as such this belongs to the executive branch, save that the mode of the collection can also be established through a law.

ARTICLE 32—Every obligation of the state towards its creditors is inviolable.

This is a consequence of article 27, which declares all properties inviolable. Nevertheless, this consequence must be clearly expressed in the constitution so that the weak are further protected against the strong. The state is usually stronger than its creditors, and it is not the first time that it has abused its strength to commit thefts and robberies with impunity, as it never lacks the legal cavils to cover itself with.

Who can summon the public power when it decides to perpetrate invasions of private property? And using what other power can we summon the public power? In the constitutions so far given to Europe, this was never considered; and for this reason, thefts in the form of rigorous legality were never lacking. In opposition to this, in our constitution the administrative power is in the hands of the judicial branch, which is strong for the number of its judges and is the legitimate representative of the justice of the people. This branch is superior to any other in the order of justice, and it can straighten the torts of all the other powers. Even the creditors of the state and all those individuals and societies that believe they have received some unjust damage from the state can turn to it.

The failures of the state, the abolition of its eroded paper or coin currency which it issued, are treasons committed against the human community, and they have to be rendered impossible. It is never the case that the state, which is the union of the citizens under one complex power, cannot pay. All citizens are held accountable. Therefore, the citizens have to be subject to the weight of the debts of the state in fair proportion to their income and through taxation (article 30); the payment of the debts may stay suspended for some time, but the debts themselves can never be cancelled.

Such principles of justice protect the credit, as the credit represents an inestimable asset. It is a means to face more easily the commitments that have been undertaken; it is a favorable condition for finding benefits through better deals during times of need; it is a source of public and private wealth.

ARTICLE 33—Intellectual property is guaranteed.

We defined intellectual property as the right to make economic profit from the works of ones own intellect (writings, artistic prints, useful inventions) through the reproduction and the distribution of those works. I do not think it is useful to analyze whether this definition is proper.

This right of intellectual property—is it a natural right, that is, a right of reason? At first glance, it does not look that way. Rather, it seems that he who, for example, buys a copy of a book then can—as the object belongs to him—make the use he wants of that object and thus even reproduce it.

But this difficulty is dissolved by the theory of the right of property.[43] This right consists in the tie of things with people, and that tie which is of an eudemonistic nature has within it something physical and something intellectual and moral, as we have extensively examined in *Filosofia del diritto*. When this tie exists between the thing and the person, then the person suffers—he suffers pain each time others separate him from that thing by force. Now, since the moral law forbids the causing of any sorrow to our peers, the moral law thus dictates something in conflict with the right of property. But the tie that constitutes property is not always equally formed in all periods of humanity; and this is the reason for the modification exerted on the property right through the different periods of the civilization and development of humankind.

The property tie that is most easily formed and evident concerns material things. This property tie existed at the beginning of mankind; it precedes civil society while the physical force of the individual up to a certain point is sufficient to protect it. In a state of greater civilization, man begins to desire that even the invention of his intellect becomes his exclusive property. But as long he despairs of actually being able to reserve intellectual property to his exclusive use and profit, he does not do that and he does not say: *These things are mine.* He does not dare say that, as he sees the impossibility of reserving such use and profit in the fact that his peers do not dispose of intellectual property at will either. Only a civil society that has reached a certain degree of progress can satisfy this natural desire; and it satisfies it when it guarantees the profit of intellectual work to the authors of that work. Then the property right concerning intellectual work begins to exist, since only then does man dare say: *These things are mine*, and with that reasoning man takes possession—and he feels offended and in sorrow if the advantage he expects from that possession is taken away. This right, therefore, is born as a consequence of the social force which sanctions it. This is not because the right of property stems from force, but because it stems from a judgment used by man for appropriating things. Man does not pass this judgment if he sees that he cannot prevent his peers from freely using the things he has appropriated. So, the right that is called literary property has its foundation in human nature, as any other right has, and its title is creation, that is, production. But this right does not come into being, at least fully, except in civil society and through its laws that sanction it, and through its force that protects it. And it is only then that men acquire the persuasion of being able to appropriate the economic advantages coming from the work and the invention of their intellects.

One can return to the objection postulated at the beginning: If a book that I purchase is mine, how can I not make the use I want of it, and thus why can I not reproduce it? To that we respond that the purchase of the physical book must not alter the integrity of the right that the author has on the book itself, since this is an anterior right which cannot be destroyed by a posterior right. Now we must reconcile the use of this posterior right with the preservation of the former. The use of the posterior right must be limited in such a way as not to threaten who has the anterior right.

Still to be determined are the limits of the right of intellectual property. This kind of property, belonging to different periods of civilization, is of an entirely personal nature. However, we do not believe that it can be passed on through heredity, although we believe that it must be fully held during the life of the author, since the title of this property is the invention from which it is reasonable that the inventor gets all the possible advantages without being molested by others. But as the inventor ceases, so does the primary title, thus the right ceases.

ARTICLE 34—The citizens of legal age have the right to send petitions even collectively to the chambers if the object of a petition is the formation of a law. The petition is sent to the executive branch if it concerns the implementation of a law, and to the judicial branch if it concerns the administration of justice. No petition can be presented personally to the chambers.

This article is in tune with article 47, which limits the rights of the chambers to receive petitions to those used to demand the formation of a law; and the same right is granted to the executive and judicial branches for the petitions concerning their attributions.

One of the unshakable principles on which the constitutional system is founded is the division of the three branches: All modern constitutions have stemmed from this principle. So every time we confuse the three branches, one of them invalidates the others, and there is incoherence with and opposition to the constitution. The invading branch then becomes despotic and the freedom proclaimed by the constitutional charter is effectively destroyed.

The chambers in all modern constitutions have invaded the three branches. They accept petitions no matter what their purpose is, and it is up to their arbitrary judgment to satisfy those petitions or to remit them to the minister. They have therefore open permission to invade the executive branch and the state does not find any sort of guarantee against these invasions.

The chambers also issue sentences, passing under the false denomination of law. We have seen in Italy the repetition of this invasion of the judicial branch, as we have seen it elsewhere. The parliament of Turin condemned the moral bodies to extinction and assigned their assets to the government. This is not a *law* but a *sentence*. In fact, the law is always a general prescription, it does not concern any individual, any entity, nor does it concern any right that actually and factually exists. The tribunals are in charge of the application of the law to things and people, and this application is called *sentence*. It is not legitimate to change definitions, and to do so becomes a public lie. To give the title of law to a sentence is to cheat the nation. Through similar lies and fraud the people have always been tyrannized. In our case, tyranny is exercised by the chambers instead of the king and this is one of those little games that make the written constitution illusory in perception and false in facts.

It is singular to observe how little thought has been given to date on putting a brake on the despotism of the parliaments. It is singular to observe the incoherence through which, while we declare that the chambers are nothing but a part of the legislative branch, on the other hand we give them the ability to receive unlimited petitions, no matter what the subject is—whether pertaining to the legislative, executive or judicial branch. The reason for that can be found in the attitudes and emotions that existed when those constitutions were compiled. The feared specter was the absolutism of the sovereigns; thus protection was conceived only against this enemy. There was absolutely no mistrust of the other enemy, the new power of the chambers, and thus there was no defense. And so it happened that too much was given to the new power, which in turn became despotic itself.

After our long experience, it is time to allow the legislative branch of the chamber to re-enter its natural boundaries, and within those boundaries be contained. Without that, there is no constitution and that which apparently exists cannot last. The confusion of the three branches and the invasion of them perpetrated by the chambers is one of the causes of the ephemeral life of modern constitutions.

One of the limits that therefore we want to impose on the powers of the chambers is this: that they have no power to accept petitions other than those that concern the legislative power; that is, that invoke the preparation of some law.

This limit imposed on the chambers—as in general all the limits imposed on the diverse powers of the state—are under the high protection of the judicial branch. Without these protections they could be overstepped with impunity, especially in those cases where the question concerning whether the limit does or does not exist in that particular case arises. Hence the necessity for this new tribunal, for this new supreme jurisdiction which, through juridical decisions, protects all branches against reciprocal invasions by keeping them separate and distinct.

And although only petitions that concern the legislative branch can be presented to the chambers, the right of the citizens to present petitions is held at its fullest, as they can turn to the executive or judicial branch if what they ask concerns the attribution of one or the other.

Citizens are also granted the right to present petitions to the competent powers either individually or collectively, because it is considered that the petition be exercised as a natural right that cannot be needlessly limited.

This disposition is consistent with articles 35 and 36, through which the right of the citizens to gather peacefully and to associate for honest ends is recognized. If it is legitimate for them to gather, then it must be legitimate for them to discuss together the petition to present to the various powers of the state. These very discussions are of benefit to public affairs, they contribute to the civil education of the citizens, and they make citizens fit for governmental duties to which they can later be called. They also enlighten governments on the matters upon which the discussion is held.[44]

If it is legitimate for the citizens to associate, why can they not appear associated in a petition that they present to a competent authority? To recognize in them the right of free association and then deny the right of collective petition cannot be ignored as a glaring incoherence.

Minors are not granted the right of petition, nor are those who cannot themselves exercise civil and political rights; however, petitions can be presented by those who represent them.

Finally, the reason why personal petitions are forbidden from being presented to the chambers is principally that this tends to provide security for the chambers themselves and for the independence of the deliberations they make. This does not all restrict the right of petition, as it reconciles liberty with order.

ARTICLE 35—All citizens can create associations amongst themselves, as long as they are not secret. However, upon judgment of a political tribunal, associations can be dissolved if declared immoral or irreligious, or contrary to the present statute; that is, that after a regular trial, it is declared that an abuse has been committed by its members for immoral or irreligious purposes and/or for the purposes of violating state laws.

Association is a natural right of every man.[45] A civil government is obligated to recognize the associations that citizens create amongst themselves for an honest purpose.[46]

Each association is a juridical person which holds the same unlimited right to own as the individuals who form it.[47] Furthermore, if the association could not hold that right, the right of association itself would be illusory, as the majority of associations cannot exist without a common fund.

Civil society is instituted to protect and to implement all natural and rational rights—not to destroy them nor to restrict or obstruct their exercise. Thus, the civil government must recognize and protect the right of association in all its fullness.

Nevertheless, this right does not extend to those associations whose ends are essentially illegitimate. If such associations are formed, the civil authority can and must dissolve them, as they threaten the rights of other citizens—if nothing else, the rights that citizens have to the common good which is the greatest of all rights. This power exercised by the civil authority does not come simply from the purpose of its institution, which is to protect the rights of all, but rests on an even deeper foundation, which is that of the natural right held by all men to defend human dignity.[48]

But which amongst the powers of civil society is the branch that must judge whether an association is illicit or that an association is such as to be suppressed? That branch cannot be any other than the judicial one, as it concerns a sentence that is to be applied to real individuals that are in fact associated. If they were condemned without a regular sentence that is based on justice, their personal security and their juridical liberty would be violated (article 23). No association can therefore be abolished by the parliament, which has instead the right to vote on laws, but not that of making legal decisions. This is part of that necessary limitation imposed on the power of the chambers, which we have discussed in the preceding article.

But what are the norms of justice upon which the competent tribunal, that is the judicial branch, can emanate a sentence that suppresses an association without offending the natural right of association? Those norms are contained in this very same article 35, and are reduced to two. An association can be suppressed only in these two cases:

1. When it is essentially immoral or irreligious or contrary to the statute.
2. When in spite of not being such, its members systematically abuse the association for immoral or irreligious ends, or to violate state laws.

If neither one of these two cases occurs, the association cannot be dissolved. These norms do not have much need to be demonstrated with arguments, as they only need to be declared.

A society which has an immoral end does not have the right to exist, because the right is a moral thing and assumes the legitimacy of the moral title.[49]

An association which is observant of the right held by all men to human flourishing is then entitled to have this right of association—the most precious of all—protected by civil society with the same vigilance as all other rights are protected, and even more so.

A society which has an irreligious end has in itself an immoral end; this is not a question of opinion or individual belief, as these are free before the civil law and do not constitute the object of society. In fact, if we had a citizen who did not believe in the existence of a superior being and thus would not practice any religion, he could not be punished on this basis by civil society.

But if an association to disseminate atheism were to be formed—an association that existed to destroy the religion practiced by other citizens, then this association should be suppressed by the government, as it would threaten the most precious right of all citizens, which is the right of their religion. Furthermore, such association would destroy the morality which is the foundation and the main part of religion and to which religion alone can administer an effective sanction, as morality is a sacrosanct and an inalienable right of man.[50]

Since the whole civil society is built upon morality and the respect for the laws, such an association must be abolished, also on the grounds of threatening the existence of civil coexistence. There can be no doubt that a civil society made of pure atheists never existed and cannot exist, since atheists, in order to act coherently, cannot look to anything but their temporal interest. But temporal interest alone does not unite men, but divides them, since temporal goods cannot be enjoyed but exclusively. For example, the bread I eat cannot be eaten by somebody else. Thus, temporal interests alone produce only a selfish exercise by individuals to seize goods for themselves without honest respect for somebody else's goods. It follows that a civil society composed only of atheists cannot endure.

The question concerning what associations must be excised from civil society as irreligious is more difficult when those associations do not threaten religion in general but one religion in particular.

This question offers two aspects which must be carefully distinguished. One is the objective aspect. Once considered, it becomes evident that the true religion, of which there can be but one, alone has the right to exist and to be called religion, as all the others must be called superstitions. The other aspect is subjective;

that is, it concerns the religious opinions of the citizens who are melded into civil society. Those opinions, although false, can be in good faith, and generally speaking, must be considered by a civil government.

The private man is obligated to look for the objective truth of religion, and, once having found it, to follow it. This is an obligation of conscience.

The government is obligated to respect the subjective religious opinions and persuasions of the citizens. Therefore, the rule that the government must observe and the judicial branch appropriately use to judge whether an association is irreligious and thus deserves to be suppressed cannot be but one—but it has to be applied according to the religious condition of the citizens themselves. Let us specify the particular cases.

Let us examine first the case of a nation where all citizens practice a religion that is objectively true, that is, the Catholic one. It is obvious that in this case the government cannot allow any foreigner to threaten the religion of the citizens with the introduction of another or by promoting in a Catholic society heresy and impiety. Without this, the objective right as well as the subjective right that all citizens have to preserve their religion and to defend themselves against any attempt to seduce them and to deviate them from their precious belief would not be guaranteed, although it is the maximum right and the dearest to them, and especially to their family.

Now let us assume the case that some of the citizens turn to false beliefs: What is the government to do?

Let us also assume that these false beliefs are atheistic and impious, such as hatred and offence to the divine, or even that they are beliefs that are absolutely indifferent as to the distinction between practicing a religion and practicing none—which is, in practice, atheism in disguise. In a case like this, these beliefs would be such, as we have said, as to remove the foundation of any civil society. Thus, while allowing full political liberty of objection to those who have embraced such opinions, and without molesting them with extreme penalties because of those opinions, the state nevertheless should oppose with any means possible the advancement in society of such objectors and the external acts through which those objectors would seek to spread their pernicious doctrines. And if such associations are formed, the political tribunal should suppress them.

If the above false beliefs do not deviate from religion in general but are rather heretical opinions, the government should:

1. prevent their spread with any means, as it is obligated to defend the true belief because it is true and because it is of the nation.
2. leave to these heretics the political freedom to express opinions for themselves, that is, without the application of any punishment.
3. not prevent by force the formation of an association by these heretics to exercise among themselves the cult of the new heretical belief (and not to promulgate said belief), nor could such an association be suppressed by the judicial branch. Nevertheless, all possible precautions

to prevent the spread of the belief and the outrage of true believers should be taken.

If, however, these false beliefs or the cult they prescribe implied acts that are offensive to morality, that is, that parts of morality that concern the duties of men toward each other or respect for human nature, the political tribunal should in that case condemn the associations and forbid the implementation of those acts.

It is better to state the same even in cases where the majority of citizens profess wrong beliefs and the true religion is professed only by the minority. The wise government should facilitate the propagation of the latter as the only truly moral one and as the only one useful to be professed by all. But the government must do so without offending the already established heretical sects—and even by defending them effectively from an external act that could disturb the functions of the cult that they profess (always excluding the case of the immoral acts that we mentioned before). Furthermore, the government should, in the implementation of its acts, use such temperance as to avoid the very grave indecency of an imprudent zeal that could harm rather than benefit the propagation of the religious truth. The exercise of governmental zeal should change according to the circumstances so as not to excite resentment by the heretics that may want to turn to the knowledge of the true religion.

These are the inalienable and unchangeable rights of truth and virtue. Truth and virtue are always of benefit and the only things that benefit man. Through them, an essential good to man is done and the foundation of any other good and progress is laid. All have the right to preach the truth; all have the right to teach and promote virtue. Can the man who exists in error take offence from those who make the voice of truth ring in his ear? How can he who lives in vice be enraged with those who exhort him to follow the path of virtue? But wrongness is on the side of the wrong and of those who have vice; and as those who are in the wrong profess an erroneous persuasion in good faith, that is, truly believing they possess the truth, nevertheless their rights are not infringed upon by those who, through peaceful words and sensible and charitable reasoning, try to make them wise. For if bringing man to the truth is a true benefit done to humanity—the highest of benefits—this noble exercise of charity is even more commendable because it treats religious truth as the most important of all, as the truth of religious belief is a part of morality. It is morality towards God and it is a true foundation of morality towards men and human nature. And since human nature is created for truth and virtue—and appropriately and principally for religious truth and virtue—it is created, in one word, for God. Human nature aspires to God with all its being. Thus, that which resents or takes offence at the words that teach and persuade about the true religion in a convincing way is never truly human nature. Rather, it is the individual or, better yet, the accidental dysfunction of this individual. The ill person does not complain about the medicine or the hand of those who treat him; he does not act as if the cure offends the human body, because the cure is all the helping hand wants to obtain. Instead, the ill person is temporarily sensitive in that part of the body where he is wounded or inflamed and for this reason complains. But when the illness is removed, he himself is grateful for the healthy pain that the helping hand has momentarily caused.

One may ask, what can the government do if it is not Catholic itself, or is not fully formed by men who profess the true religion? What is the government to do in this case?

The men of government must have in any case a true love for truth and morality, and must search for the former while conforming their lives to the latter.

In the second place, they shall respect all the beliefs of the governed under the aforementioned condition that there is no injury to the Divine and that there is no atheism, indifference or similar conditions, as such beliefs are contrary to justice and morality. They have to allow every belief to form an association for the exercise of the cult. They have to protect the exercise of this cult so as not to be disturbed by external violence or by insult. They must also protect the freedom of conscience of all the practicing religious who make civil society, so that no one is ever tested by civil law or ministerial ordinances to violate his conscience, but can instead completely fulfill everything that he affirms to be according to his sincere belief and the duty of his conscience.

In the third place, such a government will, in all good faith, promote and peacefully and prudently favor everything that it subjectively estimates to be most in conformity with truth and morality. That is, it will promote the moral good amongst men and the exercise of justice, humanity, charity, and amongst all the religious beliefs that which it judges in good faith to be the true one and to respect the true one—that which it believes to be most congenial to morality, and that contains or produces a morality that is purer, more elevated and more perfect. When each of those governing men has done all that sincerely, although he may be in error, he will have done his duty without damaging the rights of anyone, or the fullest liberty of conscience of all. But it will never be licit for a governing man or a government to be indifferent or atheist or offensive towards the Divine or towards any belief professed by the governed, and even less licit will it be to persecute them.

Thus, the political tribunal can only

1. suppress as irreligious those associations that offend the Divine or contain practices that are contrary to the moral duties amongst men;
2. suppress those associations that may be started by foreigners and that in good faith it judges to contain false beliefs that threaten the beliefs of the governed;
3. suppress those associations that disturb with visible acts the exercise of the worship professed by the governed;
4. not suppress as irreligious those associations of the governed that are turned to the exercise of the cult prescribed by their various beliefs and religious opinions.

This is the duty of the government, which can indirectly influence and promote the kingdom of religious truth and of the purest morality, as long as it does not infringe upon the freedom of conscience of anyone, and does not ever start from the principle that the belief of the governed, although in itself false, is professed in bad faith, as the government must even presume good faith. And this is the duty of the political tribunal, which cannot have influence in this but can only judge as irreligious an association when it belongs to one of the four categories indicated above.

And here we must make an important observation. In order for the political tribunal to exercise these offices concerning irreligious associations, it needs to know exactly what sentences, opinions or propositions are opposed to the beliefs professed by the citizens. Now, how can it know this?

The various beliefs and associations are a fact. Therefore, the only way the tribunal can know which conform and which are opposed is by interrogating them. Thus, the executive branch is not itself competent to decide on this point. Its decision must, therefore, be based only on the judgment of the authority that directly proceeds from religion. If the above-mentioned tribunal wants to know what belongs to the belief of the Israelites and what is contrary to such belief, it must interrogate the synagogue and conform to what the synagogue says. By the same token, if it wants to know the truths professed by the Catholic Church and the errors that oppose those truths, it will have to refer to the decisions of this Church and of the Roman Pope, who is the supreme master and the supreme ordinary tribunal of the Church. The executive branch itself is not able to say anything on those matters. But once it has received the decision of the Church, upon this it must, as the only valid proof, base its political judgment to repress in the manner described, the irreligious associations.

Finally, the executive branch must declare unjust an association that is contrary to the constitution of the state, such as one that violates the fundamental law upon which the state is built. However, amongst the associations that are contrary to the constitution, those that are instituted to discuss the ways and the means by which it is possible to legally obtain a reform of the constitution itself must not be listed. To the list belong only those which, given that a constitution is in force, tend to act in such a way that it is not implemented or is violated in some of its articles.

To summarize what we have said so far—the associations that must be suppressed are those anarchist ones that we have reduced to three categories, that is, those that are instituted for subtracting from civil society its two foundations of morality and religion, and those that are instituted for the purpose of violating the constitution which is the foundation of society itself.

But since these reprehensible ends can in some societies be masked under the color of other honest ends, we indicate in article 35 another category of association that must be repressed by the political tribunal without breaching the freedom of association and rather in defense of that freedom. These are those associations where it is proven that their members perpetrate a systematic abuse to obtain immoral, irreligious goals, or to damage the laws of the state. This must be absolutely prevented in order to maintain civil society and all the advantages that it brings.

At any rate, we must note that we do not suppress those associations when the abuse is not systematic but rather casual and accidental. In this last case, the abuse of using the association as an instrument of a secret and perverted intent proceeds from the evilness of some particular member, and does not demonstrate the premeditated intention of those who make the association. So reason demands that in such a case as this latter, the guilty members are normally punished and in the former case the association itself be dissolved and condemned.

ARTICLE 36—The right of peaceful and unarmed gathering is recognized when conforming to the laws that can regulate the exercise of it in the public interest. This disposition is not applicable to gathering in public places or places that are open to the public which remain totally subject to police law.

Some modern constitutions are satisfied to express the right that the citizens have to gather, without making specific mention of the right of association. But these are different rights that must both be guaranteed to the citizens. There are associations that never gather, such as the scientific one that in Italy is known as *de' quaranta*. There are temporary gatherings that are not associations.

We prescribe, therefore, that the gathering be peaceful and unarmed, since this is the first law of a civil society. This is also the first condition of civilization, that is, that the individuals who want to have their rights enforced surrender the taking of justice into their own hands and use the avenues of their rights before the tribunals. Thus the use of the force that protects the rights is reserved only to government, which has also the authority to legislate on the rights. It is the duty of the government to defend with the force of security those peaceful gatherings when they are threatened by the factious. Therefore, the weapons that citizens would bring to their gathering, as they cannot have the purpose of either defense or a sanction of justice—which are both duties and offices of the civil government—would no longer have any honest purpose in a regulated society and thus would have no other purpose but abuse for a dishonest end, which cannot be tolerated by the laws.

An inalienable right of the civil government is also that of regulating the exercise of rights of citizens, since civil society is instituted for this reason—to regulate the *modality* of the rights and thus also the right of gathering.[51]

But the constitution needs this regulation to be implemented through laws that are recognized as just, necessary and appropriate by the nation itself. The nation is represented by the three legislative branches, since civil society, as we have demonstrated, is not perfect unless governed with laws rather than mere precepts,[52] as in this way any danger of abuse is removed.

Concerning the gatherings held in public or in places open to the public, they are by nature more dangerous as they attract the uneducated populace without making any distinction between good and evil men. As a consequence, the evil ones can abuse them to the detriment of society and of the freedom of the citizen. It follows that the organization in charge of the preservation of public order, of the public security and of the defense of all rights, must know of and exercise on those gatherings a special vigilance—and that is satisfied with police laws.

There is also a juridical reason for which gatherings of citizens without any reserve and limitation in public places cannot be allowed. And the reason is that public places are not private property and they are exclusive to no one. Society possesses them as a whole, and each citizen has equal right of access. Thus, if some citizens could occupy public places at will and without limitation, they would prevent others the free use of those places, thus violating the common right of all.

ARTICLE 37—The press is free, but a law prevents its abuse. The Church preserves the right to impose censorship, but without the imposition of state penalty.

The laws that repress the abuses of the press and that determine the procedures to be used for the legal proceedings before the tribunals turn out to be extremely difficult to develop. Perfect legislation on this issue so far has not been obtained, not even in those nations where freedom of the press has been proclaimed for a long time. The evils produced by the abuse of this liberty, although they diminished as repressive laws were perfected have, however, never disappeared completely. Rather, they continued to be very grave everywhere. This is an indisputable fact.

But what is most deplorable is the improvidence of those governments that proclaimed an absolute freedom of press and implemented it even before the existence of any law that could repress and put a brake on abuse. Like a torrent without banks, the impetuous press was instantly transferred from the discipline of a rigid and captious censorship to a boundless liberty. Religion, morality, public order, reputations, laws, and the basis of society were assaulted and destroyed by the wrath and passion of a press with endless license. The varieties of damage that resulted for the Italian cause are there for us to see.

Therefore, the press must be free, but under the condition that there are repressive laws designed as much as possible to punish the crimes that can be committed through the abuse of the press. Freedom of press without restrictive laws is an absurdity. It is not civility; it is a return to a barbaric state, because in this case there is freedom without civil regulation. As crimes are repressed through the law, it is then appropriate to widen the freedom of press.

If there is one matter to which judgment through jury can be appropriately applied, perhaps that is the press. But it is obvious that jurors should be selected amongst those who know how to judge the issue. And since the imputation that is referred by the state prosecutor or by the injured party to the political tribunal in charge of the application of the law can concern different arguments, it would be appropriate to establish different colleges of jurors in support of the political tribunals.

Then this article, while proclaiming the freedom of press, recognizes that the Church has the right to impose censorship, and that right is incontrovertible. Such a right cannot logically be violated by the state, as it recognizes religion and the Catholic Church. The constitution must be honest in everything. If it recognizes the Catholic Church, then it must recognize it truly, and such as it is—that is, what was made by Jesus Christ.

Furthermore, it is entrusted to the knowledge of the Church itself whether it is necessary to institute censorship; and at any rate, the writer is not exempted from the repressive law of the state when he has the approval of the Church, nor is the state to add any criminal penalty to ecclesiastical censorship.

Thus the Church and the state remain in their natural and legitimate independence.

ARTICLE 38—Public spectacles are regulated with preventive measures established by the laws.

That public spectacles are regulated with preventive measures as this article establishes is required by public morality and from the right of parents to protect the innocence of their children.

ARTICLE 39—Freedom of teaching is guaranteed. There will be laws that regulate it and repress abuses.

It is a precious right of human nature to teach others without stumbling into prohibitions, obstacles, and government formalities that interfere, since government employees have no authority on truth and science that privileges them over other citizens, and civil authority is incompetent on such matters, where nothing else applies but pure reason and, concerning divine matters, the teaching of the Church.

Furthermore, it is a fact confirmed by indisputable experience, that the government, with the pretext of directing education, reserves to itself the monopoly of education and creates a means of very subtle despotism.

Competition and its effects on public opinion, which is the true queen of constitutional states, is able to ensure sufficient justice concerning education and the teachers.

It is nevertheless necessary to have a strong and vigilant repressive law to punish the abuse of such a precious right.

ARTICLE 40—The freedoms of commerce and of industry are fundamental principles of the economic law of the state.

Each man has the right to use his abilities to his advantage. Therefore, enterprise must be free, as it constitutes part of *juridical freedom*.[53]

Civil society has the purpose of protecting all the rights of the citizens and the group that is contained in the category of juridical freedom. This demonstrates the freedom of industry and internal commerce through an argument coming from the principles of right. These principles exclude any form of monopoly.

The same cannot be said of international commerce. A civil society could exclude, according to the right, the international products of another. This is because the members of a civil society do not enjoy the citizenship rights of another, and under this aspect, do not have social equality. If a society wants to abstain from purchasing the products of another society—or does not want to purchase except under certain conditions—that society exercises its own freedom without offending the other society's freedom. This is an indubitable principle of right: It is licit to limit someone else's liberty when this naturally comes from the exercise of one's own.[54]

Abstention from purchasing belongs to the right that each one has on his freedom. Here political economy comes into play. Political economy demonstrates that the freedom of commerce is reciprocally useful for all nations, providing, however, that an accumulation and distribution of artificial wealth does not occur in any of them, as happens when a nation is subjugated for a long time by the action of a prohibition system. And that more or less happened to all nations in Europe where art was substituted for nature by the presumption of governments, and it was believed that any good could derive from that art, while nature was wasted and put in chains. The conditions of the various European states being such, it is now necessary to lead them back to freedom of commerce gradually, allowing enough time for wealth to go back to its natural course. If we wanted to achieve that instantly and violently, that would cause very grave damage to private fortunes. Nevertheless, it is necessary that in the constitution this principle be declared—that is, that we want to achieve this freedom—trusting in the knowledge of governments on how to achieve it. The implementation is to be gradual, according to the economic conditions of the nation. This is the spirit of this article.

ARTICLE 41— All citizens can aspire to state responsibilities according to their abilities and suitability.

Article 41 calls all abilities, without distinction, to public service. In this way, it opens the way even to those who own nothing to improve their economic condition. This free competition for employment according to the merits of each finds its guarantee in article 15, where it is said that the law itself determines the way in which the king must choose and promote the employees. It is therefore national knowledge that determines the most appropriate ways to know merits, abilities, and the suitability of competitors. Article 41 obviously conforms to justice, as it is based on the same principles as article 30.

ARTICLE 42—Every citizen is a soldier. Exempted from military service are those who are enrolled in the clergy, and all those who hold a public office which is necessary to the state.

The draft is regulated by the law. The weight of the draft will be equally distributed amongst the citizens.

Writing in the constitution that every citizen is a soldier is tantamount to declaring that it is a duty of all members of society to defend the nation when the need arises. But the case that the nation needs to defend itself with the material forces of all the citizens is a very rare case and sometimes it never occurs. Nor are all citizens of the right age or in possession of that perfect organization that makes them fit for military service. Thus a draft or a selection regulated by law is necessary.

Furthermore, the nation—except for extreme cases—does not just need a militia defending it with material force, but has equal need of ecclesiastic, political and civil orders through which it can exist as an organized collective body. Thus, those who are used for the maintenance of these orders are rightfully exempted from the use of weapons as people who serve the nation with work that is no less useful or necessary. The weight of the militia is personal and real. The real weight is supported by those who pay taxes; the personal weight must be common and equal for all.

All citizens obligated by the constitution must participate in the defense of the nation when necessary against internal and external enemies.

In such a way, the rich contribute more, as they contribute with money and people—which is fair, because they receive double defense from the militia, that is, the defense of their possessions and their people.

But in order for the personal weight to be truly equal for all, it is necessary that those who cannot personally serve in the militia, can compensate for their lack of personal service with money. How this happens must be established by an appropriate law.

ARTICLE 43—The National Guard, which will be instituted on the basis set by the law, belongs to the army. The king can dissolve it and recall it and reorganize it within one year.

The National Guard must be considered as a part of the army, and thus it can be mobilized when the need of the nation arises. The power given to the king to dissolve the National Guard and to reassemble it within one year—which is necessary for the security of the state where political parties come to form within the guard itself—does not involve any danger of despotism. That is not only because the National Guard must always be completely recomposed with one year as established by law, but also because the minister that forms the royal ordinance is accountable to the parliament, and because through article 45, still to be discussed, it is specified that public force within the state cannot be used for any other end but the implementation of laws and decisions of the tribunals. On the other hand, the king under this proposed constitution can only be moved by the national spirit.

In France, the need to dissolve the National Guard to preserve public order has arisen many times. The law of March 22, 1831, reorganized with a larger and newer system the French National Guard. This institution was at first suspended in 2,490 municipalities that belonged to 17 departments. On November 25, 1832, the National Guard was returned to 390 municipalities, amongst those where it was suspended before.[55]

It is good to remind ourselves that the military as such only represents *brute force* which cannot hold the first place in well-ordered governments, but it is convenient that it operates at the service of *moral force* and that it obeys the governmental wisdom. This concept was often repeated by General LaFayette, who declared that the most important parts of the state belonged to civil power, and that the military power must obey it.[56]

This great maxim professed by such a distinguished man of war is that which saves society from domination by brute force, and it must be deeply imprinted in the pages of a wise constitution. For if constitutions with the opposite principle appear, that is, where military power is independent, or at any rate subtracts itself effectively from the authority of the government, one can justly conclude that a time of crisis has arisen and that those constitutions are inspired by a desire to change public order.

For this very reason, the military must not be privileged over other employees of the state. And thus writing in the constitution a special article stating, "military personnel cannot be deprived of their ranks, honors and pensions other than in the ways prescribed by the law" may sound arrogant, as the same thing must apply to all officers of the state both military and civilian, or to no one. Such an article, written in some Italian constitutions, seems to be offensive to civil equality, and shows that the constitution has been written under the influence of the fear of an anarchist party to which some concession had to be made.

ARTICLE 44—The army cannot be removed from its dependence on the responsible ministry.

Military ordinances made on behalf of the king are valid when signed by a minister.

Without this article, without the obedience of the military force to civil reason, we have no public order, but anarchy. Already article 14 states that the king has at his disposal all forces of land and sea. But since, according to article 7, the acts of government have no power if not signed by a minister, thus the military ordinances of the king need the signature of a minister in order to be valid. The military is thus bound in its dependence on the minister.

The ministry, which is the mandatory instrument of the executive power, must therefore hold within itself the heads of all different branches and departments including that of the army, as the army is merely to be used for the implementation of the laws that protect and order the state. To that end, it would be desirable that the minister overseeing the army is always a high general of the army itself, but without actual command, and that the generals with real command are named by the sovereign promptly and during peace time by the decree of nomination. It is also desirable that there be a head of the National Guard without actual command who belongs to the same ministry overseeing the army as well. In that way, the military power would be strictly tied to the ministry, and its brute force would obey morality, which is of paramount importance for the public tranquility that constitutes civil order.

However, the command of the troops not done through ministerial ordinances can be freely exercised by the sovereign and by the captains on duty on his behalf.

Certain constitutions guarantee to the military its honors and ranks from which personnel cannot be stripped except in cases foreseen by laws and regulations. But this disposition has the taste of a hideous privilege, stolen from the legislator by a party which wants to partially subtract the military power from the civil government with intentions that are hostile to public order.

The military ranks and honors must be maintained in the same condition as the ranks and honors of all other state employees—no more, no less. Both must depend on the trust that the sovereign and the minister responsible have in them. Without some degree of opinion about the honesty of the government, subordination is not given, and without subordination order is not given. The constitution must not be founded entirely on a perpetual mistrust of the executive power, and when we would like to base it on such an uncomfortable foundation then it cannot endure in any way. From the moment there is a responsible minister, he must employ men who have all his trust, and thus he or, better yet, the sovereign through him, must have all the liberty to select or to eliminate, without any form of juridical process, all the subordinate employees, whether they are civilian or military. Otherwise, the responsibility of the minister could not be at its fullest, as it instead must be. The power to change subaltern employees is a logical consequence of ministerial responsibility, without which it is not possible to govern.

On the other hand, if this freedom is recognized to the sovereign when selecting or rejecting his minister, how can it not be recognized when it concerns lower employees? Would not this be a new inconsistency?

Nor can the state be burdened with pensions in favor of those employees which, as they have not been found fit by the minister and sovereign, are dismissed. I repeat: The executive power must be strong; it must be whole and not diminished if it is to fully implement the good of the state. Public service is of greater importance than any benefit to particular groups.

ARTICLE 45—Laws and sentences must be carried out. Public force must be used, within the state, to implement the laws and the sentences of the tribunals and for no other purpose.

This contains two parts. With one, we are imposing the obligation to the government to use public force within the state when it is necessary for the implementation of the law and of the sentences of the tribunals, as both the laws and the sentences of the tribunals must be promptly and strongly executed in a well-ordered government. Thus, even the sentences of the political tribunals must be sanctioned by constitutional decree, and to leave them not implemented would be a crime perpetrated by the minister. The other part forbids the king and the government from using public force within the state for any end other than the implementation of the law and the sentences, and that subordinates the law to reason and removes the danger of despotism.

The article, therefore, establishes two responsibilities of the minister: One concerns the lack of use of force when force must be used; the other concerns the use of force when it must not be used. This creates a norm and a support to the supreme political tribunal to judge the ministers when they are accused before it for one of the other aforementioned causes.

ARTICLE 46—Municipal and provincial institutions and municipal and provincial territory are determined by the law. The proportional vote that is established in the following title for the election of the deputies will serve as a base also for the election of city council and provincial council members in the way that will be established by law.

Although the direct tax we are discussing is that which is paid to the state treasury—and not the provincial and municipal taxes—we must however realize that the proportion turns out to be the same, because provincial and municipal taxes follow the same law established by article 30 for all state taxes. Thus, the norm that is established to determine the measure of each electoral vote is one, and it is simple.

The disposition of this article harmonizes cities and municipalities and provinces with the general organization of the state.

The constitution must contain the seeds of all other laws. It must administer the regulating norms of each branch of the state. This article contains the basis of the laws concerning municipal and provincial institutions.

Here we must realize that in the election of the provincial and municipal council members—holding as firm the principle that the electoral vote is proportioned to the tax that a citizen pays to the state treasury—that election must be calculated uniquely on the income of the assets that the citizens possess within that municipality or province. Thus he who possesses goods in several provinces and in several municipalities becomes part of all the municipal and provincial elections, regardless of where his residence is.

10

Reasons for the Dispositions Contained in Title IV

ARTICLE 47—The legislative chambers have the power to discuss and to vote the laws which have to be submitted, once the majority in both chambers is obtained, to the sanctioning of the king who can grant or refuse his sanctioning at this discretion. The chambers can receive petitions requesting the creation of some legislative disposition while rejecting others. The petitioners must present the petitions directly to the executive or judicial power according to the nature of the contents. The chambers have the right of consulting and the right of inquiry, which is limited to the end of gathering the necessary information for the creation of the laws, or submit some accusation to the competent tribunals. The chambers cannot deny the public funds that are necessary to the implementation of both laws and sentences.

The need for this article is clear, as there is no greater need than that the various powers of the state be contained within their boundaries. Without this article, we are introducing a confusion of powers into the machine of the state and the struggle between their acts is born. The invasion of different state jurisdictions into one another leads to anarchy.

Modern constitutions never thought to provide for this supreme need and this capital vice was not an insignificant contributor to their quick deaths.

The power that is most difficult to contain within its boundaries is that of parliaments. This article has been written for that purpose and it acquires life and implementation through the political tribunal, which applies it to the various cases.

There are inconsiderate men who, if you tell them about the need to contain parliaments within their own boundaries of power that have been assigned to them by the constitution, curl up as if they were porcupines, as if one wanted with such limitation to restrict public freedoms. But these people are either so passionate it is impossible to reason with them, or they want anarchy. If it were true that parliaments must not have any restrictions, why then do all constitutions assign to them a special power? Why are the other powers not abolished and then concentrated in the parliaments? If no juridical person[57] in the state is to be omnipotent and none is to operate with arbitrary capriciousness; then all—even the juridical person represented by parliaments—must be contained within their own limits and not invade other spheres. Otherwise, order is destroyed and anarchy reigns.

The whole nation itself recognizes the limitations of individual and social morality and justice, beyond which it is not possible to go. It would be a great error to confuse the nation with the parliaments, as these represent the people and not the nation. And furthermore, the parliaments are not the people. We have seen sometimes that the parliaments have separated themselves from the people, corrupted by their own interests or dominated by the parties. It is therefore appropriate that a good constitution administers the means that are adequate to contain parliaments within the boundaries assigned to them by law and that force them to walk on the legitimate road.

This article 47, therefore, restrains the power of parliament and imposes parliament's limitations.

This power concerns primarily the discussion and the voting of the laws and it is limited by the sanctioning that the sovereign can grant or refuse to those laws.

When the sovereign refuses to sanction a law voted by the parliaments, neither the people nor any power of the state has the right to use violence against the sovereign, as that is a right of the sovereign. If the law is indeed useful, it can be proposed in another session, and it can be sanctioned by the very same sovereign or by another sovereign. A people that have not the patience to wait until the different powers of the state through harmonious operation produce useful and appropriate laws are a people not yet educated to liberty and not yet mature for the constitutional system. They are a people that are like a savage who, not understanding the functioning of a productive machine and seeing that the machine takes some time to implement its movements and to yield a product, because of the impatience in waiting some time for that product, gets angry at the machine and breaks it into pieces. Impatience and wanting the government to do everything immediately that is desirable is an irrational and animal instinct which becomes manifest in a people driven by demagogues, and that has spoiled the most beautiful institutions. Wise men know, on the other hand, that the most beautiful and useful things are done slowly and in that way they become long-lasting.

In the second place, the power of the parliament concerns the acceptance of petitions. But this power is limited the acceptance only of those petitions that ask for the formation of some law and that is because the power of the chambers is almost uniquely legislative although it must not invade either the executive power or the judicial one. The guarantees given by the constitutional system to the public good depend mainly on the exact separation of the three powers: If these are confused, the basis for such a government system is turned upside down. This is one of the vices of the constitutions that so far have been promulgated in Europe: to leave to the chambers the ability to receive petitions of any kind, even those that demand the implementation of laws or the preparation of a trial or of a sentence. These petitions, therefore, must be rejected by the chambers, and those who demand must present them directly to the executive power, that is, the king or the minister—in other words, the competent tribunals. Whenever the executive power or the tribunals do not perform their duties there is recourse to the supreme political tribunal.

In the third place, the rights of interpretation and of investigation belong to the power of the chambers. But even these rights are limited to the fact that interpretations and investigations are turned to the procurement of information necessary to form the laws or to refer some accusation to the competent tribunals.

Finally, the parliament has the right to grant public funds to the executive power—but even in this case, it is best that this executive power is limited. The parliament can deny the funds in cases, for example, of a war declared by the sovereign, public works, charitable donations, etc. But the funds cannot be denied if they are demonstrated to be necessary to the implementation of the laws or the sentences of the tribunals, and that is because, in article 45, the constitution prescribes that the laws and the sentences of the tribunals must be implemented. Hence, were the chambers to deny the money necessary for the implementation in such cases, they would be inconsistent with themselves as they have written those laws. They would violate the constitution, and thus they would have to answer to the political tribunal. The opposition that parliament can offer to the executive power must be honest and straightforward. To obstruct the implementation of the laws and of the sentences and in that way to perturb the regular operation of the government would be a means of opposition both illicit and dishonest, and therefore such behavior must be excluded by the constitution of a well-regulated government.

ARTICLE 48—There are two legislative chambers, both elected.

Why Two Chambers Are Proposed

With just one chamber, the royal dynasty and thus the nation would not be safe. Assuming the existence of only one chamber, it is impossible that this would not conflict with the king from time to time.

In such a conflict, which side would be taken by the nation? Indubitably, the nation would take the side of the chamber, which has many voices to influence it—as many voices as it has members and as many electors as those who give it its mandate. The king has nothing but his single voice.

In the second place, the interest of the largest owners and that of the smaller owners are often counterposed; thus, if there are two chambers that represent these two interests, the sovereign, by opposing one to the other with the right balance, is able to preserve his healthy authority.

Only one council of state is acceptable, since it has a purely consultative authority; only one legislative chamber becomes impossible.

Nor can it be said that the senate of ancient Rome was just one chamber, as the power of the people balanced the senate, as the power of the tribunes was balancing that of the consuls. The people as a whole were in effect the second chamber of Rome. But in the conditions of our times, the people would not balance only one chamber, as they would become one with it, since the chamber would be nothing but the people being represented. Conversely, the Roman senate represented itself, and it was a true aristocracy. To say it again, one chamber would represent only the people and the sovereign would stand alone against the union and the chamber.

Furthermore, only one chamber would be neither just nor useful to the nation for other reasons.

The interests of the large and small owners are two, and if they were represented together, the one with more votes would oppress the other and the minority would be sacrificed to the majority. It is therefore better that these two interests have an equal power and an equal vote so that one can stand against the other.

Only one chamber could vote a law too fast and without appeal, as only one vote—that of the sovereign—would exist against an imprudent deliberation. A vote against an equal vote does not resemble an appeal but a fight. One vote against two does not create a fight but an appeal sentence. Rather than thinking of abbreviating the examination of the laws, we should consider whether, in consideration of our fervid imagination—it would not be better to introduce a three-vote system or the "reading" system of the British.

Why the Two Chambers Must Both Be Elective

The upper house cannot exist where a true aristocracy is missing, such as is in Italy. In other nations where there is a true aristocracy, there is a natural fight between the aristocracy and the people. There is an aristocratic element counterposed to a servant-people looking for liberty.

When the people are content with a state of servitude, then there are parliaments chaired by the king without the representation of the third estate.

When a free people begins to exist together with the small properties brought by industry and commerce, then the third estate wants to be represented. The two chambers are born and they represent the two opposing elements. As the fight is not extinguished, it cannot explode as long as the two chambers balance each other—unless the king, who should serve as a mediator, conspires with one of them.

Where there is a free people without the feudal aristocratic element, the introduction of an upper house is the skilful introduction of a fight in the nation.

This artificial and unnatural element would be expelled sooner or later, and as long as it existed it would be a germ of revolution. Furthermore, the upper house, in its significance, is not in accord with the current condition of sovereignty. For the house, the constitutional sovereign would be compared to the kings of the Middle Ages, which feuded over conquered territories with their comrades in arms. On the other hand, it would be necessary to ignore the trend of society, or to cheat oneself very much in order not to realize that the very relics of feudal aristocracy are destined to disappear. Nor could anyone desire that they be preserved. Now, to create a form of government over an already broken basis of which time is inevitably sweeping away the pieces, cannot be a wise and far-sighted form of politics.

Nor can it be argued that two elective chambers give too much power to the people. That would be so if they were elected with equal votes; but since they are elected with a vote that is proportional to property, what happens is that the number of citizens is not what prevails but the interests themselves, exactly that complexity of rights that has to be protected. From that follows that the first chamber effectively represents that aristocracy that exists in fact, that is, the aristocracy of wealth. And that has this advantage: that the power of these modern aristocrats (if we want to call them that) is not the same for each one of them and is not connected with a name or a dynasty, and often with a title merely for its own sake; rather, it is scaled according to the truth of the thing, while being a solid and just power that excludes any deceit.

All things considered, the complexity of wealth taken altogether follows the complexity of other qualities that are valuable in the social balance such as culture, education, independence, hereditary ability (without considering particular exceptions). And no mistake is made by considering wealth as an indicator of the above-mentioned qualities, thus, by attributing to each a vote in power that is proportional to wealth, generally speaking, we also give a vote to all those other qualities that are connected with wealth and, as is often said, to abilities. Therefore, any kind of aristocracy that can be measured with this system is naturally introduced in the chambers without causing any fracture between itself and the people, and without the odiousness that comes with privileges. It mixes with the people and is subject to the same law without losing anything that is due to it.

ARTICLE 49—By dividing the population of the state by fifteen thousand, the total number of the deputies will be obtained: and if the number is odd, neglecting the fractions, it is to be increased by one.

This article establishes the total number of the deputies so that it is sufficient to represent all the interests, and at the same time it is not large enough to create confusion and unnecessary delays in the handling of state business.

The established number nevertheless is greater than that established by other modern constitutions for the reason that in this constitutional project, the upper house is missing and the deputies themselves are divided in two chambers. This contributes a lot to the goal that the interests of the nation are fully represented and handled with greater local knowledge.

In the footnote first affixed to this article 49, we have mentioned the proportion according to which the number of deputies should be established so that it would not become excessive if the population of the state were to exceed five million.

ARTICLE 50—Both chambers have an equal number of members.

The reason why the two chambers must have an equal number of members is because otherwise one chamber would prevail over the other and would tyrannize the other in favor of the interests that it represents, thus planting a new seed for revolution.

When the two chambers have a perfectly equal power, they resemble a scale in balance and the smallest weight put in one of the two dishes makes it tilt. Thus, the mediating authority of the sovereign can easily be exercised with chambers of equal power. But if one chamber is more powerful than the other, the sovereign authority must prevail over this differential power each time it judged fit to side with the less powerful chamber.

On the other hand, if the sovereign gains the support of the stronger chamber, his despotism becomes invincible—and with the most legal of forms.

We cannot have a true balance of power between an upper house or a house of senators and a chamber of deputies, as the latter claims to be the only national representative and the people believe it, as that is the one that the people have elected. Therefore, the upper house or the house of senators is considered as a power opposed to that of the nation—an exceptional and privileged power always subject to envy, and incapable of acquiring the trust of the people. Conversely, when the two chambers are both elective, they represent an equal number of rights, consist of an equal number of members, and equally enjoy public trust as they actually have equal power. And this is a new argument for the exclusion of the upper house from our constitution.

ARTICLE 51—The first chamber is elected by the major property owners, the second one by the minor ones.

ARTICLE 52—Property owners are rated major or minor in function of the direct taxation they pay to the state's treasury.

ARTICLE 53—Deputies are elected by electoral colleges, each one electing one deputy.

ARTICLE 54—Once the total sum of the direct taxes is divided by the total number of the deputies, the quota is represented by an electoral college.

ARTICLE 55—The major property owners gather in sufficient number to form a college, which pays the quota represented by the college to the state as a direct tax. If only one property owner pays the established quota to the state as a direct tax, then only he elects a deputy and can even elect himself. If two property owners pay together the above-mentioned quota to the state as a tax both elect the deputy. In the same way, colleges are united with other colleges in a way that first brings together those who pay more, and successively those who pay less. Thus, there are more electoral colleges when there are more electors who pay less in the colleges that form them.

ARTICLE 56—The first half of these colleges elects the deputies of the first chamber, the second half the deputies of the second chamber.

These six articles envelop the new electoral system, which we believe is the only one that conforms to social justice, and the only one that provides a solid foundation for the organization of civil government as well as a guarantee of its tranquility and of its duration. The electoral law must fulfill the electoral system in all its details, resolve the difficulties arising from its implementation, and prescribe the procedure of the acts through which it is executed. The statue establishes the principles. The six articles that contain those principles had to be submitted altogether to the eyes of the reader so that the judgment of the reader embraces the complexity of the system rather than its separate parts.

This system does two things:

1. It calls a greater number of citizens to vote in the election of the deputies than any other system—as we shall soon see—greater than that of the so-called universal franchise system, and greater than that so far adopted by the proclaimed French Republic.
2. It attributes to the voters not a vote of equal value, as other systems do, but a vote of a value that is proportional to the complexity of the rights that each voter represents, so that all the rights and interests that must be protected have an equal voice in the chambers. That is

> obtained by allowing the colleges formed by the citizens with fewer interests and rights to form more numerous electoral colleges as prescribed in article 54.

This electoral system is one of the two cardinal points—as we have mentioned in Chapter Three—upon which civil society must rest. This civil society is constituted according to the principles of reason and justice, which are the only source of consistency and tranquility. It is therefore necessary that we linger over the reasons for this part of the constitution, offering greater details than in other parts of this constitution. We feel that we have against us all the prejudice of our times and all the weight of popular authority that has been usurped from us by the very eloquent France, and that we ourselves, through the deplorable servility of our ingenuity, have unfortunately allowed France to usurp. Under the weight of this oppression, we hardly have eyes with which to see, nor heads with which to understand the numerous frightening events that have passed and pass before our eyes that make us aware of the full fallacy and the absolute vacuity of values of that proclaimed authority in which we trust. Finally, we Italians—and not we alone—give, or at least so far have given, blind faith to the words while denying those facts that alone are capable of telling us the truth. I therefore invoke the special attention of my countrymen. The electoral right should not be based on a census but rather the norm of property.

All those who make laws make them for themselves. This is an indubitable principle of experience and nature.

If those who make law possess nothing, it is certain that they will use the legislative power that they hold in their hands to pull property to themselves and divest those who possess it. Properties stand without defense. Thus, an electoral wealth threshold was always established.

But the electoral threshold on one hand is too much, and on the other is not enough for the sufficient protection of property. This electoral threshold is either very high or very low.

In the first case, many proprietors are without electoral suffrage. In this case, either they are sacrificed to the larger proprietors, or they attempt to acquire through revolution that electoral right they are entitled to and that they are denied. If the threshold is very low, the legislative power is at the whim of the smaller proprietors, who make use of it to divest the larger ones.

We should remember this principle, validated by the history of all governments: that a property without a voice of its own—a property that is not represented by a corresponding degree of political authority—remains undefended and thus is subjected to the dispositions that weaken it, and sooner or later it is lost.

The universal vote is the same in its consequences as the leveling of all properties; it is the agrarian law that in our times ends up in communism. And the equal vote granted to all those who have a certain wealth has the same vice that the universal vote has towards the major proprietors.

What was the proximate and most efficient cause of the Revolution of '89? The vote was granted to people and not to things.

Why, in the Middle Ages, did the Third Estate and the municipal republics arise? Because the small properties, born with industry and commerce, wanted their own representation as was right. Finally, they were able to acquire power for themselves.

Why, in mountain territories and anywhere properties are very fractioned or where the land is abundant enough to be sufficient for all, is democracy easily established and maintained? Why instead is this form of government never naturally established—or if established through violence or unnatural skill does not stick or endure—as in the countries of large estates, which are very populated and where there is therefore a great disparity of wealth? Because under the first set of circumstances, if all citizens take an approximately equal part in government, the influence they exercise upon it is proportioned through property, and this is a fair and natural thing. Instead, in the latter set of circumstances, if all take an equal part in government, the few rich ones are in a tiny minority and thus at the mercy of proletarians, which is an unjust thing that disturbs the social condition.

To summarize, the fact that properties are not safe if they do not have a corresponding political representation is to be considered a certainty—the same certainty we have when stating that the political power is not safe if not connected to a corresponding property. Those who have more political power than property take advantage of the excess of power to draw to themselves as much property. Those who have more property than political power will use the excessive property to draw to themselves as much political power. The fight is certain, although the outcome is uncertain: When the imbalance between property and power gets to a certain level, there is revolution and peace does not return until somehow the disturbed balance is restored.

Thus, if we want to give to civil society a peaceful and firm state, nothing can be done but to structure it so that for every citizen a *balance exists between property and power*, and to distribute the power so that those who have more property end up having just as much power, and those who have less property get proportionally less power. In this last case, each portion of property finds its political representation, its natural guarantee and a voice that speaks on its behalf.

The ancient Roman centuries were structured on this thought: The proletarians and the *capitecenses* relegated to the last century were very many and cast one vote only; they were not used in the army. Montesquieu correctly considers this structure of Roman centuries as one of the main causes of the greatness and endurance of Rome, since through such a structure the political power was distributed proportionally to the wealth possessed by the citizens.

To give equal electoral vote to all or almost all is exactly the same thing as putting the legislative power in the hands of the *capitecenses*, which constitute the majority, because the men in such a system are actually counted by head and not by the complexity of rights they have and that must be guaranteed.

If we go to the bottom of all the modern restlessness in society, and if we put aside the many pretexts, and the many words used to dress them, we find that we are actually talking about on one hand, stealing the property from those who have it (that is, to do in such a way that properties fall into the hands of those who don't have them in virtue of an artificial social mechanism); on the other hand, to defend properties with all means often foolish and unjust.

Let us now examine this question form another point of view which is no less important, and we will find that we end up with the same results.

If we consider the origin of the modern constitutions of the states and the spirit that presided over their formation, we find that the legislators who dictated them departed from two different principles: Some from the principle of popular sovereignty, others from the principle of a collective government that focuses in itself enlightenment and probity.

The first ones were deducing from the principle of popular sovereignty that each man was entitled to have equal part in government—almost as if sovereignty was related to men's nature and was not a consequence of social relations; they were confusing *natural equality* with *social equality*. These people necessarily produced the system of the universal franchise.

The second ones had no other goal but to widen the base of government and to obtain that many were part of it—not because they had a right, but because by calling many to participate in the *res publica*, hoped to improve and reinforce government with a greater abundance of enlightenment. These legislators could not think beyond the ancient concept of a *seigneurial* government or at least an *arbitrary* one, the nature of which is such that the person that governs—either unique or collective—indeed does so with wisdom and probity, but without recognizing in the governed any right to influence the government itself or to make it accountable. Moved by such thinking, they started imagining guarantees through which it could be obtained that deputies could be only those who had wisdom and probity, and one of these guarantees was thought to be the establishment of a wealth threshold for the electors and an even higher threshold for those eligible for election.

These two principles that inspired those who dictated modern constitutions were often melded together so that the legislators themselves could not have a precise and distinct perception of the principles under which they were operating.

The principle of one group of legislators was false, and the principle of the other was good in intention but insufficient in reality. The constitutions that hold within themselves the two principles (all the modern ones) have both vices held deeply within them but one is much tempered by the other.

That the first of these two principles is false can be clearly seen in the fact that it confuses, as we said before, natural rights with social rights.

Men are equal in terms of natural rights but that does not at all mean that they must be equal in the society they create among themselves. Civil coexistence is a society—a special society.[58] Thus, it cannot lack what is essential for all societies. The common social right based on the essence of general society therefore applies to it as well.

Now, according to the simplest elements of this universal social right, he who contributes more to the social fund must share the greatest returns and consequently he must affect more the regulation of that society in which he has a greater interest. Stating the opposite is obviously contrary to common sense and justice.[59]

Let us suppose that in a society there are several large estate proprietors, some small proprietors, some simple farmers, powerful merchants, shop owners, heads of factories, workers, and occasional workers. These people all have different interests and goods to protect and these interests are often in conflict with each other. Let us suppose now that someone proposes to write a social contract that reads as follows: "The interests of all will be regulated according to a majority of votes and all participants will have equal vote." Would this be accepted by the owners of large estates, by the powerful merchants and by the owners of factories? Certainly not, because they would be able to see clearly that the number of farmers, workers and small merchants is vastly greater and therefore they would be the only ones to actually make the law. They would establish the price of labor according to their will, they would distribute the social contribution as they pleased, and they would act in such a way that their children would be educated with the same nobility as the owners. So as these people are stronger with their arms, they would be stronger through the law they would make. To sum up, those who possess less property would legally dispose of the larger properties that are owned by the other partners. This is in fact the case of civil society. This society does not gather at all to protect the rights that each man has as a man—in fact, if this were to be its only goal, this society would not gather at all. The society gathers and has gathered to protect the complex of natural and acquired rights possessed by each man that enters that society; such a complex is not equal for all but changes more or less in amplitude, and sometimes the difference is enormous.

This system is therefore false and contrary to social justice, as it does not protect that group of rights that are reduced to and that concern property. Rather, this system can be compared to a machine that has been skillfully invented to crush the largest patrimonies and then throw the fragments to those who pick them up more avidly.

Nevertheless, this system does not lack some good elements, although poorly expressed: that of considering civil government as social government, where all the partners have a voice through which they can validly express their reasons—and this is a desirable element. But here is the core of the problem: to find a way through which, while everybody has enough strength and weight to defend his rights in society, does not, by the same token, end up having a superior strength through which to invade somebody else's rights.

I repeat, therefore, that the good element is to be kept, that is, that civil coexistence must not be governed through lordship or through abuse. Those are forms that have to be left to those states that do not participate in the benefits of Christianity, or that are not yet sufficiently developed and thus they have not been sufficiently influenced by Christianity. We have to believe that the Christian nation must be organized as a true society. But for this very reason, the citizens that form it must not be considered simply as *men* but as *partners* of the nation. Thus, the organic constitution of such a nation should not spring from natural right but from a societal right that does not destroy natural right, but adds to it and completes it. Now, in the societal rights, the partners are not and must not be equal, but must have a power that is proportional to what they contribute to the common funds of society and to the weight of the rights they want to protect in that society.

But the second principle that structures the constitution of the state uniquely with the purpose of having assemblies of men who are prudent and honest, indeed abandons that good element. It does not change the nature of the seigneurial or arbitrary government; it only changes the arbitrator and the legislator from individual to collective, hoping that the collective person governs better because endowed with greater enlightenment and probity. But for this very reason, the change is insufficient for a people that are developed and that are aware of their interests.

This group of men who are enlightened and prudent must arbitrate on the collision of opposing interests of the various classes of people that civil society is made of. When private individuals have some contentions amongst themselves because of their own interests, it often happens that they present their reasons to arbitrators who are wise and honest. But these arbitrators are chosen equally by the two parties and not imposed on them by a third party. Now, the system of proportional vote constitutes such an electoral body, where each interest can elect its own arbiter (from now on I will call him an arbiter, although I am using the term improperly). Any other electoral system is reduced to the establishment of arbiters equally for all interests, and those arbiters are imposed by a third party, that is by a special electoral body that is determined by law. The election of deputies with equal vote is nothing but a palliative to cover the vice of being imposed arbiters, leading to the belief that they are arbiters elected by the parties while the truth is that not all interests intervene proportionally to the election of their arbitrators. The community of men of good faith, to which it seems that universal equal vote or an equal vote for all who have a fixed wealth is a good thing, fall in the same error made by the plebeians which find the lottery game to be excellent, as they do not suspect any injustice at all. In both groups, the illusion comes from the same cause, that is, the inability to calculate.

Furthermore, when private people elect arbiters to settle their disputes, these arbiters are third parties who do not belong to the conflicting parties. Regardless of the probity, honesty and education of the conflicting parties, it is however not verisimilar—and generally speaking it is impossible—that one of the parties would want to name as its arbitrator the opposing party, and incidentally it is certain that to force it to do so would be unjust. Now, in a civil society that embraces all citizens and all their interests, it is not possible to find arbiters that are not parties at the same time. And wanting to impose on all classes of citizens who have opposing interests arbiters who are indeed parties because they are citizens themselves is tantamount to injustice—and such injustice grows in proportion to the size of the interests that are dealt with. This argument alone demonstrates that the deputies cannot be and must be considered as *arbiters*, but instead as *proxies* of all interests including their own, who get together almost as they would do in a family gathering to protect all with equity and without allowing that the protection granted to one brings prejudice to the others and to discuss and agree on the expedients to use in order to achieve this result.

He who acts through a proxy that he has chosen acts on his own behalf and the legal adage *qui per alium facit per se ipsum facere videtur* [he who acts through others shows forth for himself] is realized. In that way the nation governs itself. If, conversely, the interests of the nations are dealt with through arbiters that are assigned, no matter how that is done, the nation no longer governs itself and is not free. Wherever we cannot apply the system of arbiters that can take place only in private interests to the constitutional form of a free government, and the electoral system of equal vote also cannot be applied, the result is merely a government of arbiters, imposed on the nation by an improvident law.

Nor is it valuable to state that, through the quality of the electors and of those eligible for election required by law, we can hope to obtain enlightened and honest deputies, because even if the opposing parties are enlightened and honest, each however favors in good faith its own interests and convinces itself that the wrong stands in the opposite camp. Therefore, if one of the parties were to become the only arbitrator, the other would be dissatisfied and would rightfully feel oppressed. Therefore, even when the deputies who are considered arbiters would have the opinions that are those of enlightened and honest people, never could they acquire universal trust, as civil society would rightfully worry about its own interests, and would remain restless.

This is because the greatest part of the social interests remains without a valid proxy, as the deputies cannot be considered in any way as arbiters even if elected by a large number of citizens through the equal vote electoral system. Even less could we entrust this arbitration to the upper house, as it obviously represents one single interest, that of aristocracy, and thus one of the contending parties would sit as only judge of the grand social cause. This is one new reason to exclude the upper house, as it is an irregularity that perturbs the natural organism of civil society.

That the deputies and the legislators are enlightened and honest—certainly these are the most desirable and important qualities in them. But those qualities alone will never fully satisfy a mature and developed nation because it knows that an incorruptible probity is too much a *rara avis in terra* [a rare bird on the earth], because the argument that those who handle the interests of others are more enlightened and wise than those who handle their own is not very convincing. Finally, each one of us believes that we have the right of intervention in matters of one's own interests, and we are not satisfied unless we or a proxy we have elected handles these matters. It is a common and very true proverb which says that the eye of the master fattens the horse.

The purpose of evoking directly and immediately in the deputies the two very precious qualities of probity and enlightenment creates an uncertain and shaky basis. Has there ever existed a citizen who did not believe he was as honest and enlightened as all the others? Those who possess these noble qualities the least and who instead are rich in foolhardiness and imprudence attribute the qualities that they lack all the more passionately to themselves and take offence when they discover that others are preferred. Thus offended in their own self esteem and stimulated by their ambition, they become agitators to obtain what they believe is due to them. Covered by this pretext of justice that they render to themselves, they would turn the world upside down to obtain reparation for the wrong they think they have received. Those people naturally take power away from government, fill the newspapers with bitter censure and calumnies, and form those extreme and sophistic parties that tear society apart. And where does the pretext for all this come from, if not from the vice of the constitution itself, whose fundamental principle and whose spirit is to make people believe that the deputies of the people must be absolutely the most enlightened and honest people—almost as if a sure criterion existed to recognize them?

With such a vague and undetermined base, the constitution falsifies the ideals of the nation, produces a restless public opinion because of uncertainty, undermines the self-esteem of all, foments the agitation of all ambitions, of all passions, and it ends up by making the people impossible to satisfy. In fact, the logical consequences of a basis which is far from positive, which is never possible to define, which rather establishes unreachable goals, must eventually produce, on one hand, a perpetual dissatisfaction because the goals are never fully reached; on the other hand, a continuous effort to reach those goals or to get as close as possible to them and thus a restless desire for constant change and an attempt to always make new experiments. And what experiments! How dangerous, sinister and bloody! All that is necessarily and logically created if we give credit to the opinion that, with the election of the deputies established by law, we look for nothing else but enlightened and honest men capable of giving good laws to the state. Inasmuch as it is true that the enlightened and the honest ones must be deputies, the logical consequence is that the citizens who are the most enlightened and honest of all have the right to be preferred. Thus, as long as the most enlightened and honest of all citizens are not found, the people will believe that they are not justly represented according to the specious principles of the rights that are established and that are taught to the people. But is it possible to find with certainty those citizens who are the most enlightened and honest? How will that be done? How can we persuade the people that they are such? How can we prevent doubts and speculations that better candidates may yet exist—even if the chosen citizens are what we believe they are? How can we expect from several million citizens such impartiality and such lowering of popular self-esteem so as to believe that all other people are inferior in enlightenment and honesty to the few who are elected? If that is not possible, how can we prevent the people from believing that their rights have been violated, since the theme adopted by the constitution of entrusting the formation of laws to the most knowledgeable and most virtuous is not satisfied? If the people are not satisfied on these counts and if the nation is not persuaded, then there cannot be tranquility and the nation will not believe it is well-built. Thus it will look for new reforms and new constitutions.

It will be said that the conditions prescribed for the electors and delectable ones are guarantees given to the nation—guarantees that ensure that the most upright and wise deputies will be elected.

But who could believe that, since such guarantees are insufficient? Rather, what guarantees could be given about such an impossible thing? As we have seen, there is a double impossibility here: It is impossible to find, rigorously speaking, the best ones; and it is impossible to persuade the people and the nation that those are precisely the best ones. In fact, the guarantees that are offered are as vague and undetermined as is the purpose.

It is said that the electors and the electable must pass a certain wealth qualification threshold. But why establish precisely that threshold and not a higher or lower one? In which way, then, can we expect that a fixed threshold is the unquestionable means to extract the best from the electoral poll? This is completely arbitrary. Even if some verisimilitude existed, there would never be positive certainty. Thus, an unascertainable dispute about the sufficiency of the guarantees provided will open in the nation, and those guarantees will be found to be insufficient because they are insufficient indeed to reach the goal set by the legislator. And why could we not find better citizens for wisdom and virtue, even amongst those who do not have the wealth required to be elected or who do not belong to the categories established from which deputies must be elected? The question of the guarantees will not be solved so easily, therefore, as it is insolvable by nature. The nation will not be quiet; it will be restless, and it will eventually demand new and different guarantees which is the same as saying that it will demand and finally obtain through law or force a new constitution, which in turn will not be any better than the first one and perhaps worse. It will be a new experiment even more disastrous than the first one that will lead to yet more disastrous experiments.

What will happen the day when, once those risky experiments are over with, the nation is persuaded that the system of guarantees is impossible and that it is impossible to find guarantees that fit the purpose it wants to obtain?

Then, indubitably, the nation will abandon the road it has taken and will conclude that all citizens can be electors and electable, and will consider it preposterous that some of them are regarded by law as inferior to others, as every person must be considered optimal until the universal vote says differently. In that way, the nation will fall again into that system which earlier we recognized to be false and unjust—into the system which, by substituting social for natural rights, perpetrates violence to property and to all acquired rights, alters their distribution and, with an incalculable series of legal injustices and consequent popular violence, will shake society to its foundations, level the properties and end up with the communist experiment, which in itself cannot succeed, because it is contrary to all laws of nature and will indubitably be the cause of extreme disaster for the world.

Therefore, the system of those constitutions that directly aim to obtain people's deputies who are honest and enlightened, although very specious in appearance and well-intentioned on the part of its inventors, demonstrates its insufficiency in solving the great problem of the constitutional structuring of the states, and sooner or later surely leads the nation to the first system improperly called "the sovereignty of the people" which instead should be called "despotism of the populace" because it is false and disastrous as well.

I say sooner or later because such a disastrous effect will not manifest itself until the nation is fully mature for constitutional forms and for a veracious freedom. As long as this maturity is not there, the system of arbiters which holds national liberty under its domain can work without a disastrous setback, in the same way that at an even lower level of maturity, absolute monarchy could be sustained. With the system of deputies and senators as arbiters, the motion has already started and no matter how slowly it progresses, the critical time must come when the nation sees that it is inevitably led—even though it does not know how—to those disastrous consequences that we have indicated.

There is only one way to avoid so much misfortune: Eliminate the upper house, divide the deputies into two chambers that balance each other and which represent the two highest and opposed interests of the nation to which all other minor interests are reduced, that of the large and that of the small proprietors. Thus, we would deduce the electoral right from a *positive principle* that leaves nothing to vagueness and indeterminacy, and that is founded on the right of society rather than on that of nobility or arbitrariness, even less on simple natural rights. The positive principle leads to the creation of chambers made *not* of arbiters as the deputies are now, but of real *proxies* of all interests, of all citizens' rights. The chambers are made up of proxies elected by the very ones who have interests. Through election, the deputies are recognized as best of all for wisdom and probity. Here we can also find the best of all possible guarantees to presume them such, since they are chosen by the most vigilant and competent judge, which is private interests—a judge that looks not for vague abilities—for example, the ability to chirp to popular applause—but really looks for and finds suitability. In any case, any pretext for complaining is removed, since those who elect their own proxies can no longer complain about a bad choice.

The proportional vote system that we propose clearly fulfils all those conditions. Only in this system are all the interests participating in the choice of the deputies truly called up, and that choice unquestionably falls on those with the appropriate abilities. This is, therefore, the system that promises lasting tranquility and internal peace within civil societies, as it does not hold within itself any seed of discord and malcontent, as there is no seed of injustice. This is what consolidates the government and the nation with the force of all the families of the state, in short, that which organizes the civil society according to its own nature and not according to vain and artificial utopias.

The more we consider justice and truth, the more we find them fertile with useful consequences. The more we think on it, the more this system unveils new advantages. Hereinafter, we will mention only two that come spontaneously and that are of very great importance.

The first is that this system naturally prevents corruption, which is the cancer of all modern constitutional states. In fact, in it the large proprietors form colleges that are not very numerous in their members. Simply because they are large proprietors, they cannot be corrupt. The small proprietors form colleges that are very numerous, and simply because they are numerous, these cannot be corrupt. It would be too difficult, in fact, to buy the vote of colleges that are composed of thousands of people. If someone were to buy their votes at enormous expense, he would be buying only one vote, which is still an insignificant thing. For example, if the college were to consist of three or four thousand electors, to buy its one vote it would become necessary to face the expenditures that would buy tens of votes in the common system.

After all, where does the corruption come from? From the same principle that we have indicated above, from the tendency of property to capture power for itself and to put itself in balance once again with power. The corruptors can only be the proprietors, that is, those who have much money. The corrupted can only be those who lack money. The corruption, therefore, is born because of the vice of constitutions which substitute the natural laws of how things work with an artificial system contrary to that nature. This happens by giving an equal share in the basic political power consisting in the right of electing deputies to those who own little and to those who own a lot, so that the much more numerous former dispose of the sum of things at the expense of the latter. Instead, the natural law through which society works spontaneously leads to concede to citizens who possess things a greater influence in the social regime. But the nature of things, which is stronger than the artificial and arbitrary creations of man, claims its empire back. Thus, property seizes the electors that lack fortunes and through corruption rips from their hands that suffrage that has been unjustly granted to them by the law. This reasoning is equally applicable to private corruption, and to the corruption that could be exercised by the head of the state from whom any arbitrariness in the distribution and promotion of appointments is removed in this constitutional project (articles 15, 91). Many of those appointments are declared incompatible with the position of deputy (article 61). Thus, if we want to avoid this problem, we need to go back to nature and to obey its indisputable laws that are laws of natural justice as well, by establishing an electoral suffrage that is proportioned to property. Only in this way can we give peace back to the state, by eliminating the fighting between nature and law, and reconciling this with that, or better said, by acting in such a way that the law of the state is nothing other than the law of the nature of things, this time written on paper.

The second advantage is no less important. It is recognized by the most solid publicists that the laws of the state must be modified from time to time. It was therefore proposed that even the fundamental statutes were reviewed at certain intervals. But the revision of the fundamental statutes is a dangerous work, as it agitates the nation, and especially with the approach of the time of revision, parities become organized and begin to move. Furthermore, such revision makes the statute itself less certain and authoritative. It is therefore desirable that the wise legislator dictates the statue so that it remains always firm and—as much as human events allow—immutable and that it contains a flexible part in its application. In such a way, we spare the people from the aforementioned agitations and since the modifications are foreseen and regulated, as well as concerning only the application of the law and not the law itself, the two advantages of stability of the law and its adaptability to the changing conditions of the times are achieved. The electoral vote proportioned to property holds within itself these two advantages. While the principle is always the same, the application is changed according to the changes of the state and the distribution of property, as well as the greater concentration or natural fragmentation of the property. The property is not diverted from following its natural course by fundamental law, which does not violate it by forcing it to take a direction against its nature. Instead of preventing it, the law follows that nature; it follows it step by step and protects it wherever it goes. The application of the law is changed alongside the change of property.

It is well known how many fights have been started in England by the so-called *rotten boroughs* and by the new commercial cities that were not sufficiently represented in parliament. All those agitations would have been avoided if the electoral vote had been given by the constitution of that kingdom in a way proportional to property. By lacking this principle of the proportional vote, either a frequent reform of the constitution is indispensable—which is always preceded and accompanied by great agitations and efforts by the suffering parties, which encounter resistance to reform—or revolution with crimes and immorality becomes unavoidable.

The British politicians who do not belong to the aristocracy or that raise themselves above the selfish passion of aristocracy perfectly understand that to cure the wounds of that nation it would be necessary to give to all property a fair representation. The father of British political economy reasons on the advantages that would be gained by Great Britain if all its possessions were called to be represented in parliament.[60]

The Romans, our glorious ancestors, were the inventors of proportional suffrage; the Greeks either did not know it or did not find a way to apply it. To what did the Greek legislators turn to avoid the damage of a numerically equal vote?

They had to turn to the equality of the patrimonies and establish that none of the citizens could own a greater wealth than others. It is enough to read the description that Aristotle makes of the different governments adopted by Greek cities to be convinced that the *equality of patrimonies* was the common key of all those political constitutions. Aristotle himself, and Plato as well, recognize it as indispensable. Now, can we create something more unjust and more barbarian that the equality of patrimonies decreed by law and implemented through force? Rather, it is an impossible expedient, and for the very reason that it is impossible and against nature, it was insufficient to protect the Greek republics from the continuous discord that tore them apart. Yet, the provisions of those legislators demonstrates that they were deeply feeling the radical defect of personal suffrage and confirms more than ever the need for proportional and real vote to obtain the stability and the peace of the state.

In short, the modern constitutions contain within them the horrible seed of communism and thus the most terrible despotism, and therefore the subversion not only of established governments but of human society itself. Let us say it again: Nations will never stop being restless until they expel from themselves this devastating seed and nature will have reclaimed its empire. Italy has now in its hands the very happy opportunity to spare itself and other European nations from these horrible agitations. If this opportunity is neglected, if we abandon power merely to the numerousness of citizens, which is tantamount to saying to the number of limbs, to brute power—since that number represents nothing but brute force—how can we ever take it from their hands? When the bird escapes from the cage, who can run after it? Power in the hands of brute force cannot be reclaimed except with the use of a greater brute force: And where do we find that? Nothing is left then but to wait for the brute force to break by itself and to dissipate. This is the work of the revolutionary parties; this is the fight of that blood with which all the constitutions of French origins were written and then erased.

What a glory it would be if Italy, with its knowledge and by going to the root of the question, could pluck out the evil where it stands and write the remedy in its political constitution—a remedy that is for her both traditional and domestic, a remedy that made Rome so strong at home and so great abroad. What a glory it would be if Italy could display its example to other peoples![61]

Let us now move to make some observations on each of the six articles that are mentioned above.

Why the First Chamber Is Elected by the Major Proprietors and the Second One by the Minor Proprietors

We have mentioned it before: The interests collide in such a way as to demand different regulations and laws, since the laws favorable to one group are useless or create prejudice for the other. Thus, in a civil society, a separate representation and a separate legislative power must exist.

If only one interest were represented, and if only one interest made the laws, two very great problems would arise:

1. That interest would never write laws useful to other interests but without use for itself. In that way, the other interests would stand neglected and deprived of the appropriate provisions.
2. That interest, not having concern for other interests, would write many laws that would turn out to be useful to itself with prejudice against other interests which would be sacrificed to the interests of the legislator. An interest, in fact, tends to prosper or believes it can prosper on the ruins of the others.

If instead of only one interest being represented (and that interest legislated) there were also other opposing interests with representation and legislative power, and if all these interests were not separated (as would happen if they were united in one chamber), then the interest that prevailed through the number of votes and through greater activity would be the dominant one. It would tyrannize the others, and an ensuing fight might even upset the losing party and set it on the road to illegality and revolution.

Conversely, if the opposing interests are represented separately, as happens when the first chamber is elected by the major proprietors and the second one by the minor ones, then there is no danger that one interest alone makes the law or the possibility that one tyrannizes the other. Nor is there a chance that a fiery hand-to-hand combat begins, a duel to the death, since the two adversaries are not in each other's presence and they defend themselves from a distance without ever getting close.

From this order of things, laws that are more beneficial to the social well-being are created. Those laws, as we said, can be divided into two classes: Those which are useful to one interest and useless to the other, and those that are useful to one interest and both useless and damaging to the other, leaving as valid those that are useful to both and over which there would be no argument.

The first class of laws is proposed by that interest which finds it advantageous, and the other interest permits it because it is not harmed. Thus, the formation of laws that are useful to both interests is not neglected.

The second class of laws is argued over, but a natural transaction comes into play, since the two opposing interests find advantages in giving each other concessions so that the advantages and the damages are apportioned equally. We have, therefore, a practical solution of that problem that presents itself in all moral and physical collisions where one term cannot grow without diminishing the other.

And to apply these principles to the two great interests represented by the large and the small properties, it is clear that

1. the small patrimonies tend to preserve themselves and to defend themselves from the danger of being caught in the vortex of the great patrimonies and being absorbed by them.

2. the great patrimonies also tend to preserve themselves and to defend themselves from the danger of being ripped and broken into small parts.

So far, the two tendencies, although opposite, contain nothing that is unfair and dishonest in themselves.

The question of justice begins when we have to determine a legitimate way through which the small and the large patrimonies equally try to control their preservation. That can be done justly or unjustly. It could be unjust when it is sanctioned by the legality of laws—and furthermore it can be unjust in two ways: either through a violation of the natural *juridical liberty*, or through a violation of *property* itself.

The law violates the natural *juridical liberty* if, through its dispositions, it impedes those licit actions that affect the movement of property. For example, a law that imposes a limit on the enlargement of patrimonies beyond a certain sum—a law that exists in some Italian states—violates the juridical freedom in favor of the small patrimonies while damaging the large ones because it prevents licit actions through which patrimonies can be enlarged beyond a set threshold. Conversely, the law on primogeniture and deeds of trust violates juridical liberty in favor of the large patrimonies while damaging the small one because it prevents those licit actions through which large patrimonies can be divided and be passed on. In the ancient European legislations, we can find two opposite types of violations, and one called the other a compensation turned to give back the fair balance violated by the whim of the legislators. It is always the same: An unjust law calls for another one to somehow cure the wound inflicted on the nature of things and to justice. It is in that way that the baroque and complicated building of the legislations that have existed so far has been constructed.

The law violates *property* each time it touches private properties or individual or collective persons. For example, the law that imposes contributions that are not proportional to the income of the citizens is a clear violator of property. It violates it in favor of the large patrimonies if it makes all contributions (or more than what is due) fall on the small proprietors, as always happened when the law was written by aristocracy. It violates it in favor of the small patrimonies if it makes all contributions (or more than what is due) fall on the large proprietors, as always happened when the law was written by democracy.

Now, given that the small and large patrimonies have a separate representation and legislative vote, those legislative dispositions that violate the liberty of property against the small patrimonies can no longer be passed because the chamber of the small proprietors, watchful of its interests, opposes them. By the same token, those dispositions that violate the liberty of property against large patrimonies cannot be passed either, because the chamber of the large proprietors in opposition. What then happens? The state demands that dispositions are created. Therefore, the legislators are pushed on the way of justice and equity by creating laws that keep in equal account the advantages and the rights of both small and large proprietors. That is the way to create just laws.

There is another natural tendency which is common to small and large properties, aside from that of self-preservation: The tendency to grow. But in opposition to such tendencies of property, there is a tendency of the proletarians and of those who own nothing. According to this tendency, those who own nothing are induced to own something.

Even this tendency is honest—but the way of satisfying it must not be dishonest. What is the honest and just way through which proletarians may become owners and thus satisfy their natural desire? That of acquiring properties through licit actions that give them juridical title—in short, the use of their juridical liberty. Therefore, laws cannot violate the property of proletarians because they have none; but they can violate their liberty to acquire it by obstructing that liberty, which also must be defended.

Now, liberty does not need positive laws, as it does not need any administration. The laws upon which human liberty rest are all natural and written in the constitution. However, the positive laws, which cannot form liberty, can violate it. Therefore, liberty does not need legislative power. It only needs an eminent authority which is vigilant over the legislative power so that this does not overstep its jurisdiction and offend freedom. This authority protecting the freedom of proletarians is that of the supreme political tribunal in charge of containing the legislative power within the limit of rational and natural justice. In this way, the rights of all are taken care of, as all rights find a protection in the powers of the state that are instituted by the constitution.

Going back to the two legislative chambers and to the reason why they must represent the opposing interests of the large and small proprietors, what is of paramount consideration is how these two interests include all others. To say it better, these two interests are those upon which all others are founded, since none of the others can be administered and regulated if not through the administration and the regulation of those two interests.

The various comprehensive duties of the civilian power are reduced to these:

1. To have available the force through which public order is maintained, all rights are protected, and society is defended from external enemies.
2. To favor agriculture, industry and commerce.
3. To promote education, civil and polite behavior, and the moral sentiments.

Now, what is the indispensable means through which these duties can be exercised? Money. And who dispenses the money? Those who have it, and in the proportion in which they have it. It is an elementary principle of common sense and natural right that those who pay command. Those who pay must determine how they want their money spent, and in our case, how they want the state to be governed. Above them, only inviolable justice can stand. The rest is their job to determine—and this is the sovereignty of people founded in nature.

Let us examine this from another point of view. In a developed society, money represents everything. In a society that is not yet developed, nor come to civilization, *property* is still that condition that man needs to exist, educate himself, and operate. When man is more copiously provided with property, he can enjoy more, nourish other men at his service, exercise influence and charity on his peers, be loved and feared, aggrandize himself, and obtain all means necessary to his education. Therefore, to have influence on properties is the same thing as having influence on all other goods that are tied to and conditioned by property. It follows that all interests—even the dearest and the most noble—are reduced to that of property as it is the primary condition and the cause of all other interests.

From all we have said before, we can derive the following summation:

1. That all the laws touch property directly or indirectly, since those very laws cannot be written or implemented without property.
2. That the laws concerning property as a consequence have influence on all other human goods.
3. That those who contribute the property to government—this is the indispensable means to govern—must be the proprietors.
4. That the proprietors that contribute their property so that the government can exist and operate have the right to know how the government operates and to impose on it how it must operate.
5. That when proprietors are in discord on how to determine the action of government, equity dictates that their vote is proportional to the property they contribute.
6. That, since the conflict cannot arise but from the opposite and different interests of small and large properties, both interests must be equally recognized.
7. That in order to be successful in the implementation of number 6, neither the opinion of the small proprietors nor that of the large ones determines alone the law through which the government acts, but both have to act in accord.
8. Finally, that in order to obtain that accord, it is best that the two opinions have equal force, represented by the two chambers as established in this constitutional project. This is so that no one power overcomes the other, and both are obligated to keep a middle conciliatory way, and that those powers become unable to operate unless they satisfy this condition, made necessary by the organism of social power.

Why the Electoral Vote Is Attributed in Proportion to the Total Sum of Direct Tax That Proprietors Pay to the State Treasury

Civil society cannot exist without money; with it, it pays the bureaucrats and the military, as we have said, and it performs public works and so on. Nothing is done without money. Therefore, it is a society of contributors.

According to the common principles of social right, each contributor to the funds of society must sense an advantage that is proportional to his contribution.

This is a new reason that demonstrates that there is no equity in establishing an electoral vote of equal value for both the citizen who contributes much to the state and the citizen who pays little or nothing, since the influence that each person has in the formation of the laws is equal to the value of the electoral vote. If the value of the vote were the same for all electors, all electors would have the same influence. The advantage that each feels in society depends on the quality of the laws, and thus it is proportioned to the influence and the power that each exercises in the formation of legislation. Thus, if we want those who contribute more to the fund of society to get a greater advantage, it is necessary to do things in such a way that the electoral vote of those who contribute more proportionally has a greater value.

One can say that direct taxation (all that which is paid immediately as a tax) does not faithfully represent all properties or, better, all the incomes of contributors.

I answer that this is true, but that, as we have seen already, this comes uniquely from the defectiveness of the law that distributes the public burden amongst the citizens. This defect in turn comes from the defect of the legislator, that is, from the defect of the legislative power which, in absolute governments, has no interest in making financial laws that are fair and just for all, but only in making them such as to fill the treasury of the state without raising complaints amongst the population. This vicious circle must be broken through the restructuring of the legislative power so that it has interest in making a just and fair distribution of the social contributions. The law that distributes the public taxation must therefore be reformed during the first legislature in the way that we have described.

Furthermore, we have noticed that the restructuring of the law concerning public taxation is greatly facilitated by this principle of the proportional vote, since proportional voting opens the road that enables the state to enhance industrial and commercial wealth by inviting such wealth to grow spontaneously, consequently allowing the abolition or great diminishment of indirect taxation, which is not susceptible to equal distribution.

Some may think that something unjust or illiberal is committed by establishing that those who pay nothing to the treasury of the state are deprived of an electoral vote. But the worries of these people will disappear completely when they consider the issue seriously.

First, the fact that those who pay nothing to the treasury of the state are deprived of the electoral vote is a corollary of the incontrovertible principle that civil society finds its existence and its operation in the contributors.

However, this does not mean that society rejects those who contribute nothing. It just limits itself to not recognizing in them any right to vote in the nomination of the deputies.

Civil society is not against those who contribute nothing, and it cannot be anything other than a beneficial society. The fact that civil society recognizes its members (even those that contribute nothing to the social funds from which it draws existence and activity) is not prescribed by the right of nature and reason, but insinuated by the spirit of the Gospels which excludes slavery from the world. All men who are redeemed by Jesus Christ are free and brothers. Christian civil society thus recognizes the poor and freely takes them within itself while protecting them with justice and helping them with charity. However, that does not mean that society needs to give them political power as well. Such attribution would be pernicious, as it would instill in them the temptation to abuse that political power to draw to themselves somebody else's property over which they would acquire influence.

To expect that those who contribute nothing to the treasury of the state be given electoral rights is an opinion damaging to property. It would be like establishing by law the introduction of some individual into a private society of contributors and then exempting him from the obligation to contribute his share to the common treasury. This would be like a breach of property rights. Such a breach is built into the system of universal suffrage. For the same reason, there is a property violation in all the constitutions that grant an equal vote to different contributors, since he who contributes twice the amount of another has, next to the other, the equivalent of two juridical persons but is forced to have an influence equal to that of two members who contribute half of what he did. Therefore, if these statutes contain in their dispositions a violation of property, how can it be true rather than a lie that every property is inviolable? There is an open contradiction, and we will never tire of repeating that laws that are founded on contradictions cannot last, because man is a rational being. These statutes must necessarily produce the effect of agitating society until one of two things happens: either the destruction of the statutes, or the destruction of society.

Nor can it be said that those who own nothing, although they do not contribute with money, contribute with work, because in different ways all citizens contribute equally with work. That contribution, however, is not sufficient to sustain society and, after all, civil society in order to exist does not have a rigorous need for the work of those who put nothing in its treasury.

Thus, to keep these people within society, to declare them citizens, and to protect their rights, are benefits that society exercises towards them. Insofar as society derives an indirect advantage from these benefits, its operation does not lose its beneficial nature.

Let us keep well in mind that the civil society—as it is structured through the proposed constitution—by keeping within it those who contribute nothing to its treasury, does not consider them as second-class citizens and does not intend to diminish in any way the benefit given to them; nor does it want to seek compensation from them through some burden imposed on them. Its benefit is full and very sincere: The citizenship and the freedom that it grants to those without property have exactly the same value for them as they have for anyone else. Those without property are declared absolutely and perfectly equal before the law.

But what does the juridical equality of all citizens consist of? Certainly it cannot be considered—nor was it ever considered by any reputable publicist—as a material and arithmetical equality, but rather an equality of laws for all and nothing more. The equality of the laws implies an application that is proportional to the titles of fact, that is, to the circumstances to which laws are referred and which they recall. According to the verification of such claims and circumstances, the law can or cannot be applied in whole or in part. These are facts that change, and with a change of facts, the application of the law must change. That does not diminish the reality that the law is still the same for all, even for those who lack the claims of fact to which the law can be applied.

But what must be the spirit of all law of a civil and well-structured society? It can be contained in this formula: "The laws must protect and equally favor *all* the rights of the citizens." Therefore, one thing is protection which must be equal for all; another thing is the protected rights which can change in size and importance—in fact, they necessarily do so. That one citizen has a greater number of rights than another, this is in the realm of facts, not of law. Thus, this is a circumstance which does not destroy the legal or juridical equality we are discussing.

Let us now apply these principles to those of us who do not have property. These citizens possess fewer rights than proprietors: This fact must not be destroyed by the law. However, the law must be equal for all, meaning that it equally protects the fewer rights possessed by those who own nothing and the greater number of rights held by the proprietors. Let us now see whether this is obtained under this constitutional project.

We have said that all rights of citizens and man are reduced to two ends: liberty and property. The constitutional project protects both and we have seen that already. Those who do not have external and real properties possess nothing but personal property and liberty. What is needed to fully protect this group of rights? Nothing except defense. It needs to be defended so that the person does not incur damage or injury, and that no unjust obstacle is imposed on the development of his faculties, since liberty consists in the free use of these faculties. To achieve that end, it is useless to establish any administration, as a just tribunal with integrity is sufficient, as well as laws that fully declare the extent of those rights. Conversely, just laws and a tribunal are not enough to protect external property and the rights that concern it, and to prevent the property of some from coming into conflict with the property of others, and for the purpose of finding the compromise of a fair settlement of that conflict, to promote the varied and complex development of those properties, and to regulate the use without limiting it. It is necessary to establish a common administration and a common council of owners, which, debating over common interests, finds agreement on means of implementation, allowing for the prosperous proportional growth of the property of all.

Therefore, the two cardinal powers of civil society as dictated by the nature of things must be:

1. A tribunal, with good laws, that protects all personal rights and addresses the facts, because they can be offended.
2. A political-economic administration that promotes the development and the flourishing of wealth.

The first of these two powers has as a goal the defense of the rights against any violation and it concerns justice. The other one has as a goal the contemporary and collective development of those rights which are real and concern administration. This administration is what constitutes the principal and the main and special purpose of the national parliament, whereas the independent tribunals stemming from parliament must be equally fair to all.

The abstract politics (thus, vague and undefined) of the French Revolution, which however exercised and exercises a sort of tyranny on the mind, imprinted a confused concept of a national parliament. The parliament is conceived as the greatest and most solemn of powers—rather, the only national power—without any analysis, without ascertaining its functions and thus knowing its true and precise purpose. It is only known in general that the parliament is instituted for the formation of the laws. But what is not known, or rather what is not considered, is that the laws must be done in two manners. Some laws are to declare what is just and what is unjust. Others are to promote and increase public prosperity. Even the latter ones must be just, but their purpose is not pure justice. If we were to deal with just the first order of laws, then a parliament would not be necessary, since justice is already determined by eternal laws built into the conscience of all men, and those laws can be declared even by private scholars, and rather only scholars and religious men are competent and authoritative enough to make such declarations. Furthermore, in a good constitution, all those laws are already set. For laws concerning utility, however, the parliament is indispensable, and this is indeed its true and proper purpose. Thus the parliament must unite in itself the element of all the utilities of the state and no utility and no interest must be excluded.

That does not mean that the deputies are there to represent special interests. But since the public interest only results from the sum of all private interests, it follows that public interest cannot be fully represented if all private interests, large and small, are not represented at the same time. Furthermore, a power that is turned to utility must be accountable to another power that oversees the preservation of justice, so that the utilitarian instincts that naturally move the parliaments do not damage justice.

Thus, provides that the organization of the tribunals is skillfully established and it equally extends to both natural and civil as well as political rights and just and fundamental laws exist—such as those contained in Title III of this project—on which the decisions of the tribunals can rest, then the parliament is sufficiently equipped to deal with that group of rights that we have defined as personal and which are the only rights that apply to those who own nothing. Those rights are not susceptible of collective application simply because they are personal and do not need anything but free exercise. If, therefore, those who own nothing were to become part of the administrative power of the chambers, they would be called to pronounce themselves not on their own rights, which admit no administration but only defense, but on the rights of others. And to expect to have the right to decide and make laws on somebody else's business is contrary to justice.

The constitutional project establishes an order of tribunals (articles 25, 85) before which the citizens are all equal (article 22). These tribunals make decisions pertaining to all rights, no less on the individual than on the social (articles 81, 82, 84). Under these tribunals, even those who own nothing find equal protection and defense against any power and even against the chambers themselves, as they can appeal to aforementioned tribunals against the chambers' dispositions.

The decisions of these tribunals are supported by laws that guarantee equally to all the security of the person and the freedom of action, as well as the constitution.

The constitution begins with declaring as inviolable for each man the rights of nature and reason (article 2); it guarantees individual liberty (article 23); it declares the place of residence inviolable (article 24); it recognizes the right of petition, even collective (article 34), as well as the right to assemble and to associate (articles 35, 36); it guarantees literary property (article 33), freedom of press, teaching and commerce (articles 37, 39, 40). It also calls all citizens equally to cover all the public positions of the state according to their abilities and suitability, without regard to property (article 41) and to prevent the judgment on suitability from being solely the decision of the sovereign, it establishes that a law determines the ways to recognize such suitability (article 15); it does not demand any wealth threshold for the electoral eligibility of the deputies (Article 60) and to make sure that everybody can effectively be elected according to his merit, it assigns and indemnity to the deputies of the provinces (article 62). In this way, even those who own nothing can be elected as deputies if the proprietors who are entitled to the vote elect them—and they will elect them if they deserve it, since it is to the advantage of the proprietors to elect the most skilful, the most honest, and the most enlightened proxies.

With these dispositions, all citizens have the full exercise of their rights and it is even provided that those who own nothing are free and effectively guaranteed on all means of acquiring that wealth that they lack, and through that, even the electoral right itself.

These dispositions dispense me from defending the constitutional project against those who would object that too much is given to property at the expense of moral and intellectual abilities. When competition is free for all, when the door to social advantages of any kind is open to all, then abilities emerge and prevail spontaneously. This is the right that even the poor have and they can expect no more, since for those who have no goods of fortune it is sufficient that they can justly honestly acquire them with a just title, and cannot expect to steal them or to interfere in the administration of somebody else's property. According to this constitutional project, he who owns nothing can be elected deputy and, as we said, even become minister—if he is more capable than those who own. Such is the influence that abilities are entitled to have. So everyone is able to climb the social ladder, but through natural steps. In this case, ascending is just, as only those who have the right can do so. The evil of that ambition that ruins society comes from constructing ladders for the people—ladders that are not part of the design of the construction so that the people can assault the construction and even climb to the roof. Those who come to our home through the common stairs are not dangerous, but those who come in with ladders through the windows are dangerous. The electoral vote of equal value granted to all those who have a fixed wealth is one of these ladders. And as long as the ladder exists, the social construction will be exposed to thieves.

Articles 53, 54, 55, and 56, determine what I would call the mechanism of elections so that it conforms to the established principles.

Articles 53 and 55 are likely to provoke the objection that, if the major contributors of the state and progressively the minor contributors must unite in electoral colleges, some electors will be forced to travel to get to the location of the electoral college to which they belong.

Our main consideration here is that those electors who live at a noticeable distance from the place where elections are held can only be the richest contributors for whom traveling is less troublesome. As the abilities of the electors to contribute decreases, the places assigned to the collegial reunions are closer, and they can be made closer as needed by dividing electoral colleges into sections.

Furthermore, this difficulty disappears completely even with respect to the largest contributors if we consider that the electoral right can be exercised through proxy (article 59).

On the other hand, Italy needs to have mutual knowledge and interaction of citizens who are distant from each other. Only in this way can we enable that fusion of many different races that constitute this country. These races have been so far kept divided by insurmountable barriers that jealous and despotic governments built—governments that had, in the division of Italians, the foundation of their power.

The division of the electors into colleges, each electing a deputy, was wisely adopted, even by the state of Piedmont. But in this statute, we have assigned to each college an electoral district. And in our system, the electoral district would be assigned only to the colleges that have the largest number of people. Nothing forbids—indeed, it can be advantageous—the colleges with fewer members (that is, those made of the largest contributors) from gathering in the main cities of the state where most of them live.

Furthermore, the fact that each college elects only one deputy is necessary to obtain a true representation of the people.

The system adopted by the provisional government of France, where the electors vote for all deputies of the departments in the main official place is profoundly deceitful and insidious to liberty. To realize this, it is sufficient to consider this clear principle upon which a truly liberal electoral law must be founded:

> Electors must know the candidates in order to elect them. If we act in such a way that the electors are obligated to elect people they do not know, the election is not true but an illusion. Indeed, they are not electing them but give their suffrage randomly, which in itself is not an election.

Given this principle, it follows that if the electoral law does not try to cheat the nation, and truly wants the people to elect their own deputies, then it must set things in such a way that all electors can know the candidates and choose amongst the known ones those whom they trust. Only under this condition do we have true representatives of the people. The electoral law cheats the nation when, while claiming to grant the vote to all citizens, artificially it obtains that the greater number of electors—that is, the people, is forced to give its suffrage blindly, and to give it to people who are totally unknown. When the people are forced to choose amongst people they do not know, they are naturally indifferent to electing one candidate rather than another, and thus keen to be prompted by those who show up first to play masters, and to help them with their embarrassing choice of which they do not know the gravity. That is tantamount to saying that the people are at the whim of the foxy ones and the corrupters, as these are truly those who elect and no longer the misled people. What can a law that cheats and is perfidious, dictated by a party that has prevailed and wants to substitute itself for the people, do? It proclaims the universal vote. And surely, fools who believe this pompous proclamation and think that the shifty legislator truly wants a whole nation to speak and be heard, also believe that all citizens, none excluded, truly express themselves by voting their will. But let us come down to facts and see what the result is. What does that legislator who has a hidden agenda and a biased plan, and who is not at all interested in knowing the national will, do? To better throw his rope, he keeps on being generous with the people and assigns to them such extended rights and such difficult duties that the people absolutely cannot and do not know how to perform. Such are the rights and the duties given by the French provisional governments to each inhabitant of every village, of every cottage of France—to nominate all the electors of a department. It is quite clear that the farmer cannot know anybody but his local neighbors and the knowledge that he has of the people does not go beyond the limits of his poor town. Where will he find, then, ten, twelve, or even twenty people that can represent the nation in the parliament? And who can he name but uneducated peasants and herders? It will be, therefore, inevitable that he will cast his vote for those candidates who have been suggested to him and have been celebrated by the commissaries or by the emissaries of the government or of the influential party which has organized everything in the first place to govern the nation according to its whim. The despotism here is manifest: The perfidious nature and the scheming of those who want to absolutely enjoy the power of the state and to exploit the nation cannot be clearer. Austria—and I mean academic Austria—is the best for such infamous and hypocritical liberalism.

I cannot neglect to add to the observations above the wise observations on the electoral system adopted by the provisional French government made recently by Camillo Cavour, which are in agreement with ours:

> In the first place, this system states that elections are awarded only to relative majority and thus they cannot produce a true representation of the country. In the second place, the system forces electors to vote for people who are totally unknown, or known mostly through indirect relations. I will let you judge what would happen if the electors of Viù and those of Giaveno (and we would say those of Lazzate or of Misinto) should participate with their departments in the election of the deputies attributed to the province of Turin, and we would say of Milan. The French system has been intentionally created to make people choose those men who are the most fervent, the most passionate, the most clamorous. That may be considered as an infallible means to obtain a chamber that is animated by the most burning passions that agitate the nation; but also as a very fallacious means of constructing a faithful and exact representation of the true opinions, of the real interests, and of the lasting sentiments of the country.[62]

Finally, we must realize that to overcome the difficulties of execution, a better mechanism could be found. We will not insist on what we have proposed already. The substance of our thinking is that the electoral vote has a weight that is proportional to the tax paid by the citizens. We could, for example, set a certain tax sum to represent a vote having the value of one unit. In such a case, the vote of those who paid double, triple etc. as tax could have a vote with a value of two, three units, etc. In the capital and in other more populated centers, commissions in charge of collecting votes could be formed, and those votes could be sent to them via notarized note, other legal note, or through proxy. In that case, there would be no need for popular gatherings, which would avoid the problems that gatherings cause. The aforementioned commissions would perform the computation of the votes and their values, and would proclaim the deputies elected in that way.

Also, as many commissions as there would be electoral colleges could be instituted, and each of them would proclaim the deputies elected by the college.

With the computation of the value of the votes performed in this way, the proportion of this value to the tax paid would turn out to be even more exact.

ARTICLE 57—The king participates in the elections in proportion to the income of the fixed assets owned by the state, and of that of his private patrimony. The Church and all its administrative bodies, societies, or collective persons that contribute some direct tax to the general revenue of the state, participate in the same proportion.

Article 57 is merely a consequence of the principle that all properties, since they contribute to the creation of the state treasury, must be represented in the chambers. For the incomes of the fixed assets of the state, the electoral right can only be properly exercised by the king, to whom the executive power belongs.

Apart from this, the king is considered as any other citizen as far as his private property is concerned (article 19), although it is appropriate that he participates in the electoral suffrage in accordance with the law.

In other constitutions, the nomination of peers or senators is performed by the sovereign, but this turns out to be a hideous privilege. In this constitution, the sovereign has no privilege, but for that reason he enjoys the advantages of common law.

The determination of how collective persons must give the vote in proportion to the wealth they possess and that they represent to the state through the tribute to the treasury belongs to the electoral law. This is a point that must be thoroughly discussed.

To merely indicate how this could be achieved without drifting in the least from the principle that the votes must be cast by the property owners in proportion to their social contribution, I limit myself to just a few observations.

The assets belonging to moral entities are a title that gives to the moral body which owns and pays tax the right to the electoral vote. It is therefore necessary to make a distinction between the administrators of these assets and their owners. The right to the electoral vote does not belong to those administrators but to these owners. Let us address the details.

Amongst the moral bodies that own, the secular and regular clergy come first of all. The Catholic clergy has perfect hierarchy and unity. But concerning the ecclesiastic assets, the discipline of the Church changed as to the election of the people who were to be proxies and the representatives of the very Church which owned those assets. At one time, when the whole mass of ecclesiastical assets was trusted in the hands of bishops who, by means of those assets, were in charge of the maintenance of the clergy and of worship, the bishops were the only proxies of ecclesiastic wealth. But with the institution of benefits through which the ecclesiastical assets were assigned, things changed. The current practice considers as proxies of those assets the very same beneficiaries that use them. Therefore, these beneficiaries must cast a vote that is proportional to what they pay to the state for the benefit with which they are invested. Furthermore, the Chapters must cast their vote in proportion to what the assets not yet assigned pay.

Concerning the assets belonging to the industries of the churches, the vote belongs to the owners or to the patrons of the churches, or to those who keep them in good repair.

The assets belonging to charitable institutions, when they exist in such a way as to be indivisible from charitable use, belong to those who are called to receive the benefit.[63]

Among those, a class is destined to relieve the indigence of the poor—and by poor, we mean those who pay nothing to the state as direct tax. These people, therefore, must be registered in each municipality—or better, within that territory covered by the charitable organization—and must be invited to cast the corresponding electoral vote. In this way, the proletarians can also participate in the electoral vote, as they are enabled through Christian charity, which does not want them to be completely poor.

Here we do not have to involve ourselves with the other questions, which concern prudence and coexistence: "How can we collect these votes so that public order is not disturbed and yet ensure voting freedom?" Amongst the different ways, the government could use registers in which those summoned can write their votes. The registers should be open in the parish houses, providing that the Catholic clergy is called and put in charge of vigilance and partially also of the administration of the assets that belong to public charity.

Finally, all the collective bodies that possess common assets that pay tax have the electoral vote annexed, to be exercised by the members of their constituencies, which cast them in proportion to the quota they own in the common fund.

It is true that many juridical questions can be raised when it comes to the quantity of electoral right that moral and collective bodies are entitled to—and these are wholly new questions because legislation on this does not yet exist, and must be made as cases occur. However, since we have already established the existence of political tribunals which are in charge of the resolution of all doubts that can arise, it is convenient to put them in charge of this task as well. So an electoral law that is imperfect at the beginning gets perfected as time goes by through special decisions that the political tribunals make as the interested parties turn to them to enforce the right they think they are entitled to.

ARTICLE 58—No particular qualification is required by law to enjoy the electoral right, except the payment of a direct tax to the state.

ARTICLE 59—The electoral right is exercised solely by men. It can be exercised through legal representation: Fathers, husbands, tutors, and caretakers exercise it on behalf of children who are legal wards, wives, minors, and the interdicted. The missing votes in each college are supplied by the government in favor of any of the above-mentioned categories.

As property is what has the electoral right, no particular qualification is required for a citizen to be an elector, except the payment of a direct contribution to the state.

Property is a right, and consequently the electoral vote is also considered a true right of the associated property holders, to regulate how common interests are to be run, and how they contribute to the social fund. This deserves further consideration.

In other constitutions, the electoral vote is granted as if it were a grace given through the judgment of the legislator. That judgment can be directed by more or less prudential views, as we have seen already, since prudence and discretion have a very particular meaning when not concerning what is mine or yours, but concerning spontaneous generosity.

Therefore, other constitutions believe they are authorized to deprive fully of the electoral vote those who do not have a certain age, a certain wealth, certain other predetermined qualifications, and those constitutions do not believe that the slightest injustice is done to anyone. But this way of operating perfectly resembles what absolute and despotic governments do. Indeed, it overtakes them all when it comes to despotism and absolutism.

There could be one only child surviving in the richest family of the state. As the child has not yet reached legal age, he stands excluded from any participation in the electoral right. The same applies in the case of a single woman or convicted person—even if this person were to own all the properties on half the territories of the state. This is a legitimate consequence of the error of the concept that deputies represent people and not things, that is, of the error that sees them as arbiters and not proxies. In that way, we have an endless number of properties that have absolutely no weight in the electoral polls.

With the same absolutism, or rather legislative despotism, it is established that no one can cast his vote through proxy. So those who are absent, sick, old, or for any other reason cannot personally go to the poll stand deprived of the vote, no matter how rich, able or honest they are. But that represents no injury when the electoral vote in civil society is not a right of the citizens, but merely a grace dripping from the whim of those who dictate the constitution to the people.

So in establishing those who are fitter for the electoral vote, one proceeds tentatively and without any fixed principle. The lack of principle and of fixed norms is so great in all French type constitutions that in many electoral laws based on wealth qualification, the amount of that qualification is subtracted in favor of certain provinces of the state, while certain people are completely exempted, certain others are only exempted by half, and finally, it is established that the same asset can be computed as part of the wealth qualification of two different people.[64]

With such means, it is hoped that everybody is happy. But man is reasonable, and those laws that do not proceed from logical coherence and from clear and well-established principles hardly satisfy reason. There will be always a question about whether the discretion and prudence of the legislator has been imperfect. There will always be something to criticize, and improvements and reform of the electoral laws will be sought, and it will be impossible to define whether the demand for such reform is reasonable or not, as when it comes to mere prudence and discretional whim, it is impossible to find everybody in agreement. Finally, there will be doubts about whether the freedom of the legislator has been truly large enough, while others will say that it has been too large. This kind of doubt is such that it cannot be resolved. Such constitutions, therefore, necessarily spread in the minds of all citizens such a political skepticism that souls are kept in uncertainty, suspended in apprehension and agitation, and that skepticism is what throws the citizens towards an impossible optimism.

Society is despondent and weak as long as the belief in the fundamental law is shaky and discordant. Persuasion cannot be obtained—let us say it again—if the law is not logically deduced from *fixed principles* that are clear and unchangeable.

We believe that those discretional exclusions from the electoral right that establish the French type constitutions are tantamount to lesions on the sacred and inviolable right of citizens.

And as we believe that to exclude from the electoral colleges those proprietors who do not have the arbitrary qualifications established by law is a breach of rights, so do we also believe that it is a much graver breach that those citizens who represent a small group of rights are equated in the electoral right with other citizens who represent a group that is one hundred or one thousand times larger. So, in this case, we arbitrarily give too much to the small proprietor by granting him a vote equal to the large proprietor with a spirit of vicious and unjust democracy. By the same token, other dispositions of ordinary statutes—that is, the wealth qualifications for electors and the even higher wealth qualifications for electoral candidates as well as the denial to the deputies of any indemnity and the like—are clearly flawed with vicious and unjust aristocracy. Finally, the constitution that establishes the electors through discretional arbitrariness is flawed with vicious and unjust absolutism, since the despotism here is in the very root of society, and in the legislator, whoever he is, who dictated the constitution.

To avoid such obstacles, and consistent with the principle of social justice which established that each contributor must have an influence in society in proportion to his contribution, it is established in article 59 that the electoral suffrage can be cast even through legitimate proxy.

Hence if female decorum forbids women from personally participating in electoral colleges, nevertheless they exercise their right through proxy in the same way as non-emancipated children. The wives, minors, interdicted, and those who for whatever reason are impeded can equally exercise the right through the husband, the father, the tutor, the trustee, or any other person.

From this we can deduce that in the system we propose, a much greater number of citizens are called to vote than in any other system, including that of the universal vote. However, there is no danger whatsoever that society can fear the sinister consequence stemming from the nature of proportional vote.

The reason for which we state in article 59 that, in the scrutinizing of each college, no vote of any elector called to form the college is missing (and if it is missing, it must be supplied by the government), is not just to stimulate electors to participate, but also to preserve the proportional influence of the citizens in the elections. Still, this disposition stems from the very same principle of social justice. Otherwise, the electors that show up to cast their votes would acquire an influence which is both undue and disproportionate, if we did not take into account the votes of those who are missing.

Through this process, the government indeed acquires influence in the elections—but justly and through the will of those citizens who abstain from casting their vote.

The government in this case becomes their natural proxy, as it has the duty to supply always everything that is needed for the regularity of public order when that is not attended to by the citizens. In times when the people do not take any part in public affairs, then the government does everything and it does it necessarily and justly. In such times, there can be only absolute governments. But the government must progressively concede to the people a greater degree of intervention in public affairs as the people demonstrate that they are able and willing. In our case, what is the rule to know in what part the people know and want to intervene by exercising their electoral right? The rule of facts. The people know and want when, in fact, they intervene to cast their vote; and when they do not, they don't know what they want. Therefore the government has the full right and duty to fill that deficiency itself in proportion of the many or the few. So the constitution opportunely adapts itself to the degree of political maturity that is reached or will be reached by the nation.

Nevertheless, it is useful to add that the government is obligated to supply the missing votes in favor of any of the nominees not so much because its influence is overpowering—since a legitimate authority is never overpowering—but rather because to supply the missing votes in favor of those who are named by the colleges constitutes one of those guarantees which tend to exclude arbitrary favors bestowed by the power, which are already prevented through article 15.

ARTICLE 60—Those eligible for election must be Italians, of legal age, not interdicted, not in debt,, not criminally convicted. If they have been convicted for political matters, they must have been pardoned. Finally, they must not be, at the same time, employed in a capacity that is incompatible [with election].

The conditions imposed by article 60 for electoral eligibility are much wider than those established by other constitutions that have so far been adapted by Italian princes and even wider than any other known constitution. No wealth qualification is required; the age is the lowest possible, and so on.

The reason for which we can widen so much and without danger the conditions for eligibility is because, in the electoral system we have adopted, which makes corruption almost impossible, the judgment of the electors is in itself sufficient for a good choice to be made.

We have said it already: There is no more watchful eye than that of private interest, which, in our case, is called to elect. Property does not admit corruption. It is the person who gets corrupted for greed of property.

The first condition imposed for eligibility is that the candidate is an Italian. It is necessary to put this seed of Italian unity in Italian constitutions.

The magnanimous Charles Albert was already a forerunner of this disposition by according, in the electoral law he published, a preference for the Italians from other states of the peninsula over foreigners—although that preference was too slight.

For the quality of Italianness, I mean that any citizen of any Italian state can be elected as deputy if he submits to the laws and to the magistrates of the state during the time of his mandate.

Since deputies are proxies, speaking in absolute terms, it would not be repugnant if they were foreigners, as long as they had the necessary intellectual and moral abilities. But Italians—no matter to which state they belong—must not be called foreigners. So in this way we leave a greater liberty to the citizens to elect their proxies from a greater pool.

Since various portions of Italy are governed by different sovereigns, the unity of the Italian nations cannot be perfect unless the sovereigns unite in a very strict confederation and govern their states with the maximum possible uniformity of laws and habits, as if they were in one senate of principles that considers all Italians as members of the same motherland. It is therefore necessary that amongst the agreements that the princes and the people of Italy will establish amongst themselves, there is also this: that all Italians can aspire to public duties in each state. I will reason more extensively on this in a paper that I will add to this one.

The second condition for eligibility is legal age. Other constitutions want an older age and in that they are right, since the equal vote that they establish does not give sufficient guarantee for a good election. But the vote that is proportional to property already gives the highest possible guarantee. He who chooses a lawyer for some litigation chooses the best he finds; and much more so will a collective body of proprietors who are called to elect their proxies.

Having ensured in this way a good choice of deputies, now we can harvest the advantage of being coherent to the principle of letting the door open as much as possible to all abilities. Why, for example, should we not find a precocious ability where wisdom prevails on age, under the age of thirty?

As if there were a need for an example to prove what is so obvious, is it not the case that the first African elected unanimously by the people as general of the army and to the highest ranking of the Roman Republic was a mere twenty-four years old, and did he not fully justify the popular choice? If the choosing institution is a college of people greatly interested in good choice, it is very difficult for a wrong choice to be made.

The other negative qualities indicated by article 60 need no comment. Perhaps the wisdom and the religious sentiment of Italians looks in this article for a quality it does not find: the profession of Catholic religion. This is a doubt that must be resolved by the nation itself.

If we were talking about the electoral right, I would formally state that no one who pays some direct tax to the state is to be excluded from it in spite of being an infidel or non-Catholic. According to the principles adopted, excluding him would be an open injustice. However, we cannot say exactly the same when it comes to eligibility, which is not connected to property; and in the large mass of Catholics, everyone can find enlightened and honest proxies.

Certainly, we must fully recognize that Italy is a Catholic nation and that Catholicism kept alive by our fathers is the strongest cement that unites it.

In a Catholic nation, the Catholic faith is the common rule of all members who compose it and the heterodox and the infidels are the exception—an exception that is tolerated, not approved. In fact, there would be a contradiction in terms if we were to assume that Catholics approve those religions they believe to be false. They do not consider nor can they ever consider these as religion but only as corruptions of truth and as superstitions, no matter how much they respect those who practice them because they assume they are in good faith.

Therefore, Italy is either Catholic—and in that case does not approve of but tolerates with the fullness of charity other religions that are non-Catholic—or it approves of these religions and in that case it is no longer Catholic. In the latter case it would have to renounce consequently all its national religious festivities, although they make a brotherhood of the people, spreading among them the purest of joys, the most sincere agreement, the most intimate rejoicing of the soul.

In constitutional forms, the principles by which the majority may prevail are accepted. This is what makes law and it is recognized as just that the minority submits when its rights are not violated. Therefore, in those nations where the Catholics are the majority—and in Italy almost all the citizens are Catholics—it is obvious that constitutional justice allows Catholic sentiment to prevail. This sentiment seems to suggest to Catholics that they should be governed only by other Catholics. The Catholic nation—Italy first of all—has therefore the right to expect a legislation that is formed by Catholic legislators according to the spirit of its religion.

Let us add that the supreme need of every nation, and especially of Italy, is that of internal union. Disparity of religions is a seed of discord—of the most deeply rooted, irreconcilable discord. All histories prove that, especially the religious wars. That is further confirmed by the discordant Swiss state that we are watching right now. Would it therefore be prudent to introduce into the legislative chambers of Italy, just for the gain of a minimum fraction of citizens, a reason for discord?

If in the objectives of legislation we could distinguish certain matters that influence religion, education, and national morality from others that concern purely material interests—and if we could allow the non-Catholic and the infidels to deliberate only on the latter, the disorder would not be as grave and the repugnance less obvious. But such separation is impossible. Thus, if in the chambers were sitting people who did not practice the Catholic faith, then we would have such a monstrosity as that of Catholics calling non-Catholics to have a real influence—although indirect—in the holy interests of their conscience, and in those of the moral education of their children. In that way, the character imprinted on society by the Gospel would be endangered. Certainly, it would be weakened, as experience demonstrates has happened in other nations.

One could say that the non-Catholics admitted in the Italian chambers would be a minority. But who knows what is the power of minority in public debates in certain times? The minority in the chambers is still a pulpit of principles built in the country that listens. Will we also build a public and solemn pulpit of legislative spirit that is non-Catholic and infidel? If we measure the power of minority only by the number of votes it has available, it will still be able to create remarkable damage by preventing good laws or by tipping the scale toward the worse dish of the divided majority. But the power of minority does not depend just on the votes it has available; it mainly depends on the eloquence, audacity, ability to handle sophisms, and on the party that it can create in the people, especially in times when the Christian faith is lax and when new things and licenses to think and live are avidly looked for, especially in moments of turbulence and of popular foment. It is in these times that the power of minorities is explained: Revolution is always its act. A very recent example is that of France—and this example shows us a Jew becoming state minister at the Department of Justice of that very Christian realm! Therefore, it may even seem that the very security of the state demands that in the Italian chambers are not admitted those who do not practice the Catholic religion.

The admission of deputies of other religions brings with itself yet another problem. It is necessary that the deputies, all equal before the nation, treat each other with much regard. Therefore, the Catholic deputies would lose part of their liberty as they would be obligated in some cases to embrace the non-Catholic deputies, and make concessions to obtain the support of their vote on some disputed law. So, not only would we form the religious indifference which is the disease of the century, we would also weaken the freedom of Catholicism.

These considerations, over such an important point, could not be neglected, as no doubt they are those we find in the souls of a good part of the nation. Italy will have to say what it wants.

ARTICLE 61—No employee of the judicial order can be a member of the chambers. The mandate of deputy is incompatible with holding the job of a minister of the state. It is also incompatible with any employment that obligates the deputy to reside outside the capital. Once the mandate of deputy has elapsed, those who have surrendered employment to accept the mandate are to be available for employment in their field.

The freedom of the chambers on the one hand, and the freedom and independence of governmental employees on the other, make the office of deputy incompatible with several forms of employment.

That ministers cannot simultaneously exercise the office of deputy is a disposition required by the sovereign. At the same time, since most of those who propose laws on behalf of the sovereign are ministers, it seems equitable that they are not parties and judges at the same time.

By the same token, it is necessary that all those employments that imply an obligation to reside outside the capital are declared incompatible with the qualifications for deputies, as it is prejudicial to good order and public morality to allow the employees to abandon their place and transfer to the capital to become deputies.

Finally, the judicial order, which is declared to be independent, totally rejects taking part in the chambers of deputies. To the judicial order, as custodian of justice, all splendor must be given and it must be constituted as one of the main powers of the state so that it can balance the power of the chambers.

No governmental employee is prevented from being a candidate for deputy, however, as long as he surrenders his employment and remains available for another more senior post once his mandate is over.

It may be necessary that administrative posts be excluded from the eligibility, as happens in other constitutions, for fear that they can influence the elections; this danger, however, is removed by the electoral law that we propose, since the job of coordinating the elections is mainly entrusted to political tribunals, which also have to sign the mandate of the deputies.

ARTICLE 62—Deputies of provinces receive a moderate remuneration as a title of indemnity from the state. They cannot receive any gift from the electors. When it is proven that a deputy has received gifts, he is terminated as a deputy.

That deputies are indemnified as established by article 62 is fair, especially for those coming from the provinces. Without this provision, the number of those willing to accept the mandate would be too small, and many potentially able candidates would be excluded.

Furthermore, without this provision, the constitution would not be coherent with its own spirit, and especially with the intention of article 60, which does not assign any wealth qualifications for candidates.

In Belgium, it was necessary to award two hundred florins per month to deputies who did not live in the city where sessions are held.

The deputies from the provinces who abandon their families and the overseeing of their business to move to the capital and give their work in the office of deputy necessarily undergo notable expenditures. In a nation that has just started constitutional ways and that, however, still does not fully understand the importance of self-sustenance, it would perhaps be difficult to find people who are both able and unemployed in the provinces, and who could or would be willing to undertake such personal and real sacrifices without any indemnity, moved by pure love of their land. The candidates not only would be few in number, but they would mostly turn out to be young people with little interest but much ambition to show eloquence and harvest triumphs, instead of being wise and mature *paters familia.*

It has been said that the deputies are paid only where democracy dominates; but his observation, which is correct for those states which follow the equal vote system, is not in the least applicable to a state that elects deputies with a proportional vote. Here property itself is the electing power, and property is not democratic in the bad sense of the word, as long as it invites to its service all talents.

With this article we also establish that it is the state and not the electors that indemnify the deputies, as a consequence of the principle that electors together with the sovereign represent the nation and not the provinces or the colleges (article 5).

Finally, it is forbidden that deputies receive gifts from the electors during their period of office, in order to remove the danger of forming groups that are interested in procuring the local and private interest rather than the universal interest of the nation.

ARTICLE 63—If for any reason a deputy terminates his functions, the college that elected him will be called to a new election. Any deputy who does not participate in the chamber without a just and acceptable reason will be fined by an amount imposed by the chamber itself to which he belongs.

It is of paramount importance for the good order of governmental business that all employees sit at their posts. This maxim applies for every governmental office, and especially for that of deputies, as the fundamental principle of this constitution is that the justice and appropriateness of the laws depend on their proper compilation in an assembly which faithfully represents all properties of the state and, through them, all interests of the nation.

It is therefore prescribed that, if a deputy terminates his office, the government must proceed immediately to the election of a new one. And here a new case is established where the ministry becomes accountable if it neglects to assemble the electoral councils that must elect the missing deputies.

Furthermore, we impose a rigorous obligation on the deputies to participate in the sessions by sanctioning a fine, the size of which is established by the chambers, providing that the greater fine may be necessary in certain circumstances to obtain the desired effect of making the deputies attend sessions, while in other cases, a lesser fine may be adequate.

The negligence of the chambers themselves in implementing this discipline on their members must be compensated by the attorneys, who report the situation to the supreme political tribunal, which can prescribe that the chamber impose the fines if they were to neglect to do so.

ARTICLE 64—Each legislative term lasts six years. Half of each chamber is renewed every three years. The first half that is to be renewed is chosen by the king.

With this article we propose that the duration of the mandate of the deputies is six years. This is a much longer period than what is established by other constitutions. This prolongation of legislatures has the advantage of making the chambers more conservative and of decreasing the inconvenience of the nation with less frequent elections.

That the chambers are organized so that a conservative spirit is promoted, seems to be needed more in a form of government that excludes the upper house, which is destined, in fact, to represent the conservative principle. For the same purpose, it is here established that half of each chamber is renewed every three years. This assures that half of the deputies who are involved in the handling of state business remain in the chamber.

In this way, the work that is required for the elections does not agitate the nation as much, and a new protection against corruption is established.

The five years established in France for the duration of the legislatures by the constituent assemblies of 1814 and 1830 appear to the ambitious to be too long. By renewing half of the chambers every three years, the ambitious are satisfied, and so is the nation, which takes gratification in the frequent intervention in the formation of the chambers.

Conversely, if we were to establish the duration of three years for the renewal of all deputies as happens in the Spanish constitution, or fours years as happens in the Belgian constitution, we would lose the advantage of stability that is gained with six years.

The total renovation of the chambers takes place whenever the king considers it expedient (article 10).

When the chambers are completely new, the sovereign has the power to establish which deputies must cease after the first three years, and thus must be re-elected. This disposition has the advantage of preventing the dissolving of the whole chamber when, instead, it is sufficient to renew half of the chamber, and this would seem to contribute to the smoothness of government.

ARTICLE 65—The Italian language is the language of the chambers.

After the identity of religion, the identity of language is a great cement, as it is the expression and the effect of nationality. It is therefore not only established that in the chambers only one language is spoken, it would also be desirable for the chambers to be attentive to keeping the purity of the national idiom.

ARTICLE 66—The chamber sessions are public. But when 10 members make written request, the chambers can deliberate secretly.

The public nature of the chamber discussions is necessary so that electors can know in which way the deputies who are their proxies treat their interests, and thus act accordingly in future elections.

This seems to be a true constitutional cause, for which it is just that discussions are public also because deputies treating public interest in the presence of their electors are stimulated to operate honestly and energetically.

In fact, in a constitutional government the people must entrust the mandate to those they trust by electing them as deputies, and then fully abstain from government, accepting what their proxies consider right to do up to the time of new elections, when people again intervene through the election. If this maxim were not held firmly, there would be no more order in the state, and anarchy would be irreparable. To achieve order, constitutions are established and powers are assigned and delegated. Thus, the people who violate the constitution must be punished every time they are not content to elect their proxies and let them function, but instead want to get themselves in the government with physical violence or even only moral violence.

According to these principles, without which it is impossible to maintain the order founded on the constitution, all those people who cannot exercise their electoral right and that are indicated by article 59 should be excluded from participation in the chambers. The chambers' regulation should contain some disposition on this matter.

ARTICLE 67—It is illegal for one chamber to be gathered at a time when the other is not. The two chambers can never be united in one assembly to discuss or take any decision in common. Acts taken by the chambers in these two cases are nullified.

This article is the natural consequence of the principle establishing that the legislative chambers must be two (article 48), and the reasons that we brought forward to prove the need justify the present disposition.

ARTICLE 68—Each of the chambers is solely competent to judge the legality of the mandate of its own members. If the legal form of the mandate is recognized, the deputy is admitted. But if he obtained the mandate through means that are forbidden by the law, he must be judged by the competent tribunals.

Article 68 differs from other constitutions because it restricts the right of the chambers that examine the powers of the deputies to verify only the legality of the document that mandates their own members. If this document is not lacking in any legal form, the deputy must be admitted. If the deputy has extorted the mandate with forbidden means, he must be turned over to the competent political tribunal for the trial against him. He can be brought in front of such tribunals by an attorney of the chamber, that is, by the state attorney. The competent tribunal must be the appeal political tribunal of the province where the election took place, since the deputy's mandate is signed by the lower political tribunal that precedes the elections for what concerns the correct implementation of the election process, as we will explain later.

This disposition is coherent with the adopted principle of the total separation between the judicial branch represented by the double order of tribunals, and the administrative branch which is represented by the chambers.

In the other constitutions, justice is not fully represented because the political tribunals are missing. And what was done to compensate for this deficiency? The upper house was attributed with the quality of high court of justice for the crimes of the state, which is the same as saying that two powers which are naturally independent and separate were concentrated in the same hands: the political one that concerns utility and the judicial one that concerns justice. It was done in such a way that those very same who were parties were also judges. So, they put in the chambers that despotism that in absolute governments is in the hands of the sovereign. Despotism is dislocated but not removed. What better formula than this can be found to express despotism than to make the same person, individual or collective indifferently, become a party in the case and judge at the same time? The form of government therefore can not be truly free if it does not establish the full separation between the administrative political power and the judicial one by putting these two powers in different hands and forcing the former to recognize the latter—to recognize, that is, that justice stands over everything, even over the political power itself. Society, then, serves justice, and that holds its true and only possible freedom. It is built solidly because its basis is eternal.

ARTICLE 69—The chambers in accordance determine, through an internal regulation, the way that is used to exercise their tasks.

The regulation of both chambers, approved by both chambers, turns out to be more considered and more harmonious inasmuch as, since the chambers are both elected, each must have the same regulation as the other.

Thus, even when some modification is done to the regulation, it is beneficial that both chambers are involved so that they thoroughly preserve that perfect equality that was established by the dispositions of this constitution (Title 4).

ARTICLE 70—After their confirmation and before commencing their duties, the deputies take an oath of loyalty to the king and to the constitution.

The oath is a solemn act of religion. A Catholic people know and are highly persuaded that religion is the basis of civil society and the highest guarantee for the constitutional order. Therefore, these people of faith must desire that the religious act of oath is done with all possible decorum and solemnity. Let then the bishop and the clergy receive the oath of the representative of the people.

It would seem that taking the oath of serving and faithfully keeping the constitution would be sufficient without adding the promise of faithfulness to the king, whose power is already defined in the constitution. However, in these times, when the executive power is threatened and assaulted with attempts to weaken it by any means, it is of benefit that the promise of faithfulness is expressly mentioned in the formula of the oath, thus adding a further guarantee by the deputies.

ARTICLE 71—The president, the vice-president, the secretaries and the other officers of the chambers are named by the chambers from among themselves at the beginning of every session and for the duration of the session.

It is part of the freedom of the chambers that the officers of the chambers established by the regulation are elected by each of the chambers.

ARTICLE 72—The sessions and the deliberations of the chambers are neither legal nor valid if the absolute majority of their members is not present.

ARTICLE 73—The decisions are taken according to the majority of the vote.

According to the principles of the constitutional system we have established, law is to be written by the majority of the interests. Thus, the two articles above would be insufficient to achieve this result if, with article 63, we had not already established a punishment for those deputies who have been negligent in participating in the sessions. However, we could not avoid establishing the minimum quorum of deputies sufficient to validate the deliberations.

Having said that the absolute majority of the deputies is required, we also determine that the majority is not sufficient and that the total number of the deputies is required.

ARTICLE 74—For the preliminary work, each law proposal is first examined by the committees named by each chamber. Once approved by a chamber, the law proposal is transmitted to the other chamber. Once debated and approved by the other chamber, it is presented to the king for approval. Debates are carried out article by article first; then the law is voted as a whole.

ARTICLE 75—Votes are cast by the sitting and standing of members, by division, and by secret ballot.

This last means will always be used to vote a whole law, and matters concerning personnel.

ARTICLE 76—If the law proposal has been rejected by one of the three legislative powers, it can no longer be reintroduced in the same session.

These articles, which are common to other constitutions, do not contain new principles and they only establish procedures for the chambers in the discussion of state business. Therefore, it is not necessary to indulge in the explanation of reasons. Even if some modification were desired, this could not be of such a nature as to threaten the basis that we believe a durable constitution must be built on—a constitution that is just, and which engenders public prosperity and national greatness.

ARTICLE 77—The ministers and the government commissioners have free entrance in the legislative chambers and they have to be heard when they demand it. The chamber may demand the presence of the ministers in the discussions.

That the chamber can demand the presence of the ministers is a consequence of article 47, which attributes to the chambers the right of interrogation.

It is equally natural that the minister, on whom the exercise of the administrative power depends, and who is mainly entitled to propose laws (article 11), also has the right to speak in the chambers although he cannot vote, and to be present at all discussions in the chambers, including the secret ones. Concord between the minister and the chambers and the frequent communication between them is an indispensable condition for the smooth operation of state business.

ARTICLE 78—The chambers cannot receive any deputation, nor can they hear others outside of their own members, except for ministers and government commissioners.

In the constitutional system, the people are not the sovereign, which is absurd in itself. However, the people enjoy part of sovereignty which consists uniquely in the right of electing the proxies of their interests. Once the proxies have been elected, the people do not exercise any other act of sovereignty except through the proxies they have elected. They have a binding obligation through the act of election itself to leave the proxies free to operate through the time that has been established by law. Once the term has expired, new elections are called.

This procedure is established by the constitution handed down by the prince, so that at the same time, all the interests of the people have a voice in the government while order is preserved and confusion is prevented. If the people could intervene in the government without rules or order, immediately and arbitrarily, we would inevitably have anarchy and the people themselves would be sacrificed and become prey of the most audacious demagogues.

Therefore, for the purpose that the people can freely and with tranquility exercise that portion of sovereignty that has been granted and belongs to the people, without the birth of anarchy or violence, and without overstepping the borders of their legitimate power, we insist in this article 78 that the chambers cannot receive any deputation whatsoever, nor can they hear others than their own members and the government.

It is also necessary to protect the freedom of the chambers, as their power must not be invaded by any other power. Any other deputation would be superfluous to enlighten the chambers, as their members can obtain the necessary information everywhere and the freedom of the press gives to all citizens the right to let the public know their opinion of the running of public business.

ARTICLE 79—The deputies cannot be held accountable because of the opinions they voice and because of their votes in the chambers.

This disposition is considered necessary for the full freedom of the discussions. That does not prevent, however, the laws that have been passed in the chambers from being cancelled by the Supreme tribunal of justice or the chamber from being dissolved by the executive branch (article 10) if it abuses its power.

11

Reasons for the Dispositions Contained in Title V

ARTICLE 80—The judicial order is independent in applying the laws to the cases that occur.

The independence of the judiciary is universally recognized as a principle necessary for a good form of government. What is still left to be desired is that nothing in the constitution is inconsistent with that principle. The observations that we make on the double power of the upper house and those we are about to make will demonstrate whether that is true in the common constitutions.

In the above-mentioned article, it is only said that the judicial order is independent in applying the laws to the cases that occur, and that is because the legislative power does not reside with the tribunals. However, the judicial order in this constitutional project is disposed in such a way as to exercise a sort of vigilance and censorship on the legislative power itself, since if the laws written by this power offend the rights that are guaranteed by the constitution, the competent political tribunal can denounce the legislative power whenever the offended party turns to it, and it can issue a decision that *vetoes* the unjust law.

ARTICLE 81—There will be two tribunal orders. The first one will judge in matters concerning individual rights that are social and private. The other will judge in matters concerning social civil rights. The tribunals that are purely military belong to the first order.

One of the vices of existing constitutions is the overwhelming power given to the chambers. That power is usefully tempered with a proposed system of the political tribunals through which the fact that even chambers are subject to justice is solemnly recognized by the constitution.

The chambers together with the sovereign represent the nation, but the tribunals preside over justice, which must be recognized as eternal and superior to the nation.

The chambers have as a main purpose to procure what is useful, but what is useful in a constitution that is moral and Christian must be highly recognized and proclaimed as subordinate to what is just.

That justice must reign in a state that is well-ordered and free over everything and that it must have an imposing representation is a concept that can never be repeated enough. It is appropriate that there is another power, different from that which is merely political that has a superior dignity and that pronounces upon justice. This power does not have to be mixed at all with what concerns what is useful, that is, the administrative branch (article 61). It has only to decide on what is just.

Now, what is just extends to what is public no less than to what is private. It is therefore appropriate to institute political tribunals as much as it is appropriate to institute the civil ones.

For political tribunals we mean those that exercise vigilance directly over the implementation of the constitution, that guarantee the social rights recognized by the constitution, that defend the powers that are constituted in civil society and prevent reciprocal invasions. Thus, the tribunals that apply the laws of military discipline do not belong to this type.

ARTICLE 82—The supreme court for political justice has a number of judges equal to that of one chamber: These judges are selected by the people with a universal and equal vote from among candidates from both chambers who are at least forty years of age. Every ten years, the people will be asked if they want to renew the election. The legislative power, by first issuing a law decree, can consult the people even before ten years has elapsed.

The supreme court of political justice has the duty to exercise vigilance over all powers of the state so that none of them exceeds its limits and its acts do not damage justice in any way. This supreme and most holy tribunal equally protects individual and social justice, as well as the rights concerning freedom, and those that concern property. This concerns, therefore, all citizens equally, since the rights of the proletarian and of the rich are equally sacred. It is therefore appropriate and consistent that each citizen casts an equal vote for the election of these judges.

By universal vote, I mean that all those citizens who have the exercise of electoral right (article 59) are called to vote, men and *pater familias* who are not interdicted.

As these are the only ones who are called to vote, the family right and the authority given to the fathers are respected. With that, it is assumed that the fathers are, as they must be, the mind of their own family.[65]

About the way to perform such elections, abstractly speaking, the best would be the method called the list method. The application of it, however, encounters the difficulty that electors are unable to know the many people who are needed to make the supreme court. Instead, one could turn to the elector to nominate that greater or smaller number of people that the elector believes fit to this grand office, up to the total number of people the office holds. This method would have the advantage that, as the people become educated to the constitutional life, the lists would become more complete and perfection could be reached effortlessly and naturally.

Justice has affinity with religion, which is the supreme sanction of justice. It is therefore appropriate that these elections are performed under the protection of religion. All electors should be obligated to participate under the penalty of a fine. Registers should be open where the elected are recorded in each parish by the parish priest in the presence of two witnesses. The first count of the lists would be performed in each diocese with the bishops and with a certain public exposure and solemnity. The second count should be done under the auspices of the bishop of the capital in the presence of the king, in the name of which justice is administered (article 16). This procedure, as well, should receive the most possible public exposure and solemnity.

The number of judges is established to be equal to that of the deputies of one chamber, so that this august tribunal can maturely discuss the grave questions of public right that are brought before it for decision, and the tribunal acquires greater authority and power so that it can balance the power of the chambers.

It is appropriate that the members of the supreme tribunal have passed the age of the most fiery passions and thus are able to judge with mature reason. Thus, we here establish that they cannot be elected when younger than forty.

It is also necessary that the judges perfect themselves in this grave office for a very long time—and it would be even desirable that they could spend there their entire lives.

However, it could happen that, elections having not turned out happily, for whatever reason the court loses the full confidence of the people or degenerates into such a political clique that it starts to be a systematic opposition to the parliament. Therefore we establish that the executive branch, every ten years, is to consult the people to establish if changes are necessary; and that the legislative branch can consult the people even before the ten years have elapsed through a decree that has all the necessary formalities to make the law valid.

This possible refreshing of the judges of the supreme court of political justice is not in opposition to the spirit of article 91 where we will declare that the judges are immoveable, since this immovability only means that the executive branch cannot change the judges arbitrarily, to the end that they are independent from the influence of such power when administering justice.

ARTICLE 83—There will be lower courts, appeal courts and supreme courts in both orders of tribunal. For the cases reserved to the supreme court of justice, there will be a first and a second instance made up of two colleges of judges, one more numerous than the other. In the last instance, the court of justice will judge in plenary session.

The political jurisdiction which is assigned by other constitutions to the upper house has many shortcomings. Not only is it limited in the scope of matters but also it has vices in its procedure, since it has only one instance.

Justice cannot be fully administered if not under the condition that the three instances established through article 83 of this project are implemented. In this system, two decisions that agree must terminate any litigation.

In the case of restoring a lawsuit *ex noviter repertis* (discovery of new evidence) or because of a manifest error, it will be possible to resort to the supreme political tribunal, who makes the decision concerning whether the suit can be restored before those tribunals that decide in matters of private right.

In the provincial capitals it is appropriate to establish appeal political tribunals under which the political tribunal of first instance would be placed.

These tribunals are in charge of judging what is just about everything concerning political rights and their violation.

The electoral law must entrust to the first instance political tribunals the presidents of the elections, and they will have to exercise vigilance over the formation of the electoral lists and to compile and sign the mandate of the deputies in order to decide upon any question that could arise in the colleges. In this way they perform the function, under more regular forms, of the very important Censor Magistrate of Roman times—a function that has been neglected by the constitutions of modern states.

ARTICLE 84—Any individual or collective person can appeal to the competent political tribunal in cases where a decision made by political authorities might violate the rights that are guaranteed in this statute.

Each citizen must be able to turn to the political tribunals whenever he believes that his political rights have been violated. Let us assume that an elector believes that he has been put in a college that is not the one assigned to him by the law; he could turn to his appeal tribunal, and so on. As we said in article 68, before admitting the deputies, the chambers only have to examine if the deputy's mandate has all the legal forms and if it is properly signed by the political tribunal.

So when the chambers have approved a law proposal that is believed to contain some injustice, it would be up to the sovereign, before granting or denying his sanction, to turn the issue to the supreme political tribunal. If this tribunal judges the law proposal unjust, the proposal could no longer be brought for sanction to the prince, but would fall by itself without any need for the king to fight with the chambers. The chambers could no longer propose the law or modify it. The public display of the debates (article 92), the large number of judges, and the arguments formulated would be sufficient guarantees for the integrity of the decision issued by the supreme court on such a relevant matter. The people altogether, that is, public opinion, would constitute the imposing sanction for such solemn decisions. It is clear that no question on other irrelevant matters, either just or unjust, could arise.

Minorities—and, as we said, even the single citizen—could bring the decision of the chambers before the supreme tribunal even before the law is sanctioned by the sovereign. This would be the reign of justice, as only in this way can the rights of every minority against the oppression of the majority be defended.

It will never be said often enough that one of the main vices of constitutional states is that the minority is sacrificed to the majority.[66]

The political tribunals and especially the supreme tribunal constitute an intermediate link between the chambers and the king and would prevent such a grave problem.

We have already observed that minorities are those that cause the revolutions. If minorities would find a peaceful way to defend their rights, there would be no more reason to turn to the force of the people to upset the state.

Sismondi recognizes that one of the greatest difficulties encountered in the constitution of a government is that of protecting the rights of the minorities against the arbitrariness and the injustice of the majorities, and he does not find any other way other than that of introducing, between the one and the other, a spirit of moderation and reconciliation through which they can settle their differences amicably. That is splendid! Without morality, a government cannot exist,[67] and the government is more solid when the morality of the populations that it governs is greater. But the wise legislator must give a support to public morality through institutions, and such is the political tribunal that we are proposing.[68]

By nature, this tribunal is first of all a justice of the peace. Its first office is to attempt reconciliation between the litigators and, only if that is not possible, to pronounce its decisions.

This tribunal, as all other institutions, is supported by public force, as the constitution, with its article 45, establishes that the decisions of the tribunals must be implemented.

The sentiment of justice is visceral in man and the opinion on justice is invincible. The political tribunal would be supported by this sentiment of the nation. It is therefore indispensable to educate a people that want to exist with constitutional forms of true freedom about the ways of political justice. Now the political tribunals would become as authoritative pulpits that would teach people their rights. Their motivated decisions would become more authoritative and the decisions of first instance and of appeal should also be motivated to facilitate the recourse to the last instance. In this way, the judiciary political order has the office of preserving and watching over the national constitution. It is called to see that all the laws that emanate from the legislative power hold the most rigorous logical coherence with the fundamental law, which must be superior to all others—a touchstone for all. This institution contributes greatly to obtaining that the fundamental statute becomes a practical truth. In the other systems, a constitution is written and promulgated, and then forgotten, as there is no power which is expressly in charge of its protection. Therefore, the people directly take care of it and make justice. But only those nations that replace such ways with the juridical decision of the tribunals are civil. Therefore, we cannot say that a constitutional government is fully civil until a power is instituted which pronounces on the violations that are committed against the constitution. Only then is the constitution no longer a paper written without voice, but acquires life and begins to speak.[69]

ARTICLE 85—The organization of the judiciary will be determined by a law.

That the organization of the judiciary is determined by law is a consequence of article 25 which states that no one can be separated from his natural judges. This guarantee of individual liberty and of the other rights of the citizens would be illusory if the order of the tribunals could be changed at the prince's whim.

ARTICLE 86—Ministers are responsible.

ARTICLE 87—Each of the two chambers has the right to accuse the ministers.

When a chamber accuses, the other one judges, and the high court of political justice applies the law.

ARTICLE 88—A law will determine the cases where the responsibility of the ministers lie, and the ways used to prosecute them and the penalties to apply.

These three articles establish the responsibility of the ministers—a principle admitted by all the constitutions—and they provide a manner for proceeding in the related matters.

The application of the law in the trial of the ministers is attributed to the high court of justice, coherently with what we have said about the political tribunals.

However, the chambers take part in the process, one as the accuser and the other as a jury that decides in the matter. This concession has the purpose of better safeguarding the responsibility of the ministers against the influential protection of the sovereign power.

But if it is just that the state is protected against the influence that the executive power could exercise on the administration of justice so that justice could have its free course, it is equally just to protect the freedom of the tribunals against the influence of the legislative power, as this power too, being handled by man, has the same tendency of invading other powers. It is therefore unwise to entrust to the chambers a judgment upon the ministers, as the other constitutions that have been so far published do, as they still retain the clear signs of violence and of demagogic arrogance from which they originated.

ARTICLE 89—No deputy can be arrested, except for cases of flagrant or near-flagrant crime, during the time of the session, nor can he be judged in criminal matters without a previous decision handed down by the supreme court of political justice.

It is not the duty of the chambers but that of the supreme court of political justice to decide that a deputy can be arrested or tried in criminal matters. That is in conformity with the principle adopted—that any form of justice stays extraneous to the administrative political power of the chambers, as well as that of the sovereign.

ARTICLE 90—The king will name state prosecutors in political tribunals. The prosecutors will, as a matter of course, bring before the competent tribunals the perpetrators of abuses of the press, teaching, or other breaches of the social civil right within the limits that will be determined by a law.

The establishment of state prosecutors completes the political judicial system and makes it effective.

Once it is admitted that not even the government can take justice in its own hands, but if offended, is obligated to defer the issue to the competent tribunals that are impartial and independent as they are not at all involved in administration of politics, it is then necessary that the state has proxies which represent its cause in front of said tribunals.

Without this office of public proxies, laws that repress abuses of press, teaching and the like would be often eluded and they would lose their efficacy.

A law must determine the office of said proxies of the nation.

ARTICLE 91—After sitting for four years, judges cannot be removed.

The protected tenure of the judges established with this article is also necessary to make the judicial order independent from any influence from the executive power and the power of the sovereign.

ARTICLE 92—The sessions of the tribunals in civil and political matters are public. The debates in criminal matters will be public upon request of the accused.

The audiences of the tribunals in civil and political matters are declared public. In criminal causes, public exposure is invoked in favor of the accused, as it seems appropriate and conforms to humanitarian purposes that whenever the accused desires or demands that the public is not involved, that must be conceded. This respect, used for the modesty of the accused, helps to induce him to emendation, as it is more difficult that he who has been exposed to shame accepts being corrected. If the adopted procedure in the nation considers the confession of the guilty as proof of his crime, then the private trial (if the accused himself requires the privacy) decreases the obstinacy of the guilty, with which he insists on denial because of an invincible repugnance to admit his crime in front of the public.

To ensure that the implementation of justice is guaranteed even in these private debates, it could be disposed that the state prosecutor or a commission of citizens participate in them.

12

General Considerations

These are the reasons, briefly explained, of this constitutional project, deduced from the nature of civil society and from the right that presides over it.

Although the intent of the project cannot escape the reader, I will repeat it once again: The project intends to give a solid basis to the order of civil society. However, the need to look for this solid basis is in the already mentioned principle that all constitutions of the last sixty years actually constituted nothing. They never brought tranquility to any people, and the people on which they were imposed complained that they were cheated and betrayed; they became irate, they tore the constitutions apart—and not just one or two times, but very many times; in fact, as many times as the experiment was attempted. This restlessness, this reshuffling of civil societies, clearly shows to those who are not blind that people are looking for something they have not found yet. When they will have found it, they will be satisfied and they will find peace. Now this unknown thing that the people of Europe, no longer satisfied by the governments of the Middle Ages—this thing that people amongst sentiments of humanity furiously look for through conflicts and blood, will it be impossible to find? No. Rather, I believe, it can be found without difficulty, but under the condition that the prejudices with which the schools of the masters of past years are imbued are put aside, and that we Italians soar with our intelligence to a state of freedom and that we have the courage ourselves to take a new way—a way that, as far as I can see, is indicated by this constitutional project.

I am well aware that although this project contains the solid foundation that the palace of civility needs, that foundation does not exist yet. How many times have men who have fought for what they so passionately sought been blinded by their fiery passions and did not recognize that they already had what they sought, but were overlooking it! It seems to be in hand in our case. But to realize that this constitutional project is necessary to give consistency to society, it is necessary to calculate the complex and remote consequences of the two hinges upon which it turns: the vote proportional to property, and the political tribunal. Yet it seems almost indiscrete to ask passionate minds to show the patience of calculation.

Certainly, the sagacity of thought is not lacking. Rather, this is abundant here in Lombardy as well as in any other part of Italy. I will call myself fortunate if this project could attract the attention of Italians, for without attention, sagacity has no value, because attention is that which applies to questions.

At first, there seemed to be two difficulties—should I say repugnancies?—that the project evokes: Some will think that it gives too much to freedom; others that it gives too much to property. It would be a fortunate case if these two objections would arise together, for one would cancel the other out. What is true is that this project gives to all more than what was given by other constitutions. It gives more to proletarians and to proprietors. It gives and ensures to all everything that all could expect, and without distinction.

The other constitutions take away some liberties from proletarians instead of guaranteeing them. On the other hand, they take away from proprietors some of the general rights of property. For example, they take from proprietors' hands the right of administrative legislation. This constitutional project gives to all what other constitutions take away.

But if the other constitutions decrease the freedom of all and therefore even those of the proletarians and of the small proprietors, those constitutions compensate them by giving them the power of legislatively administering somebody else's properties—which is in itself a new injustice, a sinister gift to the middle and lower classes to which it is handed. When the law gives to a class of people that which belongs to another, it unsettles the social order and calls upon itself and upon its beneficiaries the wrath of vengeance.

Yet theoretical difficulties are not what this project has to fear. I know very well what this project must fear most of all. Its major enemies are indubitably those men who call themselves practical and who are very respectable in my eyes, but not much used to new things as in these new things they are not practical at all. These men, if they are practical, only know how to go down the beaten path, and this project instead requires us to open a new path.

What do the practical men we are talking about do? What do they do, those people who—if we have to define them—are so used to handling affairs in such a set way as to not recognize as valid any other possible theory except that which comes from the way they and others always handle things (whether with good or bad result is irrelevant)? They usually base their main opposition to any new project not on a deep examination of its intrinsic nature, but on some extrinsic difficulty. In our case, they will not argue, for example, on whether the constitutional statue conforms to justice or is useful to society. Instead, they will simply say that it is impractical; they will say that the formation of electoral lists requires too much care and diligence; or they will say something like that. So merely because of a detail—which is supposed and not even proven to exist—the main issue is abandoned; for a merely incidental difficulty of execution, the substance is abandoned. It is preferred that society is given one or another of the old constitutions, which so often have thrown society into the anguishes of death, and which are intrinsically unjust. All this for fear of some more solicitude that is needed to put the new law into practice and because this law, since it is new, needs a certain study and industry to practice it! As far as I am concerned, I am persuaded that the electoral law based on the principle of this constitutional project turns out to be simpler and also practically easier than any other, once it is understood. But the understanding comes with some difficulty because of the novelty of the idea. Since this new project demands some thought, brings with it some questions which need to be examined—although it has many positive aspects, here comes the cry of the practical man, lamenting its extreme complications and demanding a greater simplicity!

It is better to persuade ourselves that the problem of social organization is naturally complex. All the most famous and durable state constitutions were complex, as the wheels of the social machine are many, and many are the things that the eye of the philosopher who establishes its organism must see. If the constitution of the Venetian Republic which lasted so many centuries had been written, who wouldn't have found it very complex? The same can be said of that of the Roman Republic or of the British Empire. We should not seek what is simple, but what is perfect; not what is easy to implement, but what obtains the desired intent. Perfection is as simple as it can be: The machine of the human body has an extreme simplicity in its wonderful complexity. Would we consider the body of a snail as better because it is simpler than that of man? This constitutional project has all that simplicity it can have. It is lightened from all those endless exceptions that we meet in all other constitutions, and that are as many proofs of their imperfection.

It was the moral influence that France exercised in all of Europe, including Italy, that seeded in the minds the prejudice that the social problem is simple, thus easy to handle, and the persuasion that makes all souls confident and sure of having a prompt and optimal solution. Yes, the French have proposed this problem with their simplicity that seems to be clarity and that persuades the populace that it is capable of judgment. But it is equally true that just a few general ideas, no matter how beautiful they seem, stand suspended in the air and are insufficient to build the form of government where real elements are in opposition; it is then that in the reign of ideas we can enjoy perfect peace. It would be desirable that Italians took greater interest in the study of the British politicians and economists. Some of them understood better than anyone else the function of ballast that property has in keeping the ship of the state balanced. Harrington's utopia still deserves to be studied. There are positive truths in the writers of this nation of thinkers that admirably confirm the principles adopted in this constitutional project. That notwithstanding, Italians, do not delude yourselves that my invitation to study British politicians or economists intends to bring you back to the old vice of making you again swear by the words of other masters. No, no! Open your minds to anything but be the eventual masters of yourselves. Courage! God made you to be such.

Finally, I will sum up here in a few words the spirit of this constitution.

It is formed so that the rights of all are represented. There is no one right that has no voice through which it can be heard, defended, and be of benefit to itself. The individual and private natural rights common to all men and to all citizens are written in the constitution and they are represented by the political tribunal: This tribunal represents the people. The social rights, and the property that makes them possible, have their representation in the electoral body. The intellectual and moral capacities are represented in the parliament and the offices of the state, since the material interest that elect the deputies enjoy that full freedom to elect the proxies that are most fit and employment is given to those who deserve it the most, and a special law establishes the titles.

This constitution is the middle way between all systems. It reconciles them all, and reconciles the reasonable opinions.

There are those who always speak about the *people*. This magic word fixes everything. Let it be. But the people are not just the plebeians but are the universality of the citizens, as was finally recognized even by France in the constitution it voted. Furthermore, the people are not a confused and anti-social mass. If it were so, the concept of *people* would exclude that of order and society. Therefore, *people* means association and organization. In this sense, which is the only reasonable one, in our constitution everything is the people, as the people are the king, the people are the employees, the people are the political tribunal, the people are the parliament, the people are the electors. These are the limbs of the organized people, reducing the living body of social life to perfection. The people, therefore, are everything—but a fraction of people is not the people, as it is a limb, and not the body. Let each limb perform its function, united to the whole body, so that the whole body can live prosperously and happily.

There are those in whose minds there is nothing but the word *Republic*. Well, our constitution indeed establishes a republic in the true and healthy meaning of the word, since all the citizens and all the rights of the citizens live, operate and function harmoniously.

Others love monarchy. Well, our constitution is indeed a monarchy, since it unites in the hands of one the executive powers, giving him in that way that unity and that force which is necessary to make society one and strong, to make laws and juridical decisions effective while he stays protected from any abuse and arbitrariness through the accountability of the ministers and the censorial function of the political tribunal.

Others appreciate the aristocratic element. But even this is not missing in our constitution, where there are provisions for the protection of the rich families as well as the poor ones, and, at the same time, privilege is removed—a privilege that had birth or wealth taking the place of merit. The springs of the machine are ordered in such a way that once set in motion they must necessarily produce the effect, the effect that in society the aristocracy of personal merit appears and dominates.

As to the elections, some talk about the universal franchise as an excellent thing; others abhor it because of the inconvenience they see in it. Our constitution admits the universal vote with an extension that is greater than all those that have admitted it so far, but removes from it all the inconveniences and makes it graduated and proportional.

Some want direct election; others prefer the double degree election. Even here, our constitution holds the middle way, taking what is good from both systems by allowing that the votes be cast by proxies, those who are unable to give a direct vote through double degree; that is, through their proxies.

We have established a proportional vote, but we have not excluded the universal and equal vote. The proportional vote we have kept for the election of the parliaments representing the material interests—and those interests are not equal in all men. The universal vote we have adopted for the election of the political tribunal, representing the interest and the personal rights, which are and must be equal for all.

There are those who prefer elections by electoral district; conversely there are others who consider more important the elections in major centers. The manner we have established for the election of the parliaments, although it is done through districts, still operates in such a way that the major proprietors must gather in more remote centers, and the minor proprietors in centers that are closer.

Women's advocates are not lacking, and they state that women are unjustly excluded from elections. Since we have established that all properties must be represented, even women and children participate in the elections in a manner that is affordable and convenient, the rights of the family protected, through fathers, husbands or legitimate proxy.

Others want elections to be made by colleges, and others by means of a list. Still some want electors to gather personally, and others want electors to be listed in a register. Each of these systems has good elements in it, and we have taken those good elements from all and assigned them in the proper place. Thus we have arranged matters in such a way that the electors of the parliaments are united in colleges, each of them electing a deputy, and that, conversely, the electors of the political court enter their votes in registers and that each elects a list of judges. At the same time, we have made provisions for the possibility that each elector chooses people he knows, without obligating him to write in the lists a certain number of judges, but only those that he conscientiously knows as worthy of choice.

With this constitution, we have been driven by the very nature of things and by the integrating principle of justice; we have arranged matters in such a way as to follow a reconciliation of all systems and of all parties without adversity to any, and without blind and passionate propensities. This reconciliation was not in our original intent, but we found it in our hands as a spontaneous result which is a consequence of logical reasoning. When our work was done and we returned to it to reflect, we found it there, and that made us glad, as in a fair reconciliation of the many sentiments we believe the foundation of peace in society and happiness of men consists.

NOTES

1. From 1789 to the present, France has changed or modified the form of its government at least eleven times. The following list indicates the series of constitutions and the duration of each:

		Years	Days
I.	Constitution of September 3, 1791, which lasted until August 10, 1792, that is, not even one year	0	341
II.	Constitution of June 24, 1793. This constitution was never implemented	0	0
III.	Constitution of August 22,1795, which lasted until November 10, 1799 (18th Brumaire)	4	80
IV.	Constitution of December 13, 1799, which did not endure in its integrity until the senate consulting committee of August 4, 1802	3	235
V.	Senate consulting committee of August 4, 1802, up to May 18, 1804	1	288
VI.	Senate consulting committee of May 18, 1804, which was kept until the decree of the senate of April 3, 1814, through which the Emperor Napoleon was deposed	9	321
VII.	Constitution decreed by the senate on April 6, 1814, which was never implemented	0	0
VIII.	Constitutional charter of June 4, 1814, which lasted until March 1, 1815	0	302
IX.	Additional act to the Constitutions of the Empire of April 22, 1815, up to June 22, 1815	0	61
X.	Restitution of the charter of June 4, 1814, which lasted up to the "Three Days" of July, 1830	16	55
XI.	Constitution of August 9, 1830, which lasted until the Revolution of February 22, 1848	17	197

Therefore, the total duration of these 11 constitutions is only 55 years and 55 days, and the average duration of each was therefore five years and five days!

In a work published in January with the title *Alcune parole sopra diverse cause che passanno intorno a noi* (Some words about things happening around us), we found the table of all the constitutions given to the various states of Europe from May 3, 1791, to

August 24, 1829, therefore within a period of 38 years and three months. These amount to a number of 152, of which 12 had zero duration, that is, they were never implemented. Another 75 were already dead at the time of printing. Of the 65 surviving in 1829, none of them was older than 16 years!

Is it not therefore evident that all these temporary constitutions must intrinsically hold a vice that corrodes them and destroys them? Is it not evident that the abstract ideas of the French Revolution are insufficient to found a durable government, and rather, they reduce the lives of the states to resemble the lives of insects? Will as many and as painful experiments be replicated and lost for Italy in these solemn moments when she rises again to life as a nation? Is it not desirable and necessary that Italians do not let themselves be overwhelmed by French loquacity, by juvenile enthusiasm, by gratuitous promises and declamations of journalists? Is it not desirable and necessary that Italians study the social question by themselves with conscience and maturity, try to repair the rooted vices of the governmental forms so far blindly imitated from France, and that they come in that way to build the nation on firm foundations which are capable of resisting the impact of the centuries?

2. *Filosfia del diritto, del principio della derivazione de'diritti*, Chapter II, appendix II-IV; *diritto derivato*, I, 48–67.

3. This constitutional project can basically apply to a republican form if the king is exchanged for a president. The laws typical of the civil society upon which the project rests are the same in both cases.

4. Some article concerning succession to the throne will have to be inserted here.

5. If we want to make provisions for the case in which the territory of the population of the state increases, this article must be expressed as follows:

> **49. By dividing the population of the state by fifteen thousand, if the population does not exceed five million, the total number of the deputies will be obtained: and if the number is odd, neglecting the fractions, it is to be increased by one.**

With an increment of the population of the state, the divider will be increased by five thousand. This method shall be used each time the increment of the population reaches five million.

6. Under the definitions of direct tax, we do not mean just the land tax, but also personal and real estate tax, the tax for the exercise of offices, arts, professions and in general everything that is paid immediately to the treasury of the state as a bare title of tax.

7. About the notion of rights of nature and reason, see *Filosofia del diritto*, diritto derivato, 1–20.

8. About the rights of those who are not included in the civil association, see *Filosofia del diritto*, 1,677–1,679.

9. About the despotism of personal majorities, see *Filosofia della Politica*, *La Società ed il suo fine*, I, Chapter IX—*Filosofia del diritto*, diritto derivato Part II, 274.

10. We have demonstrated the existence of this extra-social right in *Filosofia della Politica*, La Società ed il suo fine (Society and its ends) Part I, Chapters X-XII and we have defended it against the usurpations of civil society in *Filosofia del diritto*, diritto derivato, Part I, 1,649–1,702; as well as in the whole Dirrito sociale—civile (Social Civil Right), 2,181–2,266.

We also have observed that certain juridical questions received different solutions by the writers depending on whether they were resolved only with the principles of social right, or also by applying the principles of extra-social right. We brought as an example the delicate question, "What sanction can the people use when their rights are violated by the government?" (*La Società ed it suo fine*, Part I, Chapter 11), and in *Filosofia del diritto*, diritto derivato, Part II, 2,347–2,388 we demonstrated that the *social rights* in an absolute monarchy do not authorize the people to use violence against the monarch, and we declared we wanted to abstain from dealing with the same question according to the principles of the extra-social rights.

11. This takes place even concerning the rights of nature and reason. The modalities can be changed by society even concerning such rights, as long as their value remains intact. See *Filosofia del diritto*, diritto derivato, Part II, 2,480–2,488.

12. If we examine the so-called Holy Alliance treaty that was signed between the three powers of the north in Paris on 22 September, 1815, one can be moved by the sanctity of the Christian maxims proclaimed in it, and one considers it as a solemn and magnificent testimonial that the dominations of the earth render to the Savior of the world. But when the treaty is examined more closely and one asks himself how this treaty yielded to the world only a peaceful exercise of dynastic despotism that lasted over thirty years, then one can easily discover its imperfection. While it highly speaks of the religion of Jesus Christ and of the principles that the religion teaches to monarchs as well as to their subjects, there is not even one word concerning *the Church*. But is there Christianity without the Church? Without it, there is nothing but an abstraction of the Christian religion, which is ineffective to contain the despotism of the princes on one hand, and the passions of the people on the other. The princes do not fear this abstract Christianity, which they regard as their legitimate interpreter which can admonish them, reprehend them and punish them each time they overstep the measure of justice. Thus, we see them always ready to recognize Christianity, but not so the Church. It is true that the Church could not be named in a *religious* convention between a Catholic monarch, a heretical one, and a schismatic one. But why, then, call holy this alliance? And how can we mix the name of sanctity with heresy and schism? Can we not see at the bottom of all this religious manner indifference—if not hypocrisy?

13. Here, we are not talking about a *constituent divine right*, but of a *moral divine right*. The latter, when offended, does not bring with it any invalidity. Therefore, the bishops, who are also named by civilian governments as long as they are elected and mandated by the Supreme Pontiff, are legitimate shepherds as defined by the Holy Council of Trent, section XXIII, Chapter VIII, with the distinction between *constituent divine right* and *moral divine right* the various decisions of the authors on this question are reconciled.

The constituent divine right in the institution of the bishops is the sacred institution and mission of the Church. These two things are totally independent of the people and of any other laical power, as the Holy Council of Trent teaches us with these words: *Docet insuper sacrosanta synodus in ordinatione episcoporum, sacerdotum, et coeterorum ordinum, nec populi, nec cujusvis saecularis potestatis, et magistratus consensum, sive vocationem, sive auctoritatem ita require, ut sine ea irrita sit ordinatio: quin poteus decernit, eos qui tantummodo a populo aut saeculari potestate ac magistrate vocati et institute, ad haec ministerial exercenda adscendunt, et qui ea propria temeritate sibi sumunt, omnes non Ecclesiae ministros, sed fures et latrones, per ostium non ingressos, habendos esse* (session 23, chapter 4).

But let us come to the *moral divine right*. This demands:

1. That the election of the shepherds of the Church is truly held by the Church itself, that is, by ecclesiastical power. Now, is not this freedom

immensely restricted and diminished through the nomination granted to the secular power? How can the Church make sure that the worthiest is elected? What guarantees are given or can be given by the lay power?

2. That the plebeians are not forced to receive a shepherd in whom they have no trust and that perhaps whose name or face they do not even know, nor do they know his integrity or work. The sheep must know their shepherd, said Jesus Christ (John 10). This is a natural divine right that proceeds from the nature of the institution of the shepherds. Saint Athanasius was referring to the apostolic tradition when, to prove that Gregory had unduly invaded the Church of Alexandria, observed that the election was not conducted *secundum verba pauli, congregates populis et spiritu ordinantium cum virtute Dominus Nostrum Jesu Christi* (EP. ad EP. orthod. n. 2). But we could not adhere to the opinion of these writers who want to hold with negative arguments that the first bishops of Alexandria were given to unaware people and founded on a text of Saint Girolamus who, by talking about those elections, nominates the priest but is silent with the people. We have reason to believe that Saint Athanasius knew better than anyone else the tradition of his Church. On the other hand, the people are not the electors of the bishops, and Saint Girolamus speaks uniquely and briefly of the *election* of those bishops. It is enough that the people accept and do not complain. Thus, Natale Alessandro writes: *De traditione DIVINA et apostolica observatione descendit, quod populus in electionibus sacris suffragetur suo testimonio, concedo; udicio, nego* (diss. VII, *in Saecul.*, I [*Historia ecclesiastica Veteris Novique Testamenti*, t.IV]) but through sovereign nomination the people in fact neither know anything nor can they complain without clashing with the powerful authority and with the brutal form of the lay governments. It is true that it was the Church who surrendered the nomination to the sovereigns. But it did so forced by hard circumstances, and to avoid a greater evil. To those who demand your life, you give your money—but that does not mean that the theft is not forbidden by divine law. Now things have changed, and the people are free and therefore they no longer have to fear the threats of monarchic despotism. About the inconveniences of the nomination of the bishops that have been left to the governments, see the work *Delle cinque piaghe della Santa Chiesa* (The Five Wounds of the Holy Church), chapter IV.

14. GIOBERTI, *Apologia etc.*, chapter I.

15. As to the right of interpreting the law, see *Filosofia del diritto*, diritto derivato, II, number 2446.

16. *Filosofia del diritto*, diritto Individuale, Part II, number 2347–2354.

17. What is the principle upon which the peace treaty between France and the allied powers was signed in Paris on May 30, 1814? This: that the peace is founded on *sur un juste répartition des forces entre les puissances* (about a just distribution of forces among the powers). This principle is reduced to that of utilitarianism, of which philosophy was infected at the beginning of the century. The signatory sovereigns start from the assumption that they have all the rights to apportion among themselves the forces as long as they constitute such a balance—as if they were persuaded that they were solving a problem of

mechanics rather than justice. In that way, the people had to think as diplomats and were accounted in the same way as merchants who keep the records of their scales.

18. On the reduction of all rights to the two groups of *liberty* and *property*, see *Filosofia del diritto*, diritto derivato, I, 44–67, 246–262, 287–290.

19. *Filosofia del diritto*, II, 2182–2187.

20. When, in 1841, by publishing *Filosofia del diritto*, I highlighted the injustice of imprisoning as a criminal a man who is accused of some crime before the judges render the decision. The chief of the censura of Milan, while he had the common sense to tell me I was right, warned me that I was writing against Austria! See *Filosofia del diritto*, I, 1844–1900.

21. *Filosofia del diritto*, II, 1588–1593.

22. *Filosofia del diritto*, I, 1630–1639.

23. *Filosofia del diritto*, I, 1700–1703.

24. *Statuto toscano* (Tuscan statute): article 8 "all properties are inviolable except for the case of expropriation for cause of public utility legally demonstrated and on condition of previous indemnity."

25. *Filosofia del diritto*, II, 1586–1591.

26. *Filosofia del diritto*, I, 1446–1448.

27. *Filosofia del diritto*, I, 1449.

28. *Filosofia del diritto*, II, 444–448.

29. *Filosofia del diritto*, II, 1630–1639.

30. Let Leopold II be praised that with the concordat signed with the Holy See on March 30, 1848, he has given back to the Church a part of its freedom. Article 14 gives the Church back the free administration of its patrimony. However, the last words of this article ("there shall be no alienation nor shall there be long time locations without previous consent of the sovereign") resound with the ancient unwise dynastic protections that the Church is subject to but does not desire. Those who want to know in which way the goods that belong to the Church and the ecclesiastic orders have acquired that sort of immobility that was so damaging through the intervention of lay power which under the usual pretext of protection, actually invaded their administration, may read Chapter 5 of the work entitled *Delle cinque piaghe della Santa Chiesa* (The Five Wounds of the Holy Church).

31. See proof in *Filosofia del diritto*, II, 1686.

32. We have taken France as a base for this calculation, where land properties are much more divided than in Italy, and immensely more than in England. Thus, the number of the large landowners turns out to be even less in proportion to medium-sized landowners and to the rest of the population in the other main nations of Europe.

33. *Filosofia del diritto*, II, 272.

34. The expression "sovereignty of the people" has no real meaning save this: that in the people, that is, in the *pater familias*, there is the root of the civil government but not sovereignty, which does not exist before the government is instituted. See *Filosofia del diritto*, II, 1700–1710.

35. This calculation is founded on the basis that among each group of 15 families there are two youngsters older than twenty-one as well as the *pater familias*. Assuming that the population is 36 million, we would have 12 million electors, but 2 million should not be considered because they are amongst those who do not participate for whatever reason in the elections. Amongst these, however, we must observe that there are large and small proprietors or proletarians as well.

36. We take as a basis for this calculation that the major owners of a quarter of the land are, in France, 90,000 families. This datum is provided by the best statisticians of that nation. For this datum, by taking the 90,000 *paters familia* and adding the 2/15 of children that have reached legal age, we have in fact 160,000 electors. If we had considered only the largest fortunes of France, the number of electors would have turned out to be much lower, and our argument would be more evident. But we have limited ourselves to counting amongst the largest owners all those who could be attributed with an average property of 300 acres of land. Let us add that we have assumed that all the 150,000 owners cast their vote, when in fact not all can vote, for the known reasons. We have previously assumed that those unable to cast their vote amount to 2 million over 12 million, that is, one-sixth. Therefore, by subtracting one-sixth of the number 150,000, we would be left with only 125,000 votes of the owners.

37. In fact, the 150,000 electors form only the sixtieth part of the 10 million electors.

38. The 150,000 electors that pay one quarter of the tax have one vote against 65. One-third of the others who also pay one quarter have 21 votes, that is, two-fifths. These personal votes united with the vote of the former, give 22 votes, two-fifths, which represent half of the total tax. The other half is represented by 43 votes, that is, one-fifth. If therefore, 44 personal votes are in favor of the law, it is obvious that those who pay little more that three-eighths of the tax, as they have the majority of personal votes, force those who pay little less than five-eighths of the tax to pay it against their will, which is tantamount to saying that the three-eighths puts its hands into the purse of the five-eighths.

39. *Risorgimento*, June 3, 1848.

40. See *Filosofia del diritto*, II, 1670–1685.

41. V.DROZ, *Economie Politique*, Book IV, Charter II.

42. Justice is saved when nothing is omitted from efforts to reduce the number of those principles that suddenly can no longer be rigorously applied. Nothing more can be demanded of the government, because we cannot demand the impossible of anyone. See *Filosofia del diritto*, I, I, 720–771.

43. *Filosofia del diritto*, I, 382–451, 895–1003.

44. Concerning the right of petition, even collective petition, see *Filosofia del diritto*, II, 2376–2380, 2384, 2387.

45. *Filosofia del diritto*, II, 426–438.

46. *Filosofia del diritto*, I, 439, 445.

47. *Filosofia del diritto*, II, 446–449.

48. *Filosofia del diritto*, I, 141–238.

49. *Filosofia del diritto della natura del diritto e della sua relazione col dovere* (The nature of right and its relationship with duty), Charter II, article V.

50. We discussed the fundamental rights to truth, morality, and religion in *Filosofia del diritto*, I, 48–58, 87–127, 144–238.

51. *Filosofia del diritto*, II, 1586–1593.

52. *Filosofia del diritto*, II, 2427, 2428.

53. *Filosofia del diritto*, I, numbers 245–282.

54. *Del principio della derivazione dei diritti* (Of the principle of the derivation of rights), Chapter II.

55. In the first eighteen months from the promulgation of the above-mentioned law of March 22, 1831, in France forty ordinances of dissolution of the National Guard were issued, 11 of which did not dissolve entire bodies, but only one or more companies of one municipality. The cities where the National Guard had to be dissolved more frequently

were those of the western border: Baucaire, Grenoble, Leon, Chalon-Sur-Saone, Colmar. That was because in that area of France where military and revolutionary habits prevailed, the election put at the head of the National Guard those men of action who are always at the opposition and poorly tolerate authority.

56. In the correspondence of this great man, this very important principle arises many times.

57. *Filosofia del diritto*, I, 1650–1652.

58. *Filosofia del diritto*, II, 19, 20, 471 and the following.

59. *Filosofia del diritto*, 243–254.

60. Smith, XXVIII

61. We must diligently note that it is appropriate that the electoral law for a constituent assembly—that is, for an assembly that must decide on the destiny of a nation—be conceived on principles different than those upon which an electoral law for a legislative assembly is conceived. As we propose the vote proportional to property, we propose it uniquely for the election of the deputies of the legislative chambers. Concerning a constituent assembly, we indubitably would propose the *equal universal vote*. Furthermore, on condition that it is made possible to all citizens who are consulted, we would like the vote to be universal in fact and not just in words. To that end, that is, for the purpose that all citizens, even the humblest that form the majority, know what they are doing, it is indispensable that:

1. The people be divided by electoral district, and that in each of them a college is formed.
2. The election is not to be immediate but in double degree, that is, that in each district some people are chosen that in turn elect the constituent assembly that needs to be formed.

Only in this way can all choose knowledgeably and conscientiously, as it is reasonable to assume that even the humblest people know the persons who are most prominent in their district. And although in each district it is not always possible to find people capable of holding the office of deputy of the constituency with dignity, people who are sufficiently enlightened on how to elect those deputies cannot be lacking. In this way, the people are not obligated to do more than they can, and they are not obligated to elect people unknown to them; that is, to elect in appearance but not in truth. Mere formalities and nice words are cheats. If we want to truly know the will of the people, it is appropriate to ask them in that manner so that they can answer by themselves, and not try to put in their mouth what we want them to say, because in that case, the electors are not the people but the prompters.

62. *Il Risorgimento*, May 21, 1848.

63. As to the nature of the goods destined for public charity, see *Filosofia del diritto*, II, 828–864, 943–955.

64. The Sardinian electoral law in article 9 says: "To the renter of rural properties who makes the rented goods fruitful, personal and at his own expense is assigned in the electoral census a fifth of this tax, providing that the location is obtained through a public act and lasts no less than nine years, without the necessity of subtracting that fifth from the electoral census that is computable to the proprietor." Thus, the same fifth in the electoral census is attributed to two different electors.

65. For what we intend as *pater familias*, see *Filosofia del diritto*, II, 1552 and also1700–1727.

66. I extensively dealt with the tyranny of majority in my work: *La società ed il suo fine* to which I refer the reader if he would like to see a treatise on this important issue.

67. This truth is demonstrated in the work: *Della sommaria cagione per la quale stanno o rovinano le società* (The principle cause of the ruination of societies).

68. See *Filosofia del diritto*, II, 2648.

69. Among the moderns, Mario Pagano recognized the necessity for a magistrate who oversees the maintenance of the laws. Carlo Botta in his *Storia d'Italia* refers to and praises the thought of Pagano with these words: "This constitution was mainly the work of Mario Pagano, and amidst the servile imitation of the provisions of France we could see some new provisions of no little importance and of evident utility. Amongst them there was mainly the censorial power committed to a tribunal of five that had the duty of vigilance so that the bad customs were corrected and the good ones were preserved. There was also an ephorate—an overseer—that had the faculty of seeing the constitution in all its parts always preserved intact, and that the magistrates could not overstep the limits of the powers conceded to them by the constitution; that those who exceeded due moderation were recalled and that would cancel all the acts emanating from that lack of moderation; that it would propose the reforms of the constitution demonstrated necessary by the experience of the senate so that the act that was cancelled by decree of the ephors—even if it became a law promulgated by the legislative body—was binding on no one and to make sure that even the legislative body itself would obey. The ephors were to sit only fifteen days a year, and if they had to sit more, that would be a state case; that they could not exercise any other office; that they would stay in power only for one year; that they were elected by the people in every department of the republic, and that one department could only elect one ephor; that they could be elected to an archontate which was the supreme power for the execution of the laws, no sooner than five years after the termination of the ephorate, that they could belong to the legislative body no sooner than three years after such termination; and that once their mandate was terminated they could never carry the title of ephor. These procedures for the ephorate are worthy of much praise and are fit to prevent in republics as well as in kingdoms that have republican features many contests and civil subversions. Certainly, where confirmed by the authority of the time, they could bring great benefit to the free states."

APPENDIX

Works by Antonio Rosmini in Italian

Breve esposizione della filosofia di Melchiorre Gioja, Studi critici su Ugo Foscolo e Melchiorre Gioja. A cura di Rinaldo Orecchia, Padova, Cedam-Casa editrice Dott. Antonio Milani, 1976, 87–191.

Della naturale costituzione della società civile, Filosofia della politica, Rovereto, Tip. Giorgio Grigoletti, 1887.

Filosofia del diritto. A cura di Rinaldo Orecchia, vol. 6, edizione nazionale delle opere edite ed inedite di Antonio Rosmini-Serbati, Padova, Edizioni Cedam, Casa Editrice Dott. Antonio Milani; vol. I: 1967, XX–258; vol. II: 1968, 259–590; vol. III: 1969, 591–846; vol. IV: 1969, 847–1195; vol. V: 1969, 1195–1438; vol. VI: 1969, 1439–1676.

Grande dizionario antologico del pensiero di Antonio Rosmini. A cura di Cirillo Bergamaschi, Roma, Centro Internazionale di Studi Rosminiani, Città Nuova, Edizioni Rosminiani, 2001.

Introduzione alla Filosofia, Opere edite e inedite di Antonio Rosmini-Serbati, Vol. II. A cura di Ugo Redano, Roma, Anonima Romana Editoriale, 1934.

La società ed il suo fine, Filosofia della Politica. A cura di Sergio Cotta, Milano, Rusconi, 1985, 153–707.

Opere inedite di politica. A cura del Prof. G. B. Nicola, Milano, Stab. Tipo. Lit. G. Tenconi, 1923.

Principi della scienza morale, en Principi della scienza morale e Storia comparativa e critica dei sistemi intorno al principio della morale. A cura di Dante Morando, Opere edite e inedite, Vol. XXI, Milano, Fratelli Bocca, Editori, 1941.

Saggio sul Comunismo e il Socialismo, Filosofia della Politica, Vol. IV, Opuscoli Politici. A cura di Gianfreda Marconi en Opere edite e inedite di Antonio Rosmini, Edizione critica promossa da Michele Federico Sciacca, Roma, Centro Internazionale di Studi Rosminiani, Città Nuova Editrice, 1978, 81–121.

Saggio sulla definizione della ricchezza, Filosofia della Politica, Vol. IV, Opuscoli Politici. A cura di Gianfreda Marconi en Opere edite e inedite di Antonio Rosmini, Edizione critica promossa da Michele Federico Sciacca, Roma, Centro Internazionale di Studi Rosminiani, Città Nuova Editrice, 1978, 12–45.

Saggi di Scienza Politica, Scritti inediti. A cura di G. B. Nicola, Torino- Milano, G. B. Paravia & C., 1933.

Storia comparativa e critica dei sistemi intorno al principio della morale, en Principi della scienza morale e Storia comparativa e critica dei sistemi intorno al principio della morale. A cura di Dante Morando, Opere edite e inedite, Vol. XXI, Milano, Fratelli Bocca, Editori, 1941.

Works by Rosmini in English

Anthropology as an Aid to Moral Science, translated from Antropologia in Servizio della Scienza Morale by Denis Cleary and Terence Watson, Rosmini House, Durham, U.K., 1991.

The Summary Cause for the Stability or Downfall of Human Societies, vol. 1 of The Philosophy of Politics, translated from *Della sommaria cagione per la quale stanno o rovinano le umane societa*, ibid., 1994.

Society and Its Purpose, vol. 2 of The Philosophy of Politics, translated from *La societa ed il suo fine*, ibid., 1994.

The Essence of Right, vol. 1 of The Philosophy of Right, translated from Filosofia del diritto, ibid., 1993.

Principles of Ethics, translated from Principi della Scienza Morale, ibid., 1988.

Rights of the Individual, vol. 2 of The Philosophy of Right, ibid.

Rights in Civil Society, vol. 6 of The Philosophy of Right, ibid., 1996.

Society and its Purpose, vol. 2 of The Philosophy of Politics, translated from *La societa ed il suo fine*, ibid.

Universal Social Right, vol. 3 of The Philosophy of Right, ibid., 1995.

Works on Rosmini's Intellectual Life and Thought

Luigi Bulferetti, *Antonio Rosmini nella Restaurazione*, Felice Le Monnier, Firenze, 1942.

Giorgio Campanini, *Antonio Rosmini e il problema dello Stato*, Morcelliana, Brescia, 1983.

Mario D'Addio, *Libertà e appagamento. Politica e dinamica sociale in Rosmini*, Edizioni Studium, Roma, 2000.

Antonio Giordano, *Le polemiche giovanili di Antonio Rosmini*, Centro Internazionale di Studi Rosminiani, Stresa, 1976.

Umberto Muratore, *Antonio Rosmini. Vida y pensamiento.* BAC, 2000.

Pier Paolo Ottonello *L'attualità di Rosmini*, Studio editoriale di cultura, Genova, 1978.

Pietro Piovani, *La teodicea sociale di Rosmini*, Cedam, Padova, 1957.

Michele Federico Sciacca, *Metafísica, gnoseologia y moral. Ensayo sobre el pensamiento de Antonio Rosmini*, Gredos, Madrid, 1963.

Giole Solari, *Rosmini inedito. La formazione del pensiero politico*, Centro Internazionale di Studi Rosminiani, Stresa, 2000.

Francesco Traniello, *Società religiosa e società civile in Rosmini*, Morcelliana, Brescia, 1997.

Danilo Zolo, *Il personalismo rosminiano*, Morcelliana, Brescia, 1963.

INDEX

ABOUT THE AUTHOR

Antonio Rosmini was a Catholic priest and philosopher. Born in Rovereto in the Austrian Tyrol in 1797, he later founded a religious order, the Institute of Charity, and wrote numerous theological and philosophical works. Rosmini died at Stresa, Italy, in July 1855.

ABOUT THE TRANSLATOR

Alberto Mingardi is Director General of Istituto Bruno Leoni, a research institute based, in Milan, Italy, and Senior Fellow of the Brussels-based Centre for the New Europe. His writing has appeared in various popular publications, including the *Financial Times* and the *Wall Street Journal*. His scholarly interests concerns nineteenth-century classical liberalism, from Antonio Rosmini to Herbert Spencer.